Endorsements

"The rich and multidimensional analysis of the Chinese carmaker Geely presented in these pages will be of great value for all researchers and practitioners interested in the current major transformations of the global automotive sector."

Tommaso Pardi
Director of Gerpisa
Senior Researcher at the CNRS (IDHES) and at the
Ecole Normal Supérieure of Paris-Saclay

"This book on Geely opens a window of inspiration for international corporates to understand the dynamics and ambition of Chinese automobile companies, and for Chinese firms to learn the possible trajectories of globalization. The academic analysis is a plus for business leaders if you wish to empower your intellectual reflection."

Dr. Yudong CHEN
President of Bosch China, China

"For those seeking to understand the rise of the Chinese auto industry in detail, this is a good place to start."

Daniel T JONES
Founder and Chairman of Lean Enterprise Academy,
Co-author of *The Machine that Changed the World*, UK

"A fascinating & enjoyable journey into China's new automotive world. For readers hungry to know more about GEELY and the wider auto market in China. From Zhejiang to China, from China to the world — every page is full of excitement."

Freeman H SHEN
CEO and Founder at WM Motor Co., China

"The book is a must-read for experts, scholars, professionals involved in global businesses and firms' international expansion. It shows the pattern of development of a new global player, Geely, in a very competitive industry such as the automotive sector. Along different stages of the Go Global policy developed by the Chinese government, Geely has succeeded to grow both domestically and at the international level. Acquisitions have become the strategic tool to rapidly acquire knowledge and know-how and to improve internal competitive advantages. The catch-up process of Geely has been fast, and high level of efficiency and innovation capacity were reached. Through Geely's history, readers can well understand the process of technological upgrade adopted by Chinese firms, which are now at the frontier of innovation thanks to integration of the automotive technology with Internet of Things, artificial intelligence, new users' experience towards smart and mobility solutions."

Dr. Professor Francesca SPIGARELLI
Director of China Center, Department of Law,
University of Macerata, Italy

GEELY
DRIVES OUT
The Rise of the New Chinese Automaker in the Global Landscape

GEELY DRIVES OUT

The Rise of the New Chinese Automaker in the Global Landscape

Hua Wang
Emlyon Business School, France

Giovanni Balcet
University of Turin, Italy

Wenxian Zhang
Rollins College, USA

W♭ World Scientific

NEW JERSEY · LONDON · SINGAPORE · BEIJING · SHANGHAI · HONG KONG · TAIPEI · CHENNAI · TOKYO

Published by

World Scientific Publishing Co. Pte. Ltd.

5 Toh Tuck Link, Singapore 596224

USA office: 27 Warren Street, Suite 401-402, Hackensack, NJ 07601

UK office: 57 Shelton Street, Covent Garden, London WC2H 9HE

Library of Congress Cataloging-in-Publication Data
Names: Wang, Hua (Professor of innovation management), author. | Balcet, G. (Giovanni), author. |
　　Zhang, Wenxian, 1963–　author.
Title: Geely drives out : the rise of the new Chinese automaker in the global landscape /
　　Hua Wang, Emlyon Business School, France, Giovanni Balcet,
　　University of Turin Italy, Wenxian Zhang, Rollins College USA.
Description: Singapore ; Hackensack, NJ : World Scientific Publishing Co. Pte. Ltd., [2021] |
　　Includes bibliographical references and index.
Identifiers: LCCN 2021015323 | ISBN 9789811234422 (hardcover) |
　　ISBN 9789811234439 (ebook) | ISBN 9789811234446 (ebook other)
Subjects: LCSH: Zhejiang ji li kong gu ji tuan you xian gong si. |
　　Automobile industry and trade--China--History--21st century.
Classification: LCC HD9710.C64 Z457 2021 | DDC 338.8/876292220951--dc23
LC record available at https://lccn.loc.gov/2021015323

British Library Cataloguing-in-Publication Data
A catalogue record for this book is available from the British Library.

For any available supplementary material, please visit
https://www.worldscientific.com/worldscibooks/10.1142/12213#t=suppl

Desk Editors: Jayanthi Muthuswamy/Lixi Dong

Typeset by Stallion Press
Email: enquiries@stallionpress.com

Printed in Singapore

Dedication

From Hua Wang:
To my wife Lily and children Henry and Hugo, to compensate for the time when I'm not by your side.

From Giovanni Balcet:
To my mentors and to my students, who motivated my research work. To my lovely family who always supported me.

From Wenxian Zhang:
To my high school and college classmates, whose friendships have made my life journey a pleasant experience.

From all of us:
To the leaders, pioneers, dreamers and doers of the Chinese automobile industry.

Foreword

This book is the result of a long-term collective effort. As the director of the GERPISA Network of Research, I have witnessed the evolution of this work through several international colloquiums. I am now delighted to see that it has grown into a remarkable book. The rich and multidimensional analysis of the Chinese carmaker Geely presented in these pages will be of great value to all researchers and practitioners interested in the current major transformations of the global automotive sector. During this period, Geely has become the most important privately owned Chinese carmaker and one of the fastest growing transnational players in this extremely competitive industry, notably through the successful acquisition of Volvo in 2010 and the more recent entry in the major capital investment of Daimler. By unpacking and explaining the different factors that have contributed to this successful trajectory, the book makes a key contribution to the study of the "new frontiers of the automotive industry" that we have put at the core of our last international programme of research.[1]

Nevertheless, it would not make justice to this book to say that it is "just" about Geely. Through the prism of this surprisingly resourceful company, which in less than 20 years has moved from the production of refrigerators to become the 13th biggest global carmaker by volume of production, Hua Wang, Giovanni Balcet, and Wenxian Zhang have cast a new light on a wide array of crucial topics in industrial economics and managerial studies that span well beyond the automotive sector. The list is long and the book makes a really good job of highlighting how each

---

[1] For an overview, see: http://gerpisa.org/node/6152.

chapter contributes both theoretically and empirically to different fields of research and key research questions. I would like here to focus on at least some of them.

First, what I really like about this book is the way it looks at the "Chinese miracle". Twenty years ago, the total production of cars in China numbered only few hundred thousands, representing less than 1% of the total world production. By 2010, it has grown to 14 million, comprising 24% of the total global production. At this time however, China was still mainly considered as one of the BRIC, a group of emerging countries that were finally seeing their automotive markets and industry growing at a regular pace. However, during the next decade, automotive production in China kept growing despite the impact of the financial crisis, while in the other BRIC countries it significantly slowed down or even dropped. By 2018, China has become by far the main automotive market and producer in the world, representing one third of the total world production of cars. It is now clear that there is something specific and unique about China that set its economic development in a class of its own.

If a lot of ground has been covered in the last years to explain the causes of this miraculous growth, most of the existing research, in particular on the automotive sector, has focused on the "visible side" of the Chinese economy: the role of central government industrial planning in shaping the automotive sector and the parallel growth of state-owned enterprises and of their joint ventures with major global carmakers. This book looks at the "hidden side" of the Chinese automotive world populated by thousands of Chinese privately owned manufacturers of cars, trucks, low-speed vehicles, and automotive parts and technologies, which have been mostly operating for years at the frontiers of legality. It is from this underworld that Geely emerged in the 2000s, mastering the art of copying foreign cars through reverse engineering and rapidly moving into their mass production with selling prices below US$8,000. The book not only follows the adventurous trajectory of Geely as it moves out from this shadowy world to fight for a spot amongst the few officially licensed Chinese carmakers but also explores the surrounding landscape. Through the notion of "quasi-open product architecture," it explains in detail how these companies with relative few resources could rely on the supply of standardized components developed through reverse engineering to produce new cars at a fast pace and low prices. It also provides an accurate account of the complex set of entrepreneurial, managerial, and technical competences that were required to succeed in this accelerated catching-up strategy. However, what set Geely apart from most of these companies has been its ability to constantly acquire new assets and competences to move toward more integral product architectures in order to upgrade its models and compete with those produced by global carmakers in China and abroad.

This extraordinary capacity of Geely of growing and expanding internationally is another key topic explored by the book. It relates to the more general question of how companies from emerging countries can become successful global players even in mature sectors, such as the automotive industry. In answering this question, the book brings together different dimensions, each one looking at some crucial factors that contributed to Geely's success.

Amongst those factors, the analysis of the role of entrepreneurship is particularly important and refreshing. In the automotive sector, the CEOs of global carmakers and mega-suppliers are all managers, mostly trained in the same universities and top business schools. They have similar competencies and tend to share similar worldviews. This relative homogeneity is even reinforced by the strong influence that financial analysts, institutional investors, and global consultants exert on the strategic options of Original Equipment Manufacturers (OEMs) and possibly explains the inertia and conservatism that generally characterized this sector. Now, one of the key factors in Geely's success has been the role of its founder, Li Shufu. The book makes a vivid portrait of Li, of his philosophy, and of his relentless search for all the possible means to sustain growth and fulfill his vision, no matter the risks and the cost. Several bold decisions made by Li, such as the acquisition in 2010 of a struggling European premium carmaker, Volvo, whose capitalization was four times that of Geely at the time, were criticized by financial analysts, but turned out to play a decisive role in the successful growth of the group. The book makes a clear and convincing statement that this type of entrepreneurial activism is a distinctive feature of the dynamic capitalistic growth of the Chinese automotive industry. In many ways, it reminds of the entrepreneurial activism of Silicon Valley's start-ups, and an interesting parallel is even developed in the book between the figures of Li Shufu and Elon Musk.

Another interesting factor that is analyzed in detail in the book is the role of finance. A significant amount of literature in social sciences has emphasized the potential negative impact of financial institutions on manufacturing companies, in particular in the automotive sector. This is an industry with huge fixed costs and small margins, where long-term strategies and planning are key to successful product development and technological innovation. Financial pressure toward the maximization of short-term profits, high dividends payments, and stock buybacks has been therefore seen as destabilizing force, having played, for instance, an important role in the bankruptcy of GM and Chrysler in 2008. However, the book shows through the case of Geely how emerging multinational enterprises can use finance as a powerful tool to achieve rapid growth and international diversification through aggressive asset-seeking and asset-acquisition strategies. Indeed, the list of companies acquired by Geely between 2010 and 2018 is impressive as well as their diversity: ranging from the premium carmakers Volvo, Lotus, and Daimler, to the low-cost Malaysian assembler PROTON, from the niche British producer of London taxis, to the cutting edge developer of flying cars Terrafugia.

Yet the books reminds us that such mergers and acquisitions can easily backfire as the recent history of the automotive sector is full of failed operations, such as the famous collapse of the Daimler–Chrysler operation, or the abortion of the Volvo–Renault alliance, of the GM–Fiat alliance and more recently the crisis of the Renault–Nissan alliance. Geely, despite being a relatively small player and an inexperienced newcomer in this industry, has remarkably succeeded in developing and integrating all these companies. The book analyzes in detail how this was possible and develops a particularly in-depth study of the Volvo acquisition. It shows how Geely, inspired again by the vision of its founder, did not rush the integration process. It first created the conditions for Volvo to grow, by providing the financial resources required to renew and enlarge the product range through the creation of a new scalable platform, and by supporting the successful industrial and commercial development of Volvo in China. It was only when the trust between the two companies had been firmly established that Geely proceeded to further integrate their operations through the creation of joint R&D centers and engineering processes, new share production platforms, and common brands (Lynk & Co).

By following this accelerated growth trajectory of Geely, the book also explores from an original angle the current major transformations that the global automotive industry is undergoing and which are now epitomized by the acronym CASE: connected, autonomous, shared, and electric vehicles. Each of these technologies has indeed the potential of transforming the automotive sector, but connected together they imply nothing less than a paradigm shift, in which the ecosystem, the frontiers, and the very nature of the automotive business are in the process of being redefined.

While all major carmakers have recently acquired both new competences and new companies to deal with these disruptive changes, it is quite clear that their transition toward Mobility as a Service (MAAS) is intended to be slow and carefully planned. What is at stake for them is to preserve both the control of the value chain, threatened by the entry of new players in each of these technological fields, and the cash flow from the "old paradigm" activities on which OEMs still depend for financing the huge investments required by the transition toward the new paradigm.

Part of the reason why this strategy seems to be working is that the diffusion of these potentially disruptive and interconnected technologies also depends on the creation of new infrastructures for fast connectivity and electric charging, and on the introduction of new political and cultural institutions to promote MAAS. Now, both in North America and Europe, national governments do not seem to have the financial resources and/or the political willingness to do so at the pace and the scale required to accelerate these transitions. But this is not the case of China. The Chinese central government has already started to massively invest in the creation of this new digital–electric ecosystem and to push radical institutional changes to reconfigure producers', consumers,' and users' approaches to the mobility of persons and goods. Chinese enterprises, in particular privately owned ones such as Geely, have also already started to invest proactively in these new technologies as a way to leapfrog toward MAAS and overtake the incumbent global players in this new technological playfield.

The book makes an excellent job of capturing all these dynamics, both at the government and at the firms' level. It shows in particular how Geely has perceived these interconnected transformations not as potential threats to its core business model, but as opportunities to further grow and diversify its assets and capabilities. As early as 2013, Geely started to develop its mobility services, which have now grown into a viable and fast-expanding car-hailing company called *Cao Cao*, and by 2015 Geely had already implemented its electrification and autonomous cars strategies, which can now rely on the development of a pure electric platform for the joint production with Volvo of the new Lynk & Co brand, on the production of the electric *smart* in China in cooperation with Daimler, as well as on the introduction of low-speed autonomous mobility services for the 2022 Asian Games of which Geely will be the main sponsor. The book analyzes how these different projects and acquisitions converge toward a comprehensive strategy to develop MAAS not to supplant the traditional business, but to further develop it.

A final but very important remark goes to the theoretical contribution of the book. Each chapter is introduced by a theoretical discussion of the topic presented: from entrepreneurship to international growth, from cross-cultural management to innovation strategy, from platform strategies to corporate culture. This rich theoretical background not only makes this book a very valuable reading for students in industrial economics, international economics, and management studies but also lays down the bricks that the three authors use all along the book to build an original approach to the study of emergent multinational companies. By combining the eclectic paradigm (ownership, location, and internationalization) developed by John H. Dunning with the "linkage, leverage, and learning" theory developed by John Mathews, the authors manage to renew the depth of the former while extending the operational grasp of the latter. The result is a complex analytical framework that integrates a multi-level analysis of emerging multinational enterprises and of their institutional environments with a dynamic approach to their strategic development and accelerated growth. A key insight provided by this book is how these companies need to constantly sustain an accelerated mode of growth through aggressive asset-seeking and acquisition in order to survive, in a way that is not very different from the trajectory of successful digital start-up companies, but with the financial constraint of being manufacturing companies that are expected to make profits! This is a very different development path from those followed, for instance, by Japanese and Korean OEMs in the 1960s and 1980s, which were evolving in protected national markets and in a relatively stable production environments in terms of product architectures and business models. Such an evolution entails the structuring of completely different productive models, where the synergies between different types of activities and new sources of profit linked to the servitization of the automotive business appear to play a central role.

This book represents a milestone in the study and characterisation of these new productive models and it opens up new fascinating questions for our future research!

Tommaso Pardi
Director, GERPISA
Senior Researcher, CNRS (IDHES) and
Ecole Normal Supérieure of Paris-Saclay

Preface

Since 2008, while the global automotive manufacturing has been faltering, the Chinese auto industry has swiftly transformed into the largest producer in the world. The growth of the Chinese automakers is a close reflection of China's powerful manufacturing economy, and Geely Auto is one such best example. This book closely examines the rise of Geely as a privately owned automaker in China. From its humble beginnings as a refrigerator component maker and motorcycle manufacturer in the late 20th century, Geely has grown to become not only a top-selling national brand in China, the largest auto market in the world, but also a significant player in the global automotive industry. The book studies the successful acquisition of Volvo, within a long-term framework of asset-seeking foreign direct investment, and then further investigates its recent strategic initiatives with Daimler, London Taxi, PROTON, and Lotus. The book reveals how the little-known carmaker is worth close examination, via its product development, organizational dynamics, corporate culture, brand development, talent and cross-cultural management strategies, as well as the entrepreneurship of its visionary founder Li Shufu. From catching up in technology to becoming a leader in product, service, and business model innovations, Geely has driven out as a new Chinese automaker on the world stage. Facing challenges in clean energy and Internet of Things, artificial intelligence, and new user experience toward smart and mobility solutions, Geely will continue to play an increasingly important role in the globalization age of the 21st century.

About the Authors

Hua Wang is Full Professor of Strategy and Innovation Management, Associate Dean of Emlyon Business School, Dean of Emlyon Business School Asia, and French Dean of Asia Europe Business School. His research interests center on innovation management, foreign direct investment, industrial clusters, globalization strategy of Chinese companies, and the automotive industry in China. He has more than 100 publications in journals, book chapters and conference proceedings, including *Management International* and *Asia Pacific Journal of Management*. He has taught courses in leading MBA and EMBA programs. He is the Executive Board Member of China *goes* Global, steering committee member of GERPISA (an international automobile industry research network), and is one of the 30 think tank members of 21st China Business Herald Automobile Center. He has served as referee for *Asia Pacific Journal of Management, Thunderbird International Business Review* (TIBR), and *International Journal of Emerging Markets*. He serves as an editorial board member of the *International Journal of Emerging Markets*, and *International Journal of Automotive Technology and Management*. Wang received a PhD from Université Pierre Mendes France. Email: hwang@em-lyon.com.

Giovanni Balcet is Professor of International Business, University of Turin, Italy; Vice Director of the Turin Centre on Emerging Economies (OEET); former Professor of International Economics and lecturer at the Master "Management of Development", ILO International Centre, Turin; and Italian Delegate at the OECD Working Group on Globalization of Industry, Paris. He was Directeur d'Etudes Associé, Maison des Sciences de l'Homme, Paris, and visiting professor in several universities in Europe and Asia. His research works are devoted to global technology, international innovation processes, joint ventures and cooperative inter-firm behavior, industrial and trade policies in the age of globalization, and the global automotive industry. His recent publications include "Internationalization, Outsourcing and Labour Fragmentation. The case of FIAT," *Cambridge Journal of Economics* (2020); "Product Innovation in Emerging Economies: Product Architecture and Organisational Capabilities in Geely and Tata," *International Journal of Automotive Technology and Management* (2018); "Emerging Countries' Multinational Companies Investing in Developed Countries: At Odds with the HOS Paradigm?" *The European Journal of Comparative Economics* (2013); "Geely: A Trajectory of Catching up and Asset-Seeking Multinational Growth," *International Journal of Automotive Technology and Management* (2012). Email: giovanni.balcet@unito.it.

Wenxian Zhang has been a member of Rollins College faculty since 1995. He is a recipient of the Cornell Distinguished Faculty Service Award and is an Arthur Vining Davis Fellow, a member of the Asian Studies Program, and a full Professor in the College of Liberal Arts in Winter Park, Florida, USA. His recent academic books related to China include *Huawei Goes Global: Made in China for the World* (Vol. 1) and *Huawei Goes Global: Regional, Geopolitical Perspectives and Crisis Management* (Vol. 2) (Palgrave Macmillan, 2020), *China's Belt and Road Initiative: Changing the Rule of Globalization* (Palgrave Macmillan, 2018), *China Through American Eyes: Early Depictions of the Chinese People and Culture in the US Print Media* (World Scientific, 2018), *China*

Visualized by Americans 1840–1911 (Peking University Press, 2017), *The Entrepreneurial and Business Elites of China: The Chinese Returnees Who Have Shaped Modern China* (Emerald, 2011), *A Guide to the Top 100 Companies in China* (World Scientific, 2010), and *The Biographical Dictionary of New Chinese Entrepreneurs and Business Leaders* (Edward Elgar, 2009). Email: wzhang@rollins.edu.

Acknowledgments

The publication of *Geely Drives Out: The Rise of the New Chinese Automaker in the Global Landscape* is the result of the collaborative efforts across the globe, as three scholars based in three continents — Asia, Europe, and North America — came together to make this collective undertaking possible. We are most grateful to the leadership team of the Zhejiang Geely Holding Group, including Shufu Li, Conghui An, Dongsheng Li, Jinliang Liu, Victor Yang, Li Li, Jenny Jin, Chenxi Wang, Liming Tang, Qiang Xu, Huangfeng Luo, Ash Sutcliffe, and Fazil Taquiddin. During our research process, most of them have met with us in person and granted us access to corporate information needed for the project. We are also in debt to Mats Fägerhag, Gang Wei, Peter Horbury, Per Ferdell, Gunilla Gustavs, Ziyu Shen, Lars Danielson, Bastien Li, and Wenjia Luo, whose personal interviews have helped us gain a more comprehensive understanding of Geely, CEVT, and LEVC operations of recent years. In addition, we have enjoyed meetings with and gained academic insights from Professors Claes Alvstam, Ramsin Yakob, and Inge Inversson of the University of Gothenburg. Furthermore, the extension of our research framework in the conclusion section has greatly benefited from the Global DBA research work of Mrs. Peihua Li.

Every research project like this requires enormous support and encouragement. We deeply appreciate the patience and good humor of our families, friends, and colleagues. We would like to thank Tommaso Pardi of GERPISA for his enthusiastic endorsement of our academic undertaking. We gained deep inspiration for this book from annual international conferences and seminars organized by GERPISA, an international network devoted to academic and policy-oriented research on the global automobile industry. This project would not have been possible without the strong support from the administrative team at Emlyon Business School, especially Ms. Allie Mao and Ms. Cecile Huang; we also would like to acknowledge the efficient research assistance provided by Ms. Xieshu Wang of the University of Turin. In addition, Ms. Lixi Dong and Ms. Jayanthi M. of World Scientific Publishing Co. have provided us professional guidance and helped us move toward the final publication, also have our sincere gratitude.

Contents

List of Figures

List of Figures

List of Tables

Part I

The Growth of the Chinese Automobile Industry and the Rise of Geely Auto

Chapter 1

Introduction: A Rising Multinational Car-maker from an Emerging Economy

Abstract

The development of Geely as a privately owned automaker is a prime example of the powerful Chinese manufacturing economy in the 21st century. As multiple theories and models in international business can be used to study Geely's globalization efforts, Chapter 1 briefly reviews the underlying academic framework to explain the growth of the Chinese automaker as a rising multinational company from an emerging economy in a highly competitive global automobile market. The chapter also conducts a comprehensive academic examination on how Geely strives to transform itself from a traditional automobile company to a global mobility services and technology solutions provider.

Keywords: Geely; international business theories and models; globalization strategies.

1.1. Introduction

Since 2008, while the global automotive manufacturing has been faltering, the Chinese auto industry has swiftly transformed into the largest producer in the world. The growth of the Chinese automakers is a close reflection of the Chinese manufacturing economy, and Geely is one such best example. In this book, we closely examine the rise of Geely as a privately owned automaker in China. From its humble beginning as a refrigerator component maker and motorcycle manufacturer in the late 20th century, Geely has grown to become not only a top-selling national brand in China, the largest auto market in the world, but also a significant player in the global automotive industry. In this scholarly endeavor, we carefully study the successful acquisition of Volvo, within a long-term framework of asset-seeking foreign direct investment (FDI), and further investigate its other strategic initiatives with Daimler, London Taxi, PROTON, and Lotus. We believe this little-known carmaker is worth close investigation, not only through its product development, organizational dynamics, corporate culture, brand development, talent and cross-cultural management strategies but also through the entrepreneurship of its visionary founder Li Shufu. From catching up in technology to becoming a leader in product, service, and business model innovations, Geely has driven out as a new Chinese automaker on the world stage. Facing challenges in clean energy, Internet of Things, artificial intelligence, and new user experience toward smart and mobility solutions, Geely will likely continue to play an increasingly important role in the globalization age of the 21st century.

1.2. The Academic Framework of Geely's Globalization Drive

In the field of international business, despite multiple efforts, there is not yet a clearly articulated and widely accepted definition of a transnational corporation (TNC) or a worldwide enterprise. According to Pitelis and Sugden (2000), a multinational corporation (MNC) is a corporate organization that owns or controls production of goods or services in at least one country other than its home country, while the International Monetary Fund (IMF) defines an MNC as an incorporated enterprise of which a direct investor, who is a resident in another country, owns 10% or more of the ordinary shares or the voting power (IMF, 2008). In their study on the internationalization of FIAT, Balcet and Ietto-Gillies (2020) define a TNC as both an agent of fragmentation of production and an integrator of activities across space, business organizations, and countries. Irrespective of the definitions used, Geely Auto has undoubtedly become an MNC; what makes its growth so intriguing is it is a rising MNC from an emerging economy in a highly competitive global automobile market.

As a successful Chinese enterprise, Geely's story has been widely reported in the Chinese media; its rise as an emerging MNC or TNC has also caught the attention of international scholars. In his chapter titled "Geely Auto, Pioneer Grassroots Automaker," Feng (2018) documented Geely's unyielding struggle for survival in the face of central authorities' regulations, while Chu (2011) explored the entrepreneurship and bureaucratic control in the Chinese automotive industry. Wang (2008) first studied Geely's product innovations in quasi-open product architecture, and Balcet *et al.* (2012) closely examined Geely's catching up and asset-seeking strategies for international growth. After Geely's purchase of Volvo, Yakob *et al.* (2018) systematically scrutinized the company's foreign acquisitions aimed at strategic asset creation and innovation upgrading. Wang *et al.* (2018) also compared Geely with Tata in terms of product innovation capabilities, since both emerging MNCs have been operating in the same industrial sector. Alvstam and Ivarsson (2014) described Geely as a hybrid emerging market MNC, while Yakob (2018, 2019) further explored the company's management capacity development through international expansion. In addition, while Alvstam *et al.* (2019) studied Geely's operations from the perspective of global value chains, Vahlne *et al.* (2017) focused on the management's role in dealing with uncertainty and risk-taking in global expansion.

Multiple theories and models in international business can be used to study the rise of Geely on the global stage. Among them, three notions have often been used to examine firms' globalization strategies, namely, the industry-based view, the resource-based view, and the institution-based view. First promoted by Porter (1980), the industry-based view argues that conditions within an industry, to a large extent, determine a firm's internationalization strategy and performance. Advocated by Barney (1991), the resource-based view proposes that it is the firm-specific differences that drive its global strategy and performance. While these two influential views have been developed primarily in the field of strategic management, Peng and Delios (2006) offer the institution-based view as the third leg that helps sustain the "strategy tripod" of international business, which suggests that institutional factors determine the international expansion strategies of firms from emerging economies.

Examining from the perspectives of the firm-advantage–based theories, while the innovation-related model considers the multinational process as an innovation for the firm, Geely's initial overseas drives fit very well the widely known Uppsala Model, which frames the internationalization as a learning process when a firm incrementally intensifies its foreign market commitments to acquire market knowledge and promote international development (Johanson and Vahlne, 1977). Moreover, the resource-based theory is also suitable in describing Geely's international endeavors to acquire and control some strategic assets, namely physical resources (production technology, raw materials, and equipment), human resources (experience), and organizational resources (managerial and institutional structure) (Barney, 1991). As outlined by its acquisitions of DSI and Volvo, the addition of valuable and strategic resources has enabled Geely to build a certain competitive advantage required to improve its business efficiency, and in turn, corporate profits.

It is an interesting fact that Geely has initially chosen to showcase its newly developed model of *Chinese Dragon* in international auto exhibits, as the company essentially symbolizes the rise of a dragon enterprise. According to Mathews (2006), a dragon enterprise is an emerging MNC with three attributes: linkage, leverage, and learning. Specifically, linkage is conceived as a primary tool for mitigating risks and uncertainty in the international markets and for acquiring resources that are unavailable in the domestic market. Leverage reflects the accessibility of external resources, as a direct result of establishing linkages between an emerging firm and its foreign partners, while learning is the end result of repeating the application of the linkage and leveraging process. Here one cannot help but notice the successful partnership between Geely and Volvo is appropriately named Lynk & Co.

Furthermore, given the significant importance of pull factors of the host countries, the Imbalance and Springboard Approach based on the host-country advantage theories can also be used to further examine some of Geely's outward FDI, i.e. a launch pad or the springboard of MNC coming from emerging economies. By the same token, the Eclectic Paradigm Model is also useful in explaining the development of Geely as an emerging MNC in recent years. Known also as the Ownership, Location, and Internationalization (OLI) model, this theory argues that the multinational nature of a firm is attributed to three main advantages, namely ownership, location, and internalization (Dunning, 1995).

Evidently, no firm can operate in a vacuum. While examining the development of an emerging MNC, national and international trends, major issues and macro-environmental factors should also be carefully considered. Accordingly, the Investment Development Path (IDP) has become one of the widely utilized frameworks for interpreting a firm's internationalization process. More specifically, by combining both firm and host-country advantage theories, IDP explains which countries are going to engage in outward FDI and how the magnitude of this activity dynamically changes with the pace of the home country's economic development (Dunning, 1997). By focusing primarily on the dynamic interactions between the flows of both inward and outward FDIs and the pace of economic development, the IDP framework recognizes the influence of the home country's governmental policies on both flows of FDI; as a result, the net FDI flow (outward minus inward) evolves at a pace that reflects the dynamic relation to economic development (Sakr and Jordaan, 2016). Within this context, five stages of economic development have been outlined, starting from the stage where a country is a net FDI receiver, and ending in the maturity stage in which a country can attain noticeably high levels of both FDI flows (Narula and Dunning, 2000).

With regard to Geely, its surge on the global stage is an excellent case in point on the validity of the IDP framework. From a broad perspective, the Chinese government has certainly played a crucial role in the country's impressive development over the last 40 years, as its pro-growth policies have had profound impact on the rise of the so-called "dragon enterprises" in the 21st century. More specifically, Geely in the beginning has greatly benefited from technology transfers brought by inward FDIs during the era of economic reform and opening up, and the company has been taking the full advantage of the going-global policy launched by the Chinese government since the global economic recession of 2008. Examining from the firm's level, the IDP framework can also be used to adequately explain some of the internationalization endeavors by Geely in recent years, including market-seeking (PROTON) and strategic-asset–seeking (Volvo, DSI, and Lotus) initiatives, which will be further explored in detail in later chapters of the book. Accordingly, based on its global orientation motives, Geely can be classified as both a strategic-asset–seeking and market-seeking emerging MNC on the international stage.

From a small, private enterprise to an active player and innovation leader, Geely has witnessed very remarkable record of growth over the past two decades. Its technological catching up and internationalization endeavors can be better illustrated in Figure 1.1. Originally developed by Balcet *et al.* (2012), this "twin trajectories" model outlines Geely's initial development via reverse engineering and technology catchup, which led to low-cost production and eventually product architecture innovation. As a latecomer, Geely learned quickly and benefited greatly from the leading multinational auto manufacturers operating in China. After the company found its footing in the domestic market and reached a stable level of commercial success, it began its ambitious overseas expansion, naturally

Figure 1.1.   Geely's growth trajectory.

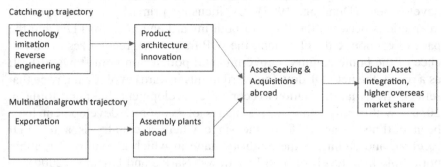

resulting in asset-seeking measures, such as the Volvo acquisition, to gain access to core technology and intellectual property rights in the global market. Through integrating both the technological catching up and international expansion strategies, Geely's trajectory of growth presents a solid case on the rise of the Chinese multinationals on the global stage in the 21st century.

1.3. The Rise of Geely in the Global Automobile Landscape

This academic work on the rise of Geely in the global automobile landscape is organized into four parts: Part I — The Growth of the Chinese Automobile Industry and the Rise of Geely Auto; Part II — Taking Geely to the World: Geely's Acquisition of Volvo; Part III — Geely's Further Expansion on the Global Stage; and Part IV — Geely's Strategic Transformation for the Future.

In Chapter 2, we offer an executive summary on the three-stage historical evolution of the Chinese automobile industry since the founding of the People's Republic of China in 1949. Focusing on the roles of government and its industrial policy, the interaction of MNCs and local car companies, we examine the future Chinese automobile industry in a context of *Made in China 2025* and the changing global geopolitical landscape, moving toward electrification, smart cars, and mobility solutions. In addition, we also discuss the hidden part of this industry, i.e. the volume-based production of low-speed cars for the "bottom of the pyramid" consumers, linking with the *de facto* dichotomy of Chinese economic structure.

In Chapter 3, we present an overview on the rise of Geely in the Chinese economic reform era. A successful global enterprise with Chinese roots, Geely is a privately held automotive group and a leading automobile manufacturer in China. From its humble beginning as a refrigerator component maker and motorcycle manufacturer in the late 20th century and catching up in technology to becoming a trailblazer in products, services, and business model innovations, Geely has survived against significant institutional and economic odds to become not only a top-selling brand and one of the most successful grassroots carmakers in China but also a rising player in the global automotive industry. A classic example of the rise of the private enterprises in the Chinese manufacturing economy, Geely has charged forward as a new Chinese automaker on the world stage.

In Chapter 4, we closely examine the entrepreneurship of Li Shufu, a visionary leader in the Chinese automobile industry. A grassroots billionaire businessman and an enduring symbol of entrepreneurship in the booming Chinese manufacture economy, Li Shufu has demonstrated to China and the world that vision and determination are the key ingredients to his remarkable success in launching and expanding Geely Auto, China's first private car company and a top-selling brand in the country, as well as a rising player in the global automotive market. Since 1997, Li has leveraged his manufacturing experience and entrepreneurial savvy to overcome multiple difficulties in a highly competitive field and risen to the challenge by putting together his dream of designing, manufacturing, and selling automobiles in China and other parts of the world.

In Part II of the book, we focus on the strategic acquisition of Volvo by Geely, the post-acquisition integration, cross-cultural management, and technology cooperation efforts between the two automakers. Chapter 5 provides an interpretative analysis on drivers, features, and results of the crucial acquisition by Geely. The purchase of Volvo Cars, concluded in 2010 and the culmination of an active search and a complex bargaining process, was a milestone in the multinational expansion of Geely. It was the most significant move in Geely's long-term international asset-seeking strategy (targeting technology, knowledge, brands, and capabilities) and the starting point of a new strategy of asset creation, innovation, and global expansion. Extended autonomy and independence were given to Volvo, based on the principle "Volvo is Volvo, Geely is Geely." As a result, Volvo rapidly and successfully expanded in China, while the opening of China Euro Vehicle Technology AB (CEVT) in Gothenburg created a key instrument for technology cooperation in the post-merger integration process.

Cross-culture relations and management deeply affect the performance of multinational corporations and the success or failure of post-acquisition integration processes. Cultural differences may cause poor performance and explain failures, but they may also give opportunities for creative sharing of knowledge, innovation, and synergies. In Chapter 6, we compare Swedish and Chinese corporate cultures, applying an analytical framework to the case of Geely and Volvo, and discussing relevant intercultural issues. We also illustrate the gradualist approach applied by Geely and explain how cross-culture cooperation successfully operated at CEVT in Gothenburg, creating convergences and synergies. We find that the initial negative coverage by Sweden's local media and skepticism by the civil society, trade unions and policy-makers eventually evolved into positive appreciation when local communities have observed tangible benefits from the presence of Geely in their territories.

In Chapter 7, we shift our focus to business cooperation, which needs to be supported and implemented by appropriate institutions. Since its establishment in 2013, CEVT represented the most impressive and fruitful instrument for the cooperation process between Geely and Volvo. Evolving from the previous "asset-seeking" strategy stage, based on imitation, learning, and technological catching up, CEVT opened a new stage that we can define as "asset augmentation" and "strategic asset creation," speeding up innovation in products and processes. We study the evolving strategies of CEVT and its original trajectory: from CEVT to the launch of the new Compact Modular Architecture (CMA) platform and finally to the new brand Lynk & Co in 2017, a globally focused car brand and a turning point of Geely's integration with Volvo.

In Part III of the book, we continue our review of Geely's other notable global expansion initiatives that include the recent equity investment in Daimler and its acquisitions of London Taxi, PROTON, and Lotus. In Chapter 8, we analyze the motivation and key process of Geely's indirect acquisition of Daimler's stake. Examining the complex financial operation by Geely, we outline the sophistication of acquisition by Geely, including its deep understanding on the regulations of host country (Germany in this case). With focus on the cases of two joint ventures, one on premium ride-hailing and another one on the *smart* car, we further study Geely's strategy upgrading, expanding from the traditional car toward intelligent electric vehicles and mobility services. In addition, we also highlight the phenomenon of reverse technology transfer, a platform developed by Geely to be used by the *smart* car of Daimler, and we provide a comprehensive review on Daimler's complex presence in China.

In Chapter 9, we study the progressive acquisition by Geely of London Taxi Company, as a part of its evolving strategy of asset-creating FDI developed in different stages. A first step in this trajectory took place in 2006, with the acquisition of shares from Manganese Bronze Holding (MBH), owner of London Taxi. This investment, a first acquisition in Europe, aimed at acquiring a highly valuable and globally recognized niche brand and improving the international exposure of Geely. Following the establishment of a joint venture, in 2008, taxicab production started in Shanghai. After full acquisition in 2013, it evolved into an asset-augmentation strategy, oriented to new electric vehicle technologies and products. Significantly, London Taxi was renamed London Electric Vehicle Company (LEVC). This evolutionary trajectory showed a remarkable capacity of Geely to absorb, integrate, and augment foreign assets within its international network, creating synergies with its firm-specific resources. Moreover, it was able to leverage from international partners to acquire new organizational capabilities.

In Chapter 10, we study Geely's strategic investment in PROTON and Lotus, with a key focus on its expansion in the Southeast Asian market. Due to intense domestic competition and market stagnation in recent years, Geely regards internationalization as a key growth strategy and an opportunity to expand its operations overseas. In 2017, Geely Auto entered into a new partnership to bring Malaysia's first national carmaker PROTON and the iconic British sports car brand Lotus under its corporate wings. While its expansion in Malaysia is seen as mainly market-seeking, its acquisition of Lotus is largely a strategic-asset–seeking move. As an example of the so-called dragon enterprises rising from China, Geely has essentially become a globalized enterprise with businesses covering the entire automotive industrial chain.

Part IV consists of the remaining chapters of the book, which concentrate on Geely's platform strategies, corporate culture, brand development, new mobility initiatives, and its transformation for the future. In Chapter 11, we provide a much-needed summary on the general introduction of product architecture and quasi-open product architecture by Chinese carmakers. After noting that Geely's first-stage development was mainly based on reverse engineering, we further investigate the complex process of changing platform strategy by Geely during the 2010s, i.e. Geely's own platform upgrading (FE, KC, NL), and the co-development of new Compact Modular Architecture (CMA) platform with Volvo at the same time. The chapter illustrates Geely's future ambition on the internalization of platform development capacity in B-segment Modular Architecture (BMA) and Sustainable Experience Architecture (SEA). We conclude the chapter with the hypothesis of future rationalization of platform strategy by the broader implementation of Volvo's platforms in CMA, SEA, and Scalable Product Architecture (SPA) to Geely's car brands when two entities further consolidate their assets in the coming years.

In Chapter 12, we examine the corporate cultures and brand development initiatives of Geely Auto over years. As Geely enters a new stage of development, the company has made great efforts to develop its corporate culture by clearly defining its vision and core values, and through a shared mission, the firm has united all different subsidiaries under the banner of Geely Holding for one common goal: transforming itself into a prominent automaker and technology leader in the global automobile industry. Guided by the notions of *making refined cars for everyone* and *making the safest, most environment-friendly and most energy-efficient vehicles*, Geely has also paid close attentions to its brand development, and after some experiments, the company has formulated a single-brand strategy that has contributed to the rise of Geely as a leading national auto brand in China in recent years.

In Chapter 13, we extend the analysis of Geely on its business model innovation, and its ambitious expansion toward Mobility as a Service (MaaS). We review Geely's four categories of mobility services by low-speed EVs (*Microcity*), economic EVs (*EVcoming*), mid-range cars (*Cao Cao*), and premium cars (*StarRides* with Daimler). We also examine two incremental innovations by Geely, the connection between high-speed train and ride-hailing services, and the launch of low-orbit satellites for the service of high-precision positioning, as well as two radical innovation initiatives, the high-speed train and flying cars. We conclude with the analysis of Geely Holding's organizational structure that supports the business model innovation, while questioning the necessity of rationalization and optimization.

1.4. Final Remarks

The international automotive industry is currently undergoing an important transitional period. The new era calls for not only new energy solutions in automobile design and manufacturing but also strategic partnerships and close collaborations around the world. Through our research, we find that constant innovation and improvement have become a part of Geely's corporate culture. In response to the evolving conditions in the global market, Geely has embraced a culture of change and rapid development while keeping its eyes on the future and a long-term horizon.

To become globally competitive, the company has made some significant investments in order to develop new technologies and create better experiences for its consumers. As its mission is to *Take Geely to the World*, Geely's management team, especially its chairman Li Shufu, should be recognized for facilitating its bold internationalization drives in recent years. By demonstrating a forward-looking vision for its growth and development, Li and his team have formulated some impressive globalization strategies. To better manage its strategic transformation, Geely readjusted its senior leadership team in late 2020, with Li Donghui as the CEO of the Zhejiang Geely Holding Group, An Conghui as President of Geely Holding Group and President and CEO of Geely Auto Group, Wei Mei as VP of Geely Holding for human resources and President of Geely University, Feng Qingfeng as VP for strategic innovation and technology, Cheng Yiming as VP for group legal affairs, Wei Zhiling as VP for government affairs, and Yang Xueliang as VP for group communication and public relations (Geely, 2020).

By serving both the Chinese and international markets with fuel-efficient, reliable, safe, and technologically high-value models, Geely has greatly expanded its business outreach and created a varied portfolio of automotive brands from all over the world. By focusing on new energy sources, artificial intelligence, autonomous driving, and total mobility solutions, Geely has strived to transform itself from a traditional automobile company to a mobility services and technology solutions provider. In essence, Geely is actively transforming itself from a market follower in automobile manufacturing to a new leader in total mobility solutions and digital and electric innovations on the global stage.

References

Alvstam, C. G. and I. Ivarsson (2014). The 'Hybrid' Emerging Market Multinational Enterprise — The Ownership Transfer of Volvo Cars to China. In *Asian Inward and Outward FDI: New Challenges in the Global Economy*, C. Alvstam, H. Dolles and P. Ström (eds.), London: Palgrave Macmillan, pp. 217–242.

Alvstam, C., I. Ivarsson and B. Petersen (2019). Are multinationals and governments from emerging economies configuring global value chains in new ways? *International Journal of Emerging Markets*, **15**:1, 111–130.

Balcet, G. and G. Ietto-Gillies (2020). Internationalisation, outsourcing and labour fragmentation: The case of FIAT. *Cambridge Journal of Economics*, **44**, 105–128.

Balcet, G., H. Wang and X. Richet (2012). Geely: A trajectory of catching up and asset-seeking multinational growth. *International Journal of Automotive Technology and Management*, **12**:4, 360–375.

Barney, J. (1991). Firm resources and sustained competitive advantage. *Journal of Management*, **17**:1, 99–120.

Chu, W.-w. (2011). Entrepreneurship and bureaucratic control: The case of the Chinese automotive industry. *China Economic Journal*, **4**:1, 65–80.

Feng, Q. (2018). *Variety of Development: Chinese Automakers in Market Reform*. Cham, Switzerland: Palgrave Macmillan, 153–184.

Dunning, J. H. (1995). Reappraising the eclectic paradigm in an age of alliance capitalism. *Journal of International Business Studies*, **26**:3, 461–491.

Dunning, J. H. (1997). Alliance capitalism and global business. *Journal of International Business Studies*, **28**:4, 866–868.

Geely (2020). Group management. Zhejiang Geely Holding Group. Available at: http://zgh.com/group-management/?lang=en (accessed December 6, 2020).

International Monetary Fund (2008). *Balance of Payments and International Investment Position Manual*, Washington DC.

Johanson, J. and J.-E. Vahlne (1977). The internationalization process of the firm — A model of knowledge development and increasing foreign market commitments. *Journal of International Business Studies*, **8**:1, 23–32.

Mathews, J. A (2006). Dragon multinationals: New players in the 21st century globalization. *Asia Pacific Journal of Management*, **23**:1, 5–27.

Narula, R. and J. H. Dunning (2000). Industrial development, globalization and multinational enterprises: new realities for developing countries. *Oxford Development Studies*, **28**:2, 141–167.

Peng, M. W. and A. Delios (2006). What determines the scope of the firm over time and around the world? An Asia Pacific perspective. *Asia Pacific Journal of Management*, **23**, 385–405.

Pitelis, C. and R. Sugden (2000). *The Nature of the Transnational Firm*. London: Routledge, H72.

Porter, M. E. (1980). *Competitive Strategy*. New York: Free Press.

Sakr, M. and A. Jordaan (2016). Emerging multinational corporations: Theoretical and conceptual framework. *Economic Research Southern Africa (ERSA) Working Paper* 574.

Vahlne, J-E., M. Hamberg and R. Schweizer (2017). Management under uncertainty — the unavoidable risk-taking. *Multinational Business Review*, **25**:2, 91–109.

Wang, H. (2008). Innovation in product architecture: A study of the Chinese automobile industry. *Asia Pacific Journal of Management*, **25**, 509–535.

Wang, H., C. Kimble and G. Balcet (2018). Product innovation in merging economies: Product architecture and organisational capabilities in Geely and Tata. *International Journal of Automotive Technology and Management*, **18**:4, 384–405.

Yakob, R. (2018). Augmenting local managerial capacity through knowledge collectivities: The case of Volvo Car China. *Journal of International Management*, **24**, 386–403.

Yakob, R., H. R. Nakamura and P. Ström (2018). Chinese foreign acquisitions aimed for strategic asset-creation and innovation upgrading: The case of Geely and Volvo Cars. *Technovation*, **70/71**, 59–72.

Yakob, R. (2019). Context, competencies, and local managerial capacity development: A longitudinal study of HRM implementation at Volvo Car China. *Asian Business & Management*. doi:10.1057/s41291-019-00080-4.

Chapter 2

The Automotive Industry in China: An Overview

Abstract

This chapter offers an executive summary on the three-stage historical evolution of the Chinese automobile industry since the founding of the People's Republic of China in 1949. Focusing on the roles of government and its industrial policy, the interaction of multinational corporations (MNCs) and local car companies, this chapter examines the future Chinese automobile industry in a context of *Made in China 2025* and the changing global geopolitical landscape, moving toward electrification, smart cars, and mobility solutions. In addition, the chapter also reveals the hidden part of this industry — high-volume production of low-speed cars for the "bottom of the pyramid" consumers — linking it with the *de facto* dichotomy of the Chinese economic structure.

Keywords: Chinese automobile industry; Industrial policy; FDI; MNC.

2.1. China: The Biggest Automobile Industry Since 2009

The year 2010 was a turning point in terms of the global manufacturing landscape. China overtook the US to become the world's largest manufacturing nation, accounting for 19.8% of the world's manufacturing output, compared to 19.4% by the US. According to Robert Allen (2011), a leading economic historian and the author of *Global Economic History*, China has thus closed a 500-year cycle in economic history (Marsh, 2011). From the historical perspective, the last time China took the leadership position of goods producer was around the year 1850. Then, UK ushered in the Industrial Revolution and held this position for around 50 years, followed by the US as the world's biggest manufacturing nation for around 110 years (1900–2010). Since 2010, China has taken over the leader's position by progressively improving its productivity and enhancing technology-intensive innovation, namely *Made in China 2025* program, a mid-term strategy, to illustrate the nation's ambition.

As for the Chinese automobile industry, it reached global leadership in terms of annual sales in 2009, overtaking the US market. Between 2008 and 2012, the market doubled in size, from 9.38 million to 19.3 million units. According to the China Association of Automobile Manufacturers (CAAM), 25.769 million cars were sold in 2019, despite the slowdown of nation's economy and the China–US trade conflict. This size of annual sales is roughly more than double the size of the US, around 2.9 times of Japanese industry, and far bigger than any European country's auto sector. The total volume of vehicle production of the three emerging countries, Brazil, Russia, and India, amounted to 9.82 million units, representing only 35% of that of China (Table 2.1).

Table 2.1.   Top 10 countries of vehicle production, 2000–2019.

	Country	2018	2015	2010	2005	2000
1	China	27,809,196	24,503,326	18,264,761	5,717,619	2,069,069
2	United States	11,314,705	12,100,095	7,743,093	11,946,653	12,799,857
3	Japan	9,728,528	9,278,321	9,628,920	10,799,659	10,140,796
4	India	5,174,645	4,160,585	3,557,073	1,638,674	801,360
5	Germany	5,120,409	6,033,164	5,905,985	5,757,710	5,526,615
6	Mexico	4,100,525	3,565,469	2,342,282	1,684,238	1,935,527
7	South Korea	4,028,834	4,555,957	4,271,741	3,699,350	3,114,998
8	Brazil	2,879,809	2,429,463	3,381,728	2,530,840	1,681,517
9	Spain	2,819,565	2,733,201	2,387,900	2,752,500	3,032,874
10	France	2,270,000	1,972,000	2,229,421	3,549,008	3,348,361
World		95,634,593	90,780,583	77,629,127	66,482,439	58,374,162

Source: Organisation Internationale des Constructeurs d'Automobiles (OICA). Available at: https://en.wikipedia.org/wiki/List_of_countries_by_motor_vehicle_production Accessed June 18, 2020.

Meanwhile, China's car ownership is relatively low, with only about 173 out of every 1,000 people owning a car. This ownership is markedly lower than other developing markets, such as Malaysia (433) and Russia (373), not to mention leading markets like the US (837), Australia (747), and Italy (695). China also lags far behind other major automotive markets in terms of car ownership per kilometer of expressway, which provides a further indicator of the strong potential of the domestic passenger car market.

China is preparing for the future disruptive innovation of the automobile industry, including the expansion to electric vehicles (EVs), smart cars, and mobility solutions. The Chinese government, together with multinational and local companies, is accelerating in those fields, through the standardization of guidelines and openness to trials of autonomous driving, and vehicles-to-everything communication (V2X, i.e. vehicle to vehicle and its environment), boosted by the newly launched 5G technology.

The Chinese automobile industry is a very interesting case to study both in terms of business and economy. Key topics include:

(1) The possibility of China to lead the paradigm change in the future global automobile industry;
(2) The dynamics of multinational corporations (MNCs) strategy in China;
(3) The increasing competition between Chinese and foreign companies;
(4) The emerging MNCs (EMNCs) from China — a typical case is Geely, for which we will have an in-depth study;
(5) The complex China regulation system (termed as the Chinese federalism), and its impact on the industrial policy, and the interaction of local–international institutions.

2.2. MNCs and Hundreds of Local Carmakers

Behind the impressive Chinese auto production figures, there is a landscape of over 120 carmakers, mixed with the MNCs and local players. For the passenger car segment, all the global players have established at least two Sino–foreign joint ventures, including Shanghai GM, SAIC–GM–Wuling, Shanghai Volkswagen, FAW Volkswagen, FAW Mazda, Beijing Hyundai, Beijing Benz, BMW Brilliance, Chang'an Ford, Chang'an Mazda, Chang'an PSA, Chang'an-Suzuki, Tianjin FAW Toyota,

Guangzhou Honda, Guangzhou Toyota, Guangzhou Fiat Chrysler, Guangzhou Mitsubishi, Dongfeng Peugeot Citroen, Dongfeng Nissan, Dongfeng Honda, Dongfeng Volvo, Chery Jaguar Land Rover, and Jiangling Ford, among the others.

Foreign brands dominated the market in the first decade of the 21st century. The market share of foreign car companies in the form of joint ventures (JVs) was 85% in 2009, which then progressively reduced to around 60% by the late 2010s. Among the top 10 brands by sales, 6 are foreign brands, including Volkswagen, Honda, Toyota, Buick, and Hyundai (Table 2.2). Volkswagen, the earliest player to enter the Chinese market, has the leadership position. For all the global carmakers, the China market is at the center of their long-term growth strategies.

Some Chinese carmakers, despite operating in a highly fragmented market, have demonstrated the dynamics of catching up and innovation to try and capture a bigger market share. Their market shares increased from 29% in 2010 to around 40% in 2018. Among the top 20 car brands, the market shares of Chinese brands were 35%. The leading brand is Geely, followed by Baojun and Chang'an. The market shares of the top 20 car brands out of a total 90 car brands were 76% (Table 2.2). Thus, in the "long tail" part, there are at least 45 Chinese brands.

The creation of Sino–foreign joint ventures by leading original equipment manufacturers (OEMs) like Volkswagen, and their component localization system, has positive spillover effects on the Chinese auto industry. Chinese cars, both state-owned (Chery, Chang'an, etc.) or private owned (Geely, Great Wall, etc.) underwent a long learning curve, moving from imitation to innovation and the creation of their own supply chain system. Low-cost, low-price competition is the common practice for entering the market segment of below RMB 80,000 (US$11,533). In the last decade, Chinese competitors have been constantly improving the product design and quality control, deepening their understanding of the local consumer needs, and even the business model innovation in the field of mobility solutions. The best-performing segment for Chinese carmakers vis-à-vis international brands is the sport utility vehicle (SUV). Chinese brands take 60% of market share, and the price range expands to RMB 150,000 (US$21,625). This commercial result demonstrates the increasing competitiveness of Chinese carmakers (Accenture, 2013).

Looking forward, the year 2022 will be another important milestone for the new landscape of the China automobile industry. Further opening-up policies will be implemented, especially the cancellation on the foreign

Table 2.2.   Top 20 car brands by sales in China (2018).

Ranking	Brand	Sales	%	Category
1	Volkswagen	3,129,743	17	German
2	Honda	1,452,441	8	Japanese
3	Geely	1,382,119	8	Chinese
4	Toyota	1,243,202	7	Japanese
5	Nissan	1,177,705	7	Japanese
6	Buick	1,057,452	6	American
7	Baojun	879,077	5	Chinese
8	Chang'an	851,361	5	Chinese
9	Hyundai	790,746	4	South Korean
10	Haval	766,062	4	Chinese
11	Chevrolet	673,376	4	American
12	Audi	620,300	3	German
13	GAC	53,6267	3	Chinese
14	Mercedes-Benz	513,108	3	German
15	BYD	507,127	3	Chinese
16	SAIC Roewe	479,156	3	Chinese
17	Wuling	476,539	3	American
18	BMW	465,044	3	German
19	Chery	443,702	2	Chinese
20	Dongfeng	440,413	2	Chinese
Total of top 20		17,884,940	76	—
	Chinese brands	628,2667	35	—
	European brands	4,728,195	26	—
	Japanese brands	3,873,348	22	—
	American brands	1,730,828	10	—
	Korean brands	790,746	4	—
	Sino-foreign brands	11,703,896	65	—
Total of 90 car models		23,423,936	—	—

Note: Figures only include locally produced models, excluding imported cars of the same brand, which make up only a small portion of sales in China.
Source: http://carsalesbase.com/china-car-sales-analysis-2018-brands/

ownership restriction (earlier, foreign investors could hold a maximum of 50% equity share). International players might reinforce the investment on this largest overseas market, either via increasing shares in JVs or creating sole proprietorship. Decision-making on management and technology transfer may progress quicker. The Chinese partners of JVs, almost all being state-owned companies, are facing higher pressure to weaken control and thus profitability. Chinese private companies are already experiencing polarization — as leading companies like Geely and BYD are growing and entering into international partnerships, small companies will face a higher possibility of market exit.

The above scenarios, which seem more promising to MNCs in China, needs to be nuanced. It mainly focuses on the anticipation of internal combustion cars. For the new energy vehicle, PWC (2018) predicted a market size of 5 million in 2025, and Chinese brands will take major shares through a neck-to-neck competition with global brands. Other potential battlefields where Chinese carmakers may take big market shares include mobility solutions, smart vehicles, and 5G-technology–based V2X mobility network.

2.3. A Brief Historical Review on the Industrial Development

The evolution of the Chinese automobile industry is replete with complexity (Harwit, 1995; Chin, 2010; McGunagle, 2007). Below is a quick overview on the three main stages of development.

2.3.1. *Infant stage in the planned economy (1949–1979)*

When the People's Republic of China was founded in 1949, there was virtually no automotive industry. The First Automobile Works (FAW), founded in 1953 in the northern part of China (Changchun city, Jilin Province), which was the first truck manufacturing plant, was the result of USSR's support. The production mode was a duplication of Ford's Rouge Plant in Detroit, first copied by USSR engineers during the 1930s and then transferred to China. Trucks branded *Jiefang* (Liberation) started production in 1956, with 1,600 units annually assembled. Limousines for senior officials, *Hongqi* (Red Flag), was made by craftsmanship with very limited number.

During the 1960s, several key geopolitical contexts greatly shaped the infant-stage development of the Chinese automobile industry. The deterioration and breakdown of China's relationship with the USSR in 1960 ended with the withdrawal of thousands of Soviet experts and sudden termination of contracts. The car industry had to develop in a self-sufficient way. The 1960s was the period of the Cold War for China. There were frequent boarder conflicts, including the border war with India in 1962, the involvement in Vietnam War in 1965, and later skirmishes with the USSR. To prepare for other possible wartime needs, the central government decided to build a series of heavy and medium military purpose truck plants in the remote and isolated mountain areas away from the boarder. This gave the birth to the Second Automobile Works, now commonly known as *Dongfeng* (East Wind), the Sichuan Auto Works, and the Shaanxi Auto Works. FAW played key role in technology transfer for setting up some of those plants. Together with FAW, Dongfeng — now one of the leading state-owned car groups — has JVs with Peugeot-Citroen, Nissan, Honda, and Kia.

2.3.2. *The proliferation stage in the early opening-up period (1979–2000)*

Deng Xiaoping, after the chaotic period of Cultural Revolution (1966–1976), took the leadership mantle and decided to open up the Chinese economy. This period marked the early stage of ideological and economic shift from a planned economy toward market mechanism with socialist features. Provincial and municipal governments were actively involved in boosting the local industry and economy. The number of automobile factories increased from 55 in 1979 to 114 in 1985. The proliferation of Chinese carmakers was mainly attributed to two forces: (1) a wave of decentralization of planning from central government to regional governments and (2) the thirst for different types of vehicles that was severely limited during the past planned economy period.

In the 1980s, regional governments had strong motivation to boost the industrialization in their respective regions. A range of small vehicle manufacturers invested by regional governments were established. It is also worth to mention that, in the planned economy period, the entire automobile industry was fragmented and was at the hand of different ministries. For example, the Ministries of the Weapons Industry and the Aviation Industry produced military vehicles, Ministry of Public Security assembled Police Cars, Ministry of Public Health made ambulances, etc. This particular phenomenon of decentralization is the *de facto* co-existence of relative autonomy of provinces and powerful ministries in China and is termed as Chinese federalism (Montinola *et al.*, 1995; Qian and Weingast, 1996, 1997; Qian and Roland, 1998; Blanchard and Shleifer, 2001).

During this period, jointly with regional governments, small-scale factories managed by ministries were relatively more flexible and were at the frontline of producing new vehicle types such as light trucks, mini vans, and large passenger cars. Those new vehicle types were manufactured first to satisfy the taxi market and then for institutional (company, government) clients. The passenger car for the individual was marginal at this stage. Vehicle types made by the newly established companies were complementary to those by existing players like FAW and Dongfeng.

Foreign direct investment (FDI) in the late 1980s opened a new chapter of Chinese automobile development. Right after the first JV between state-owned Beijing Automobile Industry Corporation (BAIC) and American Motors Corporation (AMC) in January 1984, named Beijing-Cherokee, Volkswagen signed a JV contract in October 1984 for the production of the Santana model at Shanghai-Volkswagen Automotive Company Ltd., in partnership with the state-owned Shanghai Automotive Industry Corporation (SAIC). In 1991, FAW-Volkswagen Automotive Company Ltd. was established. Starting from Completely Knocked Down (CKD) assembling, very soon a system of localization of components, with the strong support of local governments, was progressively implemented. This was the origin of a broad technology transfer and spillover, not only at the OEM level but also at the component supply chain level. In the 1990s, more foreign carmakers entered the China market after observing the huge commercial success of Volkswagen (Richet *et al.*, 2001).

During this period, the first China automobile industrial policy was promulgated in 1994, right after the industry was designated as one of the "pillar industries." The policy illustrated four key objectives of future development: (1) the consolidation via establishment of large groups; (2) the clarification on the regulation of Sino–foreign JVs and the stimulation on technology transfer, including the clear restriction on the tapped equity share; (3) the enhancement of the product development capacity and the components industry; and (4) the promotion of individual car ownership. The future development of the Chinese automobile industry illustrated both the positive and negative impacts of this industrial policy (Li *et al.*, 2000; Wang, 2003; Chu, 2011; Chan and Daim, 2012), but it is undeniable that the ambition of making automobile as the Chinese "pillar industry" has almost become true.

2.3.3. *Assume global production and sales leadership (2001–2020)*

China's accession to the World Trade Organization (WTO) was the nation's audacious strategy to seek entry into global markets. Prior to the accession, there were fierce debates on the pros and cons at the level of the automobile industry. The Chinese automobile industry was still identified to be at the stage of infancy and thus was highly protected by high import tariffs (to hinder the import competition) and strict request on local content requirement (to stimulate the technology transfer by foreign companies). After the accession in 2001, those two key protective measures were progressively released. The growth of the industry was immediate. Production increased by 38.8% and 36.7% in 2002 and 2003, respectively. By 2003, China already became the third largest auto market in the world. The pessimistic scenarios that were drawn up in the late 1990s gradually faded away.

The accession to the WTO and the booming of the Chinese market triggered massive FDI at all levels, including OEMs and suppliers. Regional governments provided significant capital, land, and preferential policies to stimulate investment. A wave of proliferation of new projects reached such a significant level that the central government urged to implement selected economic "cooling-down" policies, by discouraging bank lending and slowing down the speed of approval for investments. Despite the macro-economy control, the annual output of car production and sales still climbed by 14.1%, to 5.071 million units in 2004.

The automobile industry policy was revised and published in 2004. There were at least three significant changes, where the policy (1) stressed the importance of market mechanism of resource allocation, rather than government-prescriptive policies; (2) drew a holistic picture, by expanding automobile industry to its coordination with other related industries, e.g. material industries, mechanic industries, transportation infrastructure, and environmental protection; and (3) highlighted the importance of creation of indigenous intellectual property and brands, including the R&D of both EVs and related technologies like batteries. The industrial structure consolidation was still the key message, and the government fixed the clear objective of making large Chinese automobile groups become listed in Fortune 500 by 2010. This second version of the automobile industry policy mirrored the significant effort of economic reform of the Chinese government toward a "a socialist market economy with Chinese characteristics."

Government policies also exhibited significant power during the global financial crisis triggered in 2008. Stunning growth rates of 49.7% and 33.9% were realized in 2009 and 2010, respectively. This skyrocketing growth was mainly attributed to the government stimulation policies. Under the 2008–2009 national stimulus package of RMB 4 trillion (US$586 billion), the "Planning for Restructuring and Revitalization of the Auto Industry" was published in January 2009. Among various measures include the further release of constraints on the purchase process (limitation on the number of car purchases in large cities, limitation on car type, high charge on fees during the car usage), the central government allocated RMB 5 billion (US$733 million) as compensations for consumers in rural areas to replace used cars (Wang, 2015).

This is an interesting period to analyze the interaction of domestic and international institutions and its impact on industrial development. Institutions are composed of both formal legal framework (rules, law, and regulatory regimes) and informal restrictions (behavioral norm, customs, and self-imposed behavioral rules — Peng *et al.*, 2008; Peng and Pleggenkuhle-Miles, 2009). It should be noted that international institutions like the WTO also played important roles to regulate and shape the Chinese automobile industry. For example, China had to progressively conform with international standards and procedures, including "the trade-related investment measures (TRIMs)" and "the trade-related intellectual property rights (TRIPs)." It is only after the accession of the WTO that the market economy part of "socialist market economy with Chinese characteristics" has been further demonstrated.

In 2009, for the first time ever, China became the world biggest automobile market in terms of annual sales, overtaking the US market. Since then, the automobile industry constantly expanded production volumes and reached the threshold of 20 million units in 2013, approaching the threshold of 30 million in 2017 and 2018 (Figure 2.1). China marked the first sales decline in 2018 in the last 28 years, by 2.8%.

From the perspective of industrial clusters, China's automobile industry is basically composed of six major clusters: two in the North (Jilin Province and Beijing municipality), one in the Eastern coast region

Figure 2.1. Vehicle sales in China (million units, 2009–2018).

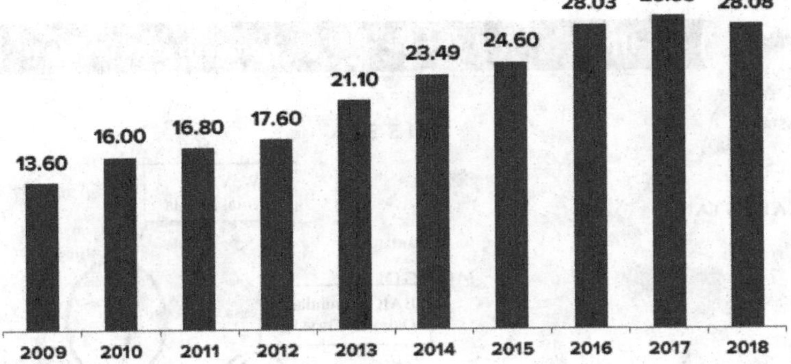

Source: China Association of Automobile Manufacturers.

(Shanghai municipality, Zhejiang and Jiangsu Provinces), one in the South (Guangdong Province), one in Central (Hubei Province), and one in the West (Sichuan Province and Chongqing municipality) (Figure 2.2). All the clusters have several key players of Sino–foreign JVs and Chinese private companies. The Eastern coast region is the biggest, accounting close to 40% of cars and auto parts. The quick development in the Central and Western regions of China's auto clusters, in line with the growing purchasing power and industrial development of those regions, is the new trend.

The persistence of small quantity production by hundreds of carmakers in China till 2020 is noteworthy, which is well below the minimum economies of scale according to the world automobile industry level. This fact is mainly attributed to the complex institutional relationship between enterprises and local governments. Regional governments in China, in the interest of supporting local economic development, and for employment stability, have strong incentive to grant subsidies and bank loans via locally controlled state-owned banks, to keep the operation of those companies, even at the stage of low-performing, or "zombie enterprises" (Jiang *et al.*, 2017).

2.4. Dual-Structure of the Market — Hidden Fact

2.4.1. *Booming of farm vehicles in the late 1990s*

In the rural areas of China, between 1980s and 2000s, there was virtually an ignored market, termed farm vehicles (FVs). The FV is a new vehicle

Figure 2.2.   Automotive clusters in China — by main JVs.

Source: Compiled by authors.

type with three or four wheels — most of the 3-wheelers is made with single-cylinder diesel engines originally designed for stationary agricultural machinery. FVs aimed to satisfy the multiple purposes of farmers (for agricultural activities and as the tool of people and good transportation) at significantly low prices (in average less than half of the conventional light trucks or vans). Easy product architecture, comprising a combination of technology of tractors and light trucks, led hundreds of small enterprises in the rural areas to rush into the business. The production volume peaked in 2002, with over 3 million FVs produced, which was three times that of conventional passenger cars in the same year. The vehicle population reached about 22 million in 2001 (Sperling *et al.*, 2005).

In contrast to the traditional Chinese automobile sector, FVs did not receive support from the government — companies that manufactured FVs were not listed or registered in the Chinese automobile industry registry. Prior to the mid-1980s, the FV was classified as a type of farm machinery, managed by the Ministry of Agriculture, and benefited from advantageous taxation comparing to conventional vehicles. The significant growth speed and volume of FV triggered the attention of the Ministry of Machinery in 1987. Since then, a series of standards and norms were fixed in terms of product specification, test method, safety, and engine emission, followed by policies published by the Ministry of Public Security in 1993 in terms of additional safety standards and vehicle registration, driver training, and driver licensing. In 2006, the term FV was officially abandoned. Since then, 3-wheel FV has been renamed 3-wheel vehicles, and 4-wheel FV as low-speed truck, thus being officially integrated into the Chinese vehicle category.

The tightening on industrial regulations and technology standards accelerated the industrial consolidation. The number of enterprises meeting the new norms of FV dropped from 204 in 2001 to 120 in 2002. Market concentration accelerated. The market share of the top 10 enterprises producing three wheelers increased from 59.5% to 65% and from 93% to 96% for top 10 four-wheeler producers. Leading companies were Shifeng and Juli, accounting for 61% of the three-wheelers market with the capacity of volume production (Wang, 2002). For example, Shifeng produced 1.35 million FVs, 1.4 million unit of engines, and 3.35 million tires in 2012.

2.4.2. *Millions of low-speed EVs in the late 2000s*

A type of low-speed EVs (LSEVs) for passengers started production around 2007 (Wang and Kimble, 2011). By nature, this is a type of electric passenger car for low-income consumers. LSEV is an interesting Chinese case of frugal innovation, tapping the market of the bottom of the pyramid (BOP) (Radjou *et al.*, 2012). The typical LSEV has a simple structure; top speed of between 40–70 km/h, a cruising distance of 80 km, 100 km, or

150 km; and costs between RMB¥20,000 and RMB¥40,000 (US$3,100 and US$6,200), much cheaper than a traditionally compact car. Different from the target consumer segment of FVs, which was mainly farmers, consumers of LSEV are mainly located in tier 3 and 4 cities, and small town and villages.

Companies producing LSEVs come from a range of different industries. Leading companies include Shifeng, which has expanded its production of FVs. Yujie, Lichi, Baoya, and Levdeo entered into this segment either from scratch or used to produce electric-powered golf carts, mini sports and entertainment vehicles, or special-purpose vehicles like post office vehicles or ambulances.

Not being officially listed as a vehicle type in China, the mechanism of statistic is not actuating comparing that of data from the Chinese automobile industry. Specialized consulting company estimated that the annual sales was over 200,000, then 400,000, and close to 700,000 between 2013 and 2015. In 2018, the annual production and sales was over one million, by over 100 companies. Shandong Province produced 695,900 LSEVs and has a cumulative ownership of 3 million LSEVs.

A similar interesting phenomenon is the duplication of Chinese federalism — a game between the central government and local authorities in the LSEV industry. Behind impressive production and sales figure, there is the evidence of support by local governments, in contrast to the various types of restriction by the central government. LESV's production and usage was first legalized in three big provinces of its production — Shandong, Hebei, and Henan — and then extended to over 100 towns or counties in over 20 provinces. Some cities of those provinces issue dedicated vehicle licenses for LESVs. The local government also provides financial support to develop the supply chain of the industry, including battery and motor. In some small cities, public charging infrastructures are developed by even providing free charging. Local LSEV associations have been created (Chen and Midler, 2016).

However, the attitude of the central government toward this grass-root industry was skeptical. After years of double-digit growth of this *de facto* LSEV industry, the central government body (the State Council and the National Development and Reform Commission) issued related regulations to tighten the technology barrier in June 2014. In November 2018, six ministries jointly published official notice to further regulate the LSEV. In addition, the central government also established a supervision mechanism on the implementation of replacing non-qualified LSEVs on the road, and this should be part of the local government official's performance evaluation. In summary, the overall principle and signal is discouragement on the further development of LSEV (Wang and Kimble, 2012).

2.4.3. *Understanding the dual-economy structure in China*

FVs and LSEVs, both having an annual market size of over one million units, are interesting illustrations of the existence of the dual-economy structure, originally elaborated by Lewis (1954), wherein an economy in developing countries have two distinct sectors — agricultural and industrial. Despite the impressive economic growth of China after the opening up in the late 1970s, the per capita annual income of rural households in 2018 was RMB 14,617.03 (US$2,107.3), less than a third of those who live in urban areas, at RMB 39,250 (US$5,658) (Figure 2.3). According to the *China Statistical Yearbook 2019*, China still has 551.62 million people living in rural areas, representing 39.40% of the Chinese population. Their low purchasing power, and inelastic needs of transportation, both for production and consumption purposes, was the strong foundation for low-cost vehicles, a huge untapped market for conventional carmakers.

On the other side of the coin, the industrialization and massive production of low-cost and low-price vehicles in the Chinese rural areas, compared to much industrialized automobile clusters in China, provides a

Figure 2.3.   Income per capita in Chinese urban and rural areas, 1990–2018.

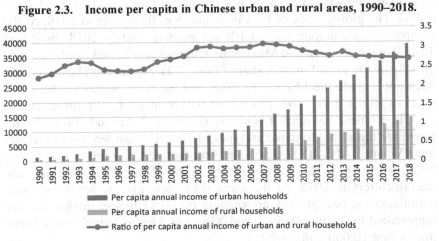

Per capita annual income of urban households
Per capita annual income of rural households
Ratio of per capita annual income of urban and rural households

Source: http://www.stats.gov.cn/tjsj/ndsj/

rich field of observation for new growth theories. This is a wave of creating indigenous automobile segment. There is neither direct involvement of FDI nor official central government support. It is a form of industrialization based on the demand of low-income people, and domestic inter-industry technological spillover from matured automobile or mechanical industries. Peoples in rural areas and small cities are both producers and consumers of those products, thus creating a new circle of industrialization and urbanization, and positively contributing to the dynamic evolution of the dual-economy structure. In the very long run, there is the possibility of moving toward economy convergence, via the increase in income level, human capital, technology intensity, and more skilled workers in the rural areas (Banerjee and Newman, 1993; Mesnard, 2001; Rapoport, 2002; Yuki, 2007). An in-depth study is worthy of analysis to determine the growth–inequality–poverty linkages and development in the long run.

2.5. Leapfrogging Toward Smart EVs and Disruptive Innovation

2.5.1. *China's leadership in EVs in the early 21st century*

China has become the biggest market of electric passenger car production. Furthermore, its market share of EVs on the road increased from 39% in 2017 to around 45% in 2018, double the size of Europe (24%), and the US (22%). The global stock of EVs is around 5 million units in 2018. At the company level, among top 20 EV car models sold in 2018, including Tesla, Nissan, Toyota, and Mitsubishi, Chinese cars models took 11 seats, or 34% of the global market share (Table 2.3). Again, the above statistic does not include the LSEVs we described earlier. Combining these two types of EVs, China's total production will be at least 2.2 million EVs.

The Chinese EV market is highly fragmented. Around 500 manufacturers are registered to make all types of EVs. Current leaders in producing EVs are BAIC, BYD, Jianghuai Automotive Corporation (JAC), and SAIC for its brand Roewe, and Chery, all listed in the top 10 global EV manufacturers in 2018. At the same time, new players having no auto manufacturing background, are rushing into the Chinese market, mainly represented by Weilai, Weima, and Xiaopeng Motors, which started selling its first 10,000 units in 2019.

Table 2.3.   Global sales of EVs by brands in 2018.

Ranking	Global Brands	Country of origin	2018	%
1	Tesla	American	245,240	12
2	BYD	Chinese	227,364	11
3	BAIC	Chinese	164,958	8
4	BMW	German	129,398	6
5	Nissan	Japanese	96,949	5
6	Roewe	Chinese	92,790	5
7	Chery	Chinese	65,798	3
8	Hyundai	Korean	53,114	3
9	Renault	French	53,091	3
10	Volkswagen	German	51,774	3
11	Hawtai	Chinese	51,736	3
12	Chevrolet	American	50,682	3
13	JAC	Chinese	49,883	2
14	Geely	Chinese	49,816	2
15	JMC	Chinese	49,312	2
16	Toyota	Japanese	45,686	2
17	Mitsubishi	Japanese	42,671	2
18	Dongfeng	Chinese	39,945	2
19	Kia	Korean	37,746	2
20	Volvo	Chinese	35,994	2
	Others	—	384,300	19
	TOTAL	—	2,018,247	100
	Chinese brands in top 20	—	683,070	34

Note: EV includes Plug-in and Pure EV models.
Source: https://insideevs.com/global-sales-in-december-full-year-2018-2-million-plug-in-cars-sold/, https://zhuanlan.zhihu.com/p/55130209

Major Chinese companies in the EV industry are exhibiting different forms of leapfrogging. BYD — which stands for "Build Your Dreams" — exercises a type of stage-skipping/leapfrog, jumping over a stage and moving straight to a more advanced stage, based on the matured technology on the market, while continuing its own innovation. Beginning from scratch in 1995, as a battery manufacturing company, BYD became the world's largest producer of NiCd batteries by 2002. In parallel, BYD moved into conventional cars industry and very quickly to the production of hybrid and electric vehicles, by combining its know-how in battery technology (Kimble and Wang, 2012; Wang and Kimble, 2013). In 2011, BYD established a 50-50 JV with Daimer AG with registered capital of 600 million yuan (US$88 million) for the production of electric vehicles exclusively for the Chinese market. As for Geely, we will discuss in detail in the following chapters. China is on the stage of expansion in the whole value chain of the EV industry. Battery, the key component, has seen rapid development, and now generates the biggest world volume production. Two leading manufacturers, CATL and BYD, are now in world's top five, squeezing out Panasonic and LG. Regional industrial clusters were quickly created with the joint forces of companies and regional government support (Zhao, 2019). To stimulate industrial development, foreign carmakers are also mandated to source locally produced batteries. Daimler created a JV with BAIC in 2017 for battery manufacturing with a total investment of RMB 5 billion (US$721 million), both to ensure quality and control costs. Volkswagen initiates the intention on the acquisition of 20% equity of one Chinese battery company in 2020. SAIC-GM started the assembling of battery since 2018 and created the world's second largest battery laboratory in Shanghai.

2.5.2. *Betting on the Chinese market by MNCs*

Expanding to the EV market segment (and future smart and connected vehicles) is perceived as the megatrend of disruptive transition. Global carmakers are readjusting their strategies of technology roadmap and investing massively in the EV industry in China, comparing to their home markets (Poliscanova and Hildermeier, 2018). The Volkswagen group led the investment by creating €10 billion joint venture with Jianghuai, an important move in line with the strategy of producing 80 new EV models by 2025. Nisaan-Renault-Dongfeng committed an investment of €8 billion for opening a new EV factory. Daimler AG-BAIC's new venture is valued at €1.6 billion for creating a new EV production facility in Beijing. Mercedez teamed with Geely in January 2020 for the creation of a 50-50 JV with registered capital of RMB 5.4 billion (US$780 million) to produce all-electric smart cars both for domestic and global markets starting from 2022.

According to the statistics, between 2017 and 2018, investment in EV in China jointly made by global carmakers was €21.7 billion, while investment in the EU zone was only €3.2 billion, seven times less. We hypothesize that global players are not reactively implementing the Chinese automobile industrial policy but proactively considering China as the future global EV export hub.

2.6. Future Chinese Automobile Industry — National Strategy in a New Geopolitical Landscape

The development of EVs in China was based on three national strategies: secure energy safety; reduce emissions; and engage in technology leapfrogging to combat the bigger sales of internal combustion engine vehicles, which leads to a higher dependency on imported fossil fuels and creates the bigger challenge of air pollution caused by automobiles (Fang and Zeng, 2007; Nordqvist, 2007). China is counting on the development of EV and future smart vehicles as the way of leapfrogging.

The initial development of EVs began with the Eighth Five-Year Plan (1991–1995). During the period of the Tenth Five-Year plan (2000–2005), the EV officially became a national priority. The central government formulated dedicated preferential policies, and financial subsidies (both to producer and consumers) were allocated (Zhao, 2006; Wang and Kimble, 2011). In 2009, China announced mid-term quantified objective of EV industry by 2012: reaching a production capacity of 500,000 units, representing 5% of the total annual market for passenger car sales. While this objective was forced to scale down the initial target, it has lowered the technology barrier by 2012. An updated objective by the Ministry of Industry and Information Technology (MIIT) was to request the industry to reach a cumulative sales figure of 500,000 units by 2015 (Kimble and Wang, 2013).

To further encourage EV production, the government introduced a fleet quota system in September 2017, which took effect in April 2018. This system imposed to all carmakers and importers a minimum percentage of new energy vehicles (NEVs) relative to their total production or imports. This quota was 10% in 2019 and 12% in 2020. Companies failing to meet the target are required to purchase NEV credits from other carmakers that exceeded production quotas. China's new aim is to have seven million EVs registered by 2025.

The quick development of EVs in China in the late 2010s pushed industry policy further, upgrading from significant incentives to the reduction of subsidies. The reduction in subsidies for EVs started in 2016. In March 2019, MIIT, Ministry of Technology, and the National Development and Reform Commission (NDRC) jointly published the notice on the phasing out of government subsidies on EVs. The objective is to cut subsidies by 50% in 2019 and completely phase them out in 2020. The measure is to further stimulate the technology improvement (e.g. higher performance battery), and partial elimination of low-efficient companies. However, the negative growth rate of China's automobile industry in 2019 alerted the government to reassess the pace of implementation. In January 2020, the MIIT minister announced the necessity of revision, toward a milder pace of subsidy reduction, so as to mitigate the shock of industry downturn.

The Chinese government's ambition of leapfrogging goes beyond the EVs and expanded to smart cars (connected vehicles, autonomous drive, vehicles to everything or v2x) and personal mobility embedded in the smart city. The government is formulating forward-looking policies to shape the future industrial and national competencies. Those domains are possible sources of paradigm shift (Teece, 2019). New automobile technologies are emerging in conjunction with 5G, another emerging strategic industry announced in the *Made in China 2025* plan. China vows to make breakthroughs in 5G mobile communication. Connected cars and smart cities are industrial projects slated to use 5G technology. A pilot project in Xiong'an, a new city 129 km southwest of Beijing, is being implemented by combining the forces of China Mobile, China Telecom, Baidu (web giant), and automobile companies. For broader application, 5G technology will extend to the smart factory and smart city traffic management. The joint force of 5G and the automobile industry is creating a new ecosystem of future automobile industry, and it is a process of creating new competitive advantage. The Chinese government's mid- to long-term vision driven by five-year economic development plans and industry policies, are serving as the early indicators and assurance of business risks. Corporates are protected to innovate in a safer environment. At the superficial level, this central-government–driven approach in China seems significantly different from the Western approach, while it mirrors the capitalism spirit on creative destruction and industrial innovation (Greenspan and Wooldridge, 2018). China is actively participating in both the global industry and geopolitical competition.

References

Allen, R. (2011). *Global Economic History: A Very Short Introduction*. Oxford: Oxford University Press.

Accenture (2013). China's Automotive Market. How to Merge into the Fast Lane with Consumer and Digital Marketing Insights. Available at: https://www.readkong.com/page/china-s-automotive-market-accenture-5030463 (accessed July 18, 2020).

Blanchard, O. and S. Andrei (2001). Federalism with and without political centralization: China versus Russia. *IMF Staff Papers*, **48**, Special Issue.

Banerjee, A. and A. Newman (1993). Occupational choice and the process of development. *The Journal of Political Economy*, **101**:2, 274–298.

Chan, L. and T. Daim (2012). Sectoral innovation system and technology policy development in China: Case of the transportation sector. *Journal of Technology Management in China*, **7**:2, 117–135.

Chen, B. and C. Midler (2016). The electric vehicle landscape in China: Between institutional and market forces. *International Journal of Automotive Technology and Management*, **16**:3, 248–273.

Chu, W. (2011). Entrepreneurship and bureaucratic control: The case of the Chinese automotive industry. *China Economic Journal*, **4**:1(February), 65–80.

Chin, G. (2010). *China's Automotive Modernization: The Party-State and Multinational Corporations*. London: Palgrave Macmillan.

Fang, Y. and Y. Zeng (2007). Balancing energy and environment: The effect and perspective of management instruments in China. *Energy*, **32**:12, 2247–2261.

Greenspan, A. and A. Wooldridge (2018). *Capitalism in America: A History*. New York: Penguin, 2018, p. 486.

Harwit, E. (1995). *China's Automobile Industry: Policies, Problems, and Prospects*. Armonk, New York: M.E. Sharpe.

Jiang, X., S. Li and X. Song (2017). The mystery of zombie enterprises — Stiff but deathless. *China Journal of Accounting Research*, **10**:4 (December), 341–357.

Kimble, C. and H. Wang (2012). Transistors, electric vehicles and leapfrogging in China and Japan. *Journal of Business Strategy*, **33**:3, 22–29.

Kimble, C. and H. Wang (2013). China's new energy vehicles: Value and innovation. *Journal of Business Strategy*, **34**:2, 13–20.

Lewis, A. (1954). Economic development with unlimited supplies of labor. *The Manchester School*, **22**:2, 139–191.

Li, J., E. Weldon and A. Tsui (2000). *Management and Organizations in the Chinese Context: An Overview*. New York: Macmillan Press.

McGunagle, D. (2007). *The Chinese Auto Industry: Taming the Dragon*. Saarland, Germany: AV Akademikerverlag Gmbh & Colorado. KG, p. 116.

Marsh, P. (2011). China noses ahead as top goods producer. *CNBC*, March 14. Available at: https://www.cnbc.com/2011/03/14/china-noses-ahead-as-top-goods-producer.html (accessed July 15, 2020).

Mesnard, A. (2001). Migration temporaire et mobilite intergenerationnelle. *Louvain Economic Review*, **67**:1, 59–88 [in French].

Montinola, G., Y. Qian and B. Weingast (1995). Federalism, Chinese style: The political basis for economic success in China. *World Politics*, **48**:1, 50–81.

Nordqvist, J. (2007). Reining China's industrial energy — challenges of promoting expedient measures in a Chinese actor environment. *Energy Policy*, **35**:6, 3270–3279.

Poliscanova, J. and J. Hildermeier (2018). EU playing catch-up: China leading the race for electric car investments. *Transport & Environment*. Available at: https://www.transportenvironment.org/sites/te/files/EV%20investments%20paper%20FINAL_210618.pdf (accessed July 18, 2020).

Peng, M., D. Wang and Y. Jiang (2008). An institution-based view of international business strategy: A focus on emerging economies. *Journal of International Business Studies*, **39**:5, 920–936.

Peng, M. W. and E. G. Pleggenkuhle-Miles (2009). Current debates in global strategy. *International Journal of Management Reviews*, **11**:1, 51–68.

PWC, (2018). The Opening-Up of Chinese Automotive Industry and its impact. https://www.pwccn.com/en/automotive/chinese-automotive-industry-opening-up-impact.pdf (accessed March 15, 2020).

Qian, Y. and B. Weingast (1996). China's transition to markets: Market-preserving federalism, Chinese Style. *The Journal of Policy Reform*, **1**:2, 149–185.

Qian, Y. and B. Weingast (1997). Federalism as a commitment to preserving market incentives. *Journal of Economic Perspectives*, **11**:4, 83–92.

Qian, Y. and G. F. Roland Jr (1998). Federalism and the soft budget constraint. *American Economic Review*, **88**:5, 1143–1162.

Radjou, N., P. Jaideep and S. Ahuja (2012). *Jugaad Innovation: Think Frugal, Be Flexible, Generate Breakthrough Growth.* New Jersey: John Wiley & Sons.

Rapoport, H. (2002). Migration, credit constraints and self-employment: A simple model of occupational choice, inequality and growth. *Economics Bulletin*, **15**:7, 1–5.

Richet, X., H. Wang and W. Wang (2001). Foreign direct investment in the Chinese automobile industry. *China Perspective*, **38**:(November–December), 40–47.

Sperling, D., Z. Lin and P. Hamilton (2005). Rural vehicles in China: Appropriate policy for appropriate technology. *Transport Policy*, **12**:2 (March), 105–119.

Teece, D. (2019). China and the reshaping of the auto industry: A dynamic capabilities perspective. *Management and Organization Review*, **15**:1 (March), 177–199.

Wang, H. (2002). The Coexistence of Two Automotive Systems in China. *The Tenth GERPISA International Colloquium — Coordinating Competencies and Knowledge in the Auto Industry*, June.

Wang, H. (2003). Policy reforms and foreign direct investment: The case of the Chinese automotive industry. *Journal of East-West Economics and Business*, **6**:1, 287–314.

Wang, H. (2015). Fluctuation of the Chinese Automobile Market during and after the Financial Crisis. In B. Jetin (ed.) *Global Automobile Demand*. London: Palgrave Macmillan, pp. 113–135.

Wang, H. and C. Kimble (2011). Leapfrogging to electric vehicles: Patterns and scenarios for China's automobile industry. *International Journal of Automotive Technology and Management*, **11**:4, 312–325.

Wang, H. and C. Kimble (2012). The Low Speed Electric Vehicle — China's Unique Sustainable Automotive Technology? In A. Subic, J. Wellnitz, M. Leary, and L. Koopmans (eds.) *Sustainable Automotive Technologies*. Berlin: Springer, pp. 207–214.

Wang, H. and C. Kimble (2012). Business Model Innovation and the Development of the Electric Vehicle Industry in China. In G. Calabrese (ed.) *The Greening of the Automotive Industry*. London: Palgrave Macmillan, pp. 240–253.

Wang, H. and C. Kimble (2013). Innovation and leapfrogging in the Chinese automobile industry: Examples from Geely, BYD, and Shifeng. *Global Business and Organizational Excellence*, **32**:6, 6–17.

Yuki, K. (2007). Urbanization, informal sector, and development. *Journal of Development Economics*, **84**, 76–103.

Zhao, J. (2006). Whither the car? China's automobile industry and cleaner vehicle technologies. *Development and Change*, **37**:1, 121–144.

Zhao, W. (2019). Constructing a value chain from below: Emergence of NEV battery manufacturing and advanced cluster policy in the Pearl River Delta, China. *27th Gerpisa International Colloquium*. June 11–14, ENS Paris-Saclay, Cachan, Paris.

Chapter 3

The Rise of Geely in the Reform Era

Abstract

A successful global enterprise with Chinese roots, Geely is a privately held automotive group and a leading automobile manufacturer in China. From its humble beginnings as a refrigerator component maker and motorcycle manufacturer in the late 20th century, catching up in technology, to becoming a trailblazer in products, services, and business model innovations, Geely has survived against significant institutional and economic odds to become not only a top-selling brand and one of the most successful grassroots carmakers in China but also a rising player in the global automotive industry. A classic example of the rise of the private enterprises in the Chinese manufacturing economy, Geely has charged forward as a new Chinese automaker on the world stage.

Keywords: Geely Auto; Chinese automobile manufacturing; Li Shufu; private enterprises; China.

3.1. Introduction

Headquartered in Hangzhou, Zhejiang Province, Geely is a privately held, global automotive group and a leading automobile manufacturer based in the People's Republic of China. Geely Auto was founded in 1997 as a subsidiary of Zhejiang Geely Holding Group, which was established in 1986 by Li Shufu, a grassroots entrepreneur in the Chinese economic reform era. After more than two decades of development, Geely has grown to become not only a top-selling brand in China but also a rising player in the global automotive industry. In addition to its own brand, Geely also holds Volvo in Sweden and the London Electric Vehicle Company (LEVC), has significant ownership of PROTON in Malaysia and the UK-based Lotus, and is the largest shareholder of the German automaker Daimler-Benz. With an annual revenue of US$49.7 billion in 2018, overall assets of US$48.6 billion, and total profit of US$1.97 billion, Geely presently ranks 220 among the Fortune 500 (2019). In 2019, the group employed 124,846 people (52,400 for Geely Auto), operated 14 vehicle manufacturing plants, 9 powertrain plants, and 6 knockdown kit plants. Its vehicles have been sold through a network of over 1,000 dealers across China as well as over 450 international sales and service points covering 40 countries, mainly in emerging economies and developing countries in the Eastern Europe, Middle East, and Africa. The company saw its sales volume increase to 765,000 vehicles in 2016, 1.24 million in 2017, and 1.5 million (2.15 million for the Geely Group) in 2018 while enduring a reduced sales of 1.36 million in 2019 due to the economic uncertainty. As a classic example of the rise of the private enterprises in the Chinese manufacturing economy, Geely has survived against significant institutional and economic odds to become "one of the most successful grassroots carmakers in China" (Feng, 2018, p. 182).

3.2. Geely at a Glance: The Historic Growth and Development

Originally started as a refrigerator component manufacturer in 1986, Geely was founded by Li Shufu in the coastal region of Zhejiang Province. In 1994, after acquiring a failing state-owned enterprise (SOE), Geely launched its motorcycle manufacturing business, and within a few years, became one of the major motorcycle production bases in the country. The company entered the automotive industry in 1997 and began to make passenger vehicles the following year with its compact model production, the first private enterprise in automobile manufacturing in China. Since then, Geely, under Li's leadership, has transformed from a private, family-run business to a successful modern enterprise with top-selling national brands, a leader in technological innovations, and an emerging player in the global auto market.

When China launched its economic reforms in 1978, no one would have foreseen it would one day become the largest market for automobiles in the world. The growth of the Chinese automobile industry is in close parallel with the country's economic development, and Geely is a good case study on the struggles and triumphs of Chinese national brands in auto manufacturing. During the early stage of its development, Geely faced substantial challenges, as the market was already dominated by some large SOEs and powerful joint ventures (JVs) with significant resources from well-established foreign partners. Furthermore, the industry was closely controlled and regulated by government bureaucracies. Despite the seemingly unsurmountable roadblocks, Geely was able to find its niche: *making affordable cars for ordinary citizens* in the People's Republic of China. Unlike JVs that received technology transfers directly from international partners, Geely in the beginning had to rely on reverse engineering to gain technology know-hows. Its first few models, including *Haoqing, Merrie*, and *Uliou*, are all based largely on similar vehicles of foreign carmakers and JVs already in production. Fortunately, around that time, the relatively weak environment in intellectual property protection and a booming manufacturing economy in the country worked in Geely's favor. By keeping its costs low, Geely overcame both industrial and institutional barriers to find its place in automobile manufacturing (Balcet *et al.*, 2012). Although this strategic positioning ensured its survival and initial growth in the Chinese auto market, its focus on affordability also led to the overall impression that its products were low-cost and low-quality vehicles, a negative stereotype that Geely has strived to eliminate in later years.

China's entry into the World Trade Organization (WTO) marked a significant milestone in the history of Geely Auto, as the company finally received state approval for passenger vehicle manufacturing in 2001 and began its car production in earnest. Within a year, it became one of the top 10 automakers in the country. Ranked among the top 500 firms in China, the company quickly developed its own engine production, successfully defended itself in an intellectual property lawsuit filed by Toyota, and began to export its vehicles overseas in 2003. Along the way, its *Beauty Leopard* sports coupe also won the Special Award in Innovative Design and was collected by the Chinese National Museum. Around that time, although the Chinese automotive industry was still tightly controlled by the central administrative bureaucracy, Geely was able to adeptly manage the relationship with government agencies and secure the necessary support for its continual growth. For instance, in 2005, during a special session of the Chinese People's Political Consultative Conference, Li Shufu gave a speech titled "Independent Innovation Is the Future of the Chinese Automotive Industry" that deeply impressed Wen Jiabo, then Premier of the State Council (Wang, 2006). Afterward, the Chinese Ministry of Science and Technology held a seminar in Beijing on the so-called "Geely Phenomenon: The Path of Development for the Chinese National Automobile Industry" (Sina Auto, 2005). Through shell-borrowing, Geely was listed on the Hong Kong Stock Exchange in 2005, a strategic move to raise essential financing for further development; by 2017, Geely has become a constituent of the Hang Seng Index. Under Li's leadership, Geely committed itself to independent innovation and development, achieving major breakthroughs in engine, transmission, and other core technologies in the automobile industry. Guided by the new vision, Geely issued its "Ningbo Declaration" in 2007 to mark its strategic transformation from low-cost production to competing on technology innovation, quality, brand, and value-added services for consumers (Wang and Liang, 2017). Since then, Geely has entered a fast track of growth. The company has been ranked among the Fortune 500 in the world since 2012, and Geely Auto has also been recognized as one of the top 100 brands in China (*China Automotive News*, 2018).

Since its acquisition of Volvo in 2010, Geely has experienced a period of tremendous growth. As illustrated by Figure 3.1, the company's

Figure 3.1.   Geely operations from 2009–2019 (RMB in 000).

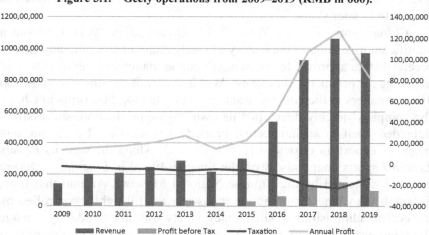

Source: Compiled by author from the annual reports of Geely Automobile Holdings Limited, 2009–2019.

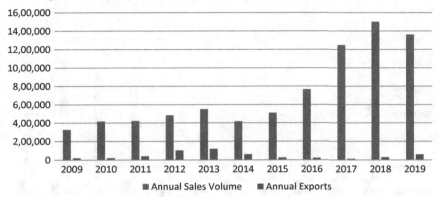

Figure 3.2. Geely's annual sales and export volumes from 2009–2019.

Source: Compiled by author from the annual reports of Geely Automobile Holdings Limited, 2009–2019.

revenue increased 692% and net profit by 626% over the last decade, while its total sales grew from 326,710 units in 2009 to 1,361,510 in 2019, making Geely the largest indigenous brand vehicle manufacturer in China in terms of sales volume and the third largest passenger brand in China (Figure 3.2), even though its annual sales decreased 9% in 2019 due to the economic uncertainty and deterioration of consumer confidence (*Geely Annual Report*, 2019). Equally impressive, Geely's total assets increased 574%, while its total equity rose 639%, and equity attributed to share-holders surged 774% over the last 10 years (Figure 3.3). However, it is notable that Geely's exports remain relatively flat over the last decade. In 2019, Geely exported 57,991 vehicles, up 109% from 2018 but only accounted for 4.3% of its total sales of the year and 8% of the country's export volumes of passenger vehicle market in 2019, which indicates that China is still the dominant market for Geely's vehicles.

3.3. Rise of Geely as an Emerging Global Enterprise

From very early on, Geely had its eyes on the overseas market and made multiple efforts in international expansion. Shortly after acquiring its official approval for passenger car manufacturing, Geely in 2003 launched a small-scale export project to the Middle East. The company showcased its new vehicles at the 2005 Frankfurt Motor Show and at the Detroit Auto

Figure 3.3.   Geely's total assets and liabilities from 2009–2019 (RMB in 000).

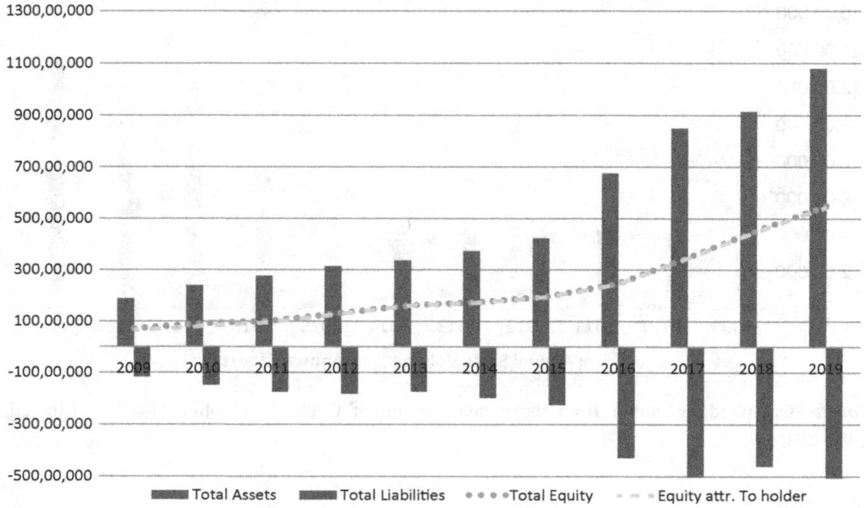

Source: Compiled by author from the annual reports of Geely Automobile Holdings Limited, 2009–2019.

Show the following year, thus making history as the first Chinese company with national brands displaying in top international auto exhibits. In 2006, Geely acquired 23% of London Taxi from Britain's Manganese Bronze and set up a JV in Shanghai to manufacture the iconic black cabs (Monaghan, 2013). Geely's next overseas acquisition was to purchase the Australian automatic transmission supplier Drivetrain System International (DSI) for AU$58 million to strengthen its gearbox production line and bring Australian technology into China (Wong, 2009), which is a major technology-oriented, asset-seeking measure that contributed greatly to enhance Geely's automobile development capabilities going forward. When the worldwide economic crisis hit the global automobile industry, Geely approached Ford in mid-2008 about a possible takeover of Volvo Cars. After some challenging negotiations, on March 28, 2010, which was reported as a "historic day" for a Chinese carmaker to acquire a foreign rival, Geely signed an agreement with Ford Motor Company to acquire Volvo for US$1.8 billion, along with US$900 million of working capital from Geely and a commitment to build a Volvo factory in China (Nicholson, 2010). Other notable international acquisitions made by Geely during the recent years include purchasing a 51% controlling stake in the UK-based Lotus to expand into the sports and racing car market (Macfarlane, 2017); acquiring 49.9% stake in PROTON of Malaysia to facilitate future growth in the lucrative Southeast Asia region (Zainul and Idris, 2017); investing a 9.69% stake in Daimler AG to foster technology partnership with the leading German carmaker (Taylor and Shirouzu, 2019); buying Terrafugia, an American maker of flying cars to explore future mode of transportation (Grady, 2017); and forming a €50 million (US$55 million) partnership with Daimler on the German start-up Volocopter, hoping to produce and sell air taxis in the coming years (Sun and Goh, 2019). Table 3.1 outlines Geely's endeavors in international expansion over the last two decades, and all these initiatives have positioned the firm as an emerging player in the global automobile market.

3.4. Geely's Corporate Structure and Operations

With global operations spanning the entire automotive value chain from design, research and development (R&D) to production, sales, and services, Zhejiang Geely Holding Group is divided into six subsidiaries (Figure 3.4): *Geely Auto Group*, which includes Geely Auto, Lynk & Co, Geometry, PROTON, Lotus, and smart vehicles; *Volvo Car Group*, which includes Volvo Cars and Polestar; *Geely New Energy Commercial Vehicle Group*, which includes the London Electric Vehicle Company and Farizon Auto (Yuancheng) Auto; *Geely Technology Group*, which includes Cao Cao, Qjiang Motor, Geespace, Aerofugia, BSKY, and other new businesses; *Mitime Group*, which is Geely's non-vehicle operations such as motorsports, tourism business, among others; and finally, *Geely Talent Management Group*, which includes its educational institutions.

The Geely Auto Group has 11 vehicle manufacturing facilities all over China in places such as Taizhou, Ningbo, Xiangtan, Chengdu, Baoji, Jinzhong, and Guiyang (Figure 3.5), with a total production capacity of 2.1 million vehicles per year, which is a substantial increase from 4 plants and an annual capacity of 200,000 units back in 2007, when the company began its strategic transformation (Wang, 2008). The company in 2020 produces *Emgrand* GL (A-class cars), *Emgrand* GT (B-class cars), X7 Sport (SUV), *Emgrand* GS (crossover SUV), *Emgrand* EV (A-Class EV), X7, GC6, and other vehicles along with a full range of powertrains using gasoline and new energy sources. Among Geely's corporate affiliates, *Geometry* is Geely's new division for electric vehicles (EV) modeled after

Table 3.1.   Chronology of Geely's global expansion.

1997	Geely Auto was established.
1998	First Geely vehicle rolled out the assembly line in Linhai, Zhejiang.
2001	Geely received the official permission from the Chinese central government for passenger car manufacturing.
2003	Geely began for the first time to export in the international market.
2004	Export volume reached 5,000.
2005	Geely was listed on the Hong Kong Stock Exchange.
	– Geely vehicles anticipated in the Frankfurt International Auto Show, the first for a Chinese indigenous brand.
	– The World Brand Lab recognized Geely among the Top 100 brands in China.
	– Geely exported over 7,000 vehicles to 30 countries and regions in the world.
	– Geely Maple entered an agreement for CKD plant in Malaysia, the first time a Chinese auto brand sought to establish an overseas manufacturing base.
2006	Geely participated in the Detroit International Auto Show.
	– The company began to sponsor the Asian Geely Formula International Open Competition, which later became China Formula Grand Prix (CFGP).
	– Geely entered an agreement with Manganese Bronze Holdings (MBH) for the joint production of London Taxi in Shanghai.
2007	Li Shufu issued the "Ningbo Declaration," marking its strategic transformation from low-cost production to competing in technology innovation.
	– Entered a CK-1CKD assembly program for Indonesia.
2009	The firm acquired the Australian automatic transmission supplier Drivetrain System International (DSI) for AU$58 million.
	– Export volume reached 19,350.
2010	The company acquired Volvo Cars from the Ford Motor Company.
	– Export volume reached 20,555.
2011	Geely established BelGee, a joint venture with BelAZ for auto manufacturing in Belarus.
	– Export volume reached 39,600.
2012	For the first time Geely entered on the Fortune 500 list (No. 475).
	– Export volume reached 101,908.
2013	Geely established China Euro Vehicle Technology AB (CEVT), a research and development company in Gothenburg, Sweden.
	– Geely acquired the remaining assets of London Taxi from MBH and restarted the production of the iconic black cab.
	– Export volume reached 118,871.
2014	The firm redefined its mission for "creating refined cars for everyone."
	– The company developed a new brand strategy, consolidated existing brands, and revealed a new corporate logo for global expansion.

Table 3.1. *(Continued)*

	– Geely entered a strategic agreement with the Export-Import Bank of China (China Exim Bank).
	– Geely acquired the UK-based Emerald Automotive.
2015	The firm launched the *Blue Geely Initiative* and the *Geely Intelligent Power*, with a central focus on the development of new energy vehicles.
	– The company announced new plant and design for electrical vehicle manufacturing in England with zero emission.
2016	Geely unveiled Lynk & Co in partnership with Volvo.
	– Geely launched Geely *20200 Strategy*, aiming to sell 2 million vehicles by 2020 and becoming a global top 10 automaker, and the most competitive and respected Chinese brand.
2017	Geely acquired 49.9% of PROTON and 51% of Lotus from DRB-HICOM.
	– Geely acquired Terrafugia, an American maker of flying cars.
	– London Taxi was renamed London EV Company, and the new factory completed in Coventry, England.
	– Geely acquired 8.2% of AB Volvo and became the largest shareholder of Volvo Group.
	– Geely and Volvo Cars sign JV agreements on technology-sharing and development of Lynk & Co
	– A new CKD factory completed, and Geely Atlas rolled out the BelGee assembly line in Belarus.
	– Became a constituent of the Hang Seng Index.
2018	Geely acquired 9.69% of Daimler AG, the largest shareholder of the German carmaker.
	– New PROTON X70 based on Geely Boyue SUV went on production in Malaysia.
2019	The firm entered a new partnership with Daimler for the transformation of smart vehicle.
	– The company unveiled its new electrical vehicle Geely Geometry in Singapore.
	– Geely and Volvo announced plan to combine combustion engine operations.
	– Geely rose to the 220th place on the *Fortune 500*.
	– Lotus unveiled Evija, the world's first pure electric British hypercar.
	– Geely and Daimler announced jointed investment in Volocopter.
2020	Zhejiang Geely Holding Group total sales reached 2.178 million in 2019.
	– Geely reported 57,991 vehicles to 17 countries through 327 sales and service outlets, a 109% increase in year-over-year export, which comprised 4.3% of the company's total sale volume and 8% of China's export market.
	– Geely launched *Geespace* to build low-orbit satellites to provide more accurate data for self-driving cars.
	– Geely and Volvo announced a proposal to merge to boost scale of operation.

Figure 3.4.   Corporate structure of the Zhejiang Geely Holding Group (reprinted with permission).

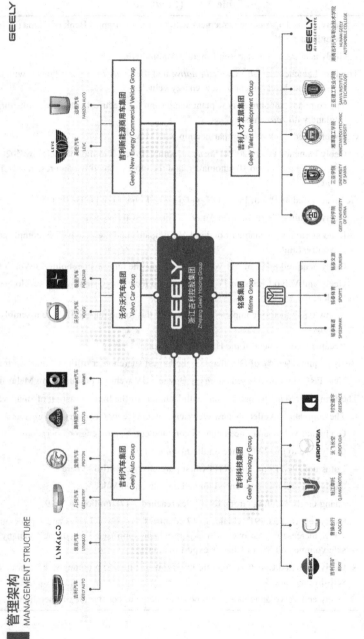

Figure 3.5. Geely's global footprint (reprinted with permission).

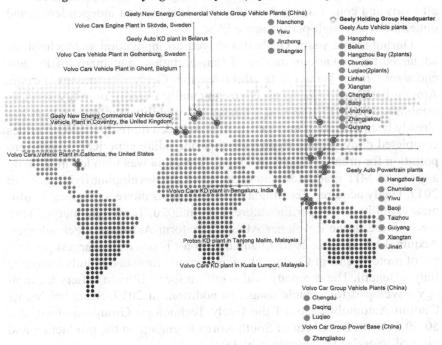

Tesla. Lynk & Co is a newly created and globally focused high-end car brand based on jointly developed technology by Geely Auto and Volvo Cars, which is owned 50% by Geely Auto, 30% by Volvo, and 20% by Zhejiang Geely Holding Group. PROTON is the national brand of Malaysia, established in the 1980s and later reverted to private ownership under DRB-HICOM (Heavy Industries Corporation of Malaysia Berhad). Through the purchase agreement reached in June 2017, Geely acquired 49.9% of ownership and management right while DRB-HICOM still retained 50.1% of PROTON. The same deal also gave Geely 51% of Lotus Cars, whereas Etika Automotive held the remaining 49% of the company shares. Within the Volvo Car Group, Geely owns 99% of Volvo Cars AB, while a group of Swedish institutional investors hold the remaining 1%. Volvo is one of the most well-known and respected premium car brands in the world, with sales in over 100 countries through 2,300 local dealers. *Polestar* is the performance vehicle division of Volvo formed to explore how the racing technology could be applied to cars on all roads and conditions in everyday life. It is now an independent brand under Volvo for high-performance EVs.

During recent years, Geely has strived for innovation and technology advancement in various modes of transportation, and many of its new endeavors have been clustered under the Geely Technology Group. Among them, *Cao Cao* is an environmentally friendly mobility services established in 2017, the first Chinese EV mobility platform, which has already been operating in over 50 cities and seen more than 500,000 rides completed daily, aiming to provide superior riding experiences with zero pollution for urban residents in China. Terrafugia was founded in 2006 by a group of MIT graduates who dreamed of the developing flying cars. In 2017, Geely acquired Terrafugia in an audacious move to explore its ultimate mobility vision for the future; then in 2020, Terrafugia merged with the Chinese drone developer AOSSCI to form Aerofugia Technologies. Acquired by Geely in 2016, Qianjiang Motor is one of the largest producers of motorcycles in China and owns several renowned brands including Italy's Benelli. The company is also known for its lithium battery technology developed for vehicle usage. In addition, in 2019, Shanghai Maple Guorun Automobile Co. of the Geely Technology Group has formed a 50-50 JV with LG Chem of South Korea to engage in the production and sales of batteries for electric vehicles.

Other notable undertakings in the Geely Technology Group include *Geespace*, a new endeavor for the development, launch, and operation of low-orbit satellites supporting near instant communications with vehicles and infrastructures that will focus on facilitating the safe rollout of autonomous vehicles; China Railway Gecent Technology (*CRGT*), a three-way partnership of China Railway Investment Co., Geely, and Tencent for a high-speed rail Wi-Fi platform that offers users integrated services ranging from parking, ride-hailing, Wi-Fi access, and mobility services to food delivery, entertainment, news, information, e-commerce, travel, and smart retail services; and Geely-Daimler Mobility Service, a 50-50 JV to provide high-end mobility services in select cities in China. The newest entity under Geely Technology is BSKY, a mining and energy group based in Guangxi Province that was first established in 1996 and acquired by Geely in 2019.

Geely New Energy Commercial Vehicle Group began with the full acquisition of the London Taxi Company from Manganese Bronze Holdings in 2013. Later, the iconic brand under Geely was renamed to

LEVC to reflect its new focus on developing and producing electric commercial vehicles with zero-emission for the modern metropolis. Geely's *Farizon* Auto (*Yuancheng*) was formed in 2016 to focus on the development of new energy commercial vehicles in China, which has already launched several long-range, environmentally friendly truck and bus solutions, including the world's first M100 methanol heavy truck, F12 hydrogen fuel cell passenger bus, and C11 pure electric city bus.

Mitime Group is the non-automotive subsidiary of the Geely Holding, representing its diversified investments in the fields of sports, speed racing, tourism, and health services. Mitime Group has dozens of subsidiary enterprises collectively valued at over 10 billion RMB with over 3,000 employees. Notable among them is Mitime Sport, a pillar of the Mitime Group, with a mission of promoting sports and healthy living to the public. In China and abroad, Mitime Sport has organized many athletic events, constructed multiple race circuits, provided high-end, sport-related support services, and promoted public participation in sports such as racing, golf, sailing, and endurance sports.

As one of the largest private higher education investment groups in China, Geely Talent Management is the last and latest group under Geely Holding, which includes the Geely University of China (Beijing), University of Sanya (Hainan), Sanya Institute of Technology (Hainan), Hunan Geely Automobile College, and Xiangtang Polytech University (Hunan). With the goal of developing Chinese automotive talent pools, over 150,000 graduates have entered the workforce since the founding of the first Geely school in the late 1990s. In 2020, over 50,000 students are enrolled at Geely-funded schools and 20,000 graduate each year.

3.5. Geely's Forward-Looking Vision and Growth Strategies

As noted earlier, when Geely Auto was founded in the late 1990s, the Chinese automotive industry was primarily dominated by large SOEs and few JVs producing automobiles with artificially inflated prices. Instead of focusing on the high-end market that required heavy capital investment and advanced technologies, Geely began to concentrate its efforts on economy vehicles. Under Li's leadership, *building affordable cars for ordinary people* became the first mission of the company, and this strategy not only contributed significantly to the initial success of Geely but also led to the general perception of Geely as a symbol of cheap and low-quality automobile manufacturer in China. After a decade of rapid development, while the automobile ownership among Chinese families has been greatly enhanced, Geely has also matured and begun to shift to a different track for sustainable growth. In 2007, the company issued its "Ningbo Declaration," outlining a new corporate strategy for competing on technology, quality, brand, and after-sale services rather than price wars (CGTN, 2018). Instead of fiercely competing in the compact vehicle sector, the new strategy has moved Geely up the market value chain through making new models for the rising middle-class households in the country. This declaration marks one of the most important transformations in the history of Geely, as the carmaker has grown from low-cost production to competing for value-added products and making safe, reliable, environmentally friendly, and energy-efficient vehicles for consumers. Up to that point, Geely Auto had functioned largely as a market follower trying to imitate successful models developed by other large manufacturers. To reach its newly defined and ambitious goals, the company has made great efforts to establish a full line of production competing in different sectors. After some soul searching, Geely has decided that the key for success and sustainable future would have to include a forward-looking vision, technology innovation, and continual investment in R&D.

To a large degree, Geely's impressive achievement over the past two decades is due to the audacious business insights of its chairman Li Shufu. As a visionary entrepreneur, he knew very well technology innovation and overseas expansion would be critical if Geely wanted to be an auto company with global influence, and acquisitions would be the most direct and cost-effective strategy for gaining new technologies, know-hows, and international market shares. Among multiple factors that contribute to the rise of Geely as a successful emerging MNC (EMNC), Li has played an especially significant role, embodying the definition of a transnational entrepreneur, i.e. "a social actor capable of bearing the risks and taking the strategic initiatives to establish, integrate and sustain the foreign operations" (Yeung, 2002). As a transnational entrepreneur, Li has actively exploited foreign investment opportunities, effectively controlled Geely's economic activities in the different markets, and strategically managed its resources across borders through creative and innovative deployment of the company's international investments. His leadership in the development of Geely will be further examined in Chapter Four.

In his letter titled "How we find room to grow in a changing world," Li has stated "The future is not for those who stand alone," and outlined his forward-looking vision for Geely:

> Focusing on the future, not just on business development and industrialization, we will continue to place emphasis on the consumer and on their experience whilst remaining committed to sustainable social development, clean energy, environmental protection, safety, privacy, and other areas affecting people's daily livelihood. Fate rewards those who work hard. The years ahead may be completely beyond what you or I predict; the best way to grasp tomorrow is to create your own future. But we must not daydream, we must advance step by step, work hard with every task, turn dreams into reality, with success being rewarded to those who are resolute (Li, 2019).

The same statement also underscores Geely's unwavering transition from high-speed development to a new stage of high-quality development. While still remaining automotive-focused at its core, the company under Li has recognized multiple challenges and great opportunities brought out by new technologies and powerful trends that are swiftly transforming the marketplace. With an ultimate goal of providing users with better transportation solutions and experiences, Geely in 2020 is positioning itself beyond a traditional automaker to also become a technology leader and service provider, a company that is willing to play an active role in reshaping the global automotive industry for a new and exciting future. During his speech at the *Third World Internet Conference* in 2016, Li delineated his vision for Geely: "There is no essential distinction between Internet companies and automakers in Internet automobile manufacturing, and Internet technologies are being already used by car companies" (Zhu, 2016).

Therefore, instead of fixing solely on high sale volumes, Geely has shifted its focus and redefined its corporate mission. As stated by An Conghui, President and CEO, "Geely Auto is still committed to its brand mission of '*Making Refined Cars for Everyone*,' which has led us to become China's leading privately-owned automotive brand. However, our vision for the future is not just to be China's leading brand, but to become the most competitive and respected Chinese auto brand in the world" (An, 2019). Unveiled in late 2016, a key component of its plan for leaping forward is its *20200 Strategy*, i.e. from 2020 onwards, Geely Auto plans to sell two million vehicles annually and enter the rank of the top 10 global auto companies, while introducing 30 new cars to the market and dramatically expanding its dealership network across to over 1,000 stores in China and over 500 globally (Li, 2016). However, the road to a bright future is by no means smooth or straightforward. Although the company experienced a banner year of growth in 2017, sales in 2018 were not on target, and its stock price plummeted as a result. With unexpected economic downturn, ongoing trade conflicts with the US, and potentially another round of global recession, many consumers have adopted a wait-and-see approach in the marketplace. Since Geely has been aggressively expanding internationally, the downward pressure has greatly tested Geely's capital chain and financial strength while increasingly raising doubt about its ambitious *20200 Strategy* (Internet Information Agency, 2019).

Despite the market challenges, Geely has charged forward with its notion for future. Another core piece of its master plan is the *Blue Geely Initiative*. First revealed in 2015, the company promises that 90% of its future sales would come from new energy vehicles, and consumers would be able to purchase hybrids at the price of traditional models from 2020 and beyond (Li, 2018). With its strong belief that the future of the auto-mobile industry resides in electric and new energy vehicles, the company has launched the *Geely Intelligent Power*, a diversified new energy strat-egy that follows four main technological pathways of hybrid, pure electric, alternative fuel, and fuel cell technologies, with the goal of making Geely a global leader in new energy mobility (Manthey, 2018). In addition to 30 new electric and hybrid models, Geely has also pledged to invest US$5 billion for EVs with an intention of launching its first fuel cell vehicle by 2025. Related to this initiative, Geely has placed great importance in the area of automotive intelligence and pushed forward its iNTEC brand of technologies, a concept to "humanize intelligent drive" with advanced tech-nologies to give occupants a greater level of safety and convenience when traveling. All things considered, despite multiple difficulties, the future looks fairly promising for Geely Auto. Equipped with leading technologies, Geely's *Emgrand* EV has created some excitement and new market poten-tials while its *Borui* GE has become the first mass-produced mild-hybrid B-segment sedan in China with great fuel efficiency.

Reflecting back from 2010, the acquisition of Volvo Cars clearly has had a profound impact on the future direction of Geely Auto, as it has significantly speeded up the technology learning and transformed the company from a market follower to an industry leader and innovator. Inspired by Volvo's human-centric focus and its remarkable track record in automobile safety, the protection and security of life has become Geely's first and foremost concern in auto design and development during recent years. Through its partnership with Volvo, CEVT has been established in Gothenburg, Sweden, and this research institute and innovation center has assembled a group of world-class engineers dedicated to making safety technology a core pillar in automobile development. This partnership has also contributed greatly to the modular development and advanced virtual engineering that enable the application of new technologies for both Volvo and Geely brands. Notable among its accomplishments is the development of universal modular scalable platforms and architectures, which allows new technologies to be developed faster and more cost-effectively. Its Compact Modular Architecture (CMA) is one such flexible and scalable system for small and mid-size cars that integrates European R&D concepts with leading technologies from around the world, and this design has become the foundation for new Volvo, Lynk, and Geely vehicles, including sedans, hatchbacks, coupes, crossovers, and SUV models. In 2020, Geely manufactured 17 major vehicle models (including the Lynk & Co) developed under 4 platforms and 2 modular architectures.

3.6. Conclusion

The growth of the Chinese automakers in the reform era is a close reflection of the country's powerful manufacturing economy, and Geely Auto is one such best example. From its humble beginning as a refrigerator component maker and motorcycle manufacturer in the late 20th century, Geely has grown to become not only a top-selling brand in China, the largest auto market in the world, but also a significant new player in the global automotive industry. In addition to its successful acquisitions of Volvo Cars, London Taxi, DSI, and the US-based Terrafugia in recent years, the company also holds substantial investments in Daimler, Malaysian carmaker PROTON, and UK-based sports car brand Lotus, among others. From catching up in technology to becoming a trailblazer in products, services, and business model innovations, Geely has charged forward as a new Chinese automaker on the world stage. With a bold and forward-looking vision, Geely has strived to become an industry leader and worked aggressively toward the future with its electric and fully connected vehicles, and its business model innovation toward mobility solutions has become an inspiration for both Chinese and Western competitors.

While Geely has become a globalized enterprise today, it sees itself as a Chinese corporation competing on the global market. Therefore, *Take Geely to the World* has become the motto of the company, and its current mission is to *make the safest, most environment-friendly and most energy-efficient vehicles*. Moreover, with a well-defined core value of *Happy Life, Geely Drive*, its vision statement simply asserts: *Let the world be filled with happiness and prosperity*. In brief, the rise of Geely as a private auto-maker in China over the past two decades has been a quite impressive feat. Under the entrepreneurial leadership of Li Shufu, Geely has grown to be a successful global enterprise with Chinese roots.

However, Geely's path for future growth and success is not necessarily secure. Despite its multiple efforts in global expansion, China is still the prime market for Geely vehicles, as its total exports amounted to less than 5% of annual production. Although the country has been the largest automobile market in the world for more than a decade, the industry still remains highly fragmented compared to that of more developed nations. In fact, the sales of the top 10 models in China in 2020 represent less than 15% of the total market shares. The low concentration of sales in the top models not only is a clear indication of rough competition in the auto sector, the fragmentation of the market also further hinders sustainable growth. For the Chinese auto industry to fully compete with the leading automobile manufacturers in the world, advanced technology and further industry consolidation, efficiency, and the economy of scale will all be required, which will present tough challenges to private enterprises such as Geely. So far, Li Shufu has a proven track record of thriving in the so-called "market economy with Chinese characteristics." Nonetheless, the relationship with policy-makers and bureaucracy is always a delicate task and an act of balance and managing expectations in China. Undoubtedly, the Chinese government and its relevant economic development policies will still have profound impacts on the growth of the Chinese auto industry in general and Geely in specific. As the country's automobile manufacturers face tremendous paradigm shifts around electric, connected, shared, and autonomous vehicles, an enterprise's relationship with authorities will determine whether it can receive preferable treatment and vital financial support, which will be key for its continual growth and success.

On February 10, 2020, Geely and Volvo jointed announced that both firms are considering combining their businesses to achieve the economy of scale and accelerate technological and financial efficiencies between the two automakers (*Automotive News*, 2020). If such a proposed merger is finalized, it would certainly create a strong global group capable of competing with other leading automakers in the world. In addition, Geely made an ambitious announcement in March 2020 to launch *Geespace*, its own low-orbit satellite program to aid autonomous driving (*New Mobility Weekly*, 2020). On August 6, 2020, in his keynote speech on the "Ten years of Geely-Volvo Globalization" for the 14th *China Goes Global* academic conference, while talking about changes in globalization tendency and how companies should respond, Li Shufu outlines his vision of continual global innovation for Geely: "The automobile industry is a globalized industry. Geely has always adhered to two rules in its process of globalization: firstly, complying with laws and regulations without playing tricks; and secondly, never stopping technological innovation" (Emlyon, 2020).

References

An, C. (2019). Our Vision: Message from the CEO. Geely Auto. Available at: http://global.geely.com/our-vision/ (accessed September 14, 2019).

Automotive News. "Volvo, Geely Plot Merger to Boost Scale." February 10, 2020. Available at: https://www.autonews.com/automakers-suppliers/volvo-geely-plot-merger-boost-scale (accessed February 14, 2020).

Balcet, G., H. Wang and X. Richet (2012). Geely: A trajectory of catching up and asset-seeking multinational growth. *International Journal of Automotive Technology and Management*, **12**:4, 360–375.

CGTN (2018). Faces of reform and opening up: Li Shufu leads china's largest private auto company to go global. December 22. Available at: https://news.cgtn.com/news/3041444d30494464776c6d636a4e6e62684a4856/share_p.html (accessed September 14, 2019).

China Automotive News (2018). Automakers listed on *Fortune*'s top 500 Chinese companies. July 18. Available at: http://autonews.gasgoo.com/china_news/70014912.html (in Chinese, accessed September 2, 2019).

Emlyon Business School (2020). The 14th China *goes* Global Conference held successfully for dialogue on post-pandemic global trends. August 7. Available at: http://en.em-lyon.com.cn/news/view/261 (accessed September 29, 2020).

Feng, Q. (2018). *Variety of Development: Chinese Automakers in Market Reform*. Cham, Switzerland: Palgrave Macmillan, pp. 153–184.

Fortune Global 500 (2019). Zhejiang Geely Holding Group. Available at: https://fortune.com/global500/2019/zhejiang-geely-holding-group/ (accessed March 26, 2020).

Geely Auto (2019). Geely Annual Report 2019. Zhejiang Geely Automobile Holding Limited. Available at: http://geelyauto.com.hk/core/files/financial/en/2019-02.pdf (accessed April 24, 2020).

Grady, M. (2017). Report: Terrafugia sold to Chinese conglomerate. AV Web, July 5. Available at: https://www.avweb.com/recent-updates/business-military/report-terrafugia-sold-to-chinese-conglomerate/ (accessed September 14, 2019).

Internet Information Agency (2019). Sales & share price plummeted, Geely '20200 Strategy' to be screwed? January 14, 2019. Available at: http://english.news18a.com/news/english_129937.html (accessed September 14, 2019).

Li, I. (2016). Geely announces '20200' strategy. *China Automotive Review*, November 18. Available at: https://cbuwordpress.azurewebsites.net/index.php/Geely-announces-20200-Strategy/ (accessed September 14, 2019).

Li, F. (2018). Geely to ramp up digitalization, new energy efforts. *China Daily*, March 21. Available at: http://www.chinadaily.com.cn/a/201803/21/WS5ab19e3ba3106e7dcc143fbb.html (accessed September 14, 2019).

Li, S. (2019). Letter from Chairman: How we find room to grow in a changing world. Zhejiang Geely Holding Group. Available at: http://zgh.com/letter-from-the-chairman/?lang=en (accessed September 14, 2019).

Macfarlane, A. (2017). Lotus Has a new Chinese owner. *CNN Business*, May 24. Available at: https://money.cnn.com/2017/05/24/autos/lotus-geely-china-proton/index.html (accessed September 14, 2019).

Manthey, N. (2018). Geely presents wide-ranging electric vehicle strategy. *Electrive*, May 30. Available at: https://www.electrive.com/2018/05/30/geely-presents-wide-ranging-electric-vehicle-strategy/ (accessed September 14, 2019).

Monaghan, A. (2013). China's Geely saves London cab maker Manganese Bronze." *Telegraph*, February 1. Available at: https://www.telegraph.co.uk/finance/newsbysector/industry/9843178/Chinas-Geely-saves-London-cab-maker-Manganese-Bronze.html (accessed September 14, 2019).

New Mobility Weekly Roundup (2020). Geely building satellites to aid autonomous driving. March 4. Available at: https://www.newmobility.global/autonomous/geely-building-satellites-aid-autonomous-driving/ (accessed April 23, 2020).

Nicholson, C. (2010). Chinese carmaker geely completes acquisition of Volvo from Ford. *New York Times*, August 2. Available at: https://www.nytimes.com/2010/08/03/business/global/03volvo.html (accessed September 14, 2019).

Sina Auto (2005). Geely phenomenon: The path of development for the Chinese national automobile industry. November 10. Available at: http://auto.sina.com.cn/news/2005-11-10/1459149757.shtml (in Chinese, accessed September 2, 2019).

Sun, Y. and B. Goh (2019). Geely to bring air taxis to China in tie-up with Daimler-backed volocopter. *Reuters*, September 9. Available at: https://www.reuters.com/article/us-geely-daimler-investment/geely-to-bring-air-taxis-to-china-in-tie-up-with-daimler-backed-volocopter-idUSKCN1VU0BX (accessed July 16, 2020).

Taylor, E. and N. Shirouzu (2019). Daimler to develop smart brand together with Geely. *Routers Business News*, March 28. Available at: https://www.reuters.com/article/us-daimler-geely-electric/daimler-to-develop-smart-brand-together-with-geely-idUSKCN1R90NG (accessed September 14, 2019).

Wang, H. (2008). Innovation in product architecture: A study of the Chinese automobile industry. *Asia Pacific Journal of Management*, **25** (2008), 509–535.

Wang, L. (2006). Chinese Henry Ford. *Economic Observer*, December 30. Available at: http://auto.sina.com.cn/news/2006-12-30/0947242108.shtml (in Chinese, accessed September 2, 2019).

Wang, Q. and D. Liang (2017). *The New Manufacturing Era*. Beijing: CITIC Press, p. 89 (in Chinese).

Wong, K. (2009). Geely buys Australian transmission supplier. *South China Morning Post*, March 28. Available at: https://www.scmp.com/article/674856/geely-buys-australian-transmission-supplier (accessed September 2, 2019).

Yeung, H. W.-C. (2002). Entrepreneurship in the international business: An institutional perspective. *Asia Pacific Journal of Management*, **19** (2002), 29–66.

Zainul, I. and I. Idris (2017). Chinese carmaker's partnership with Proton to create more job opportunities. *The Star*, May 25. Available at: https://www.thestar.com.my/news/nation/2017/05/25/geely-to-make-malaysia-its-global-hub-proton-now-on-firm-footing-proton-now-on-firm-footing-chinese (accessed September 2, 2019).

Zhu, L. (2016). What did the big names say during the 3rd WIC? *China Daily*, November 18. Available at: http://usa.chinadaily.com.cn/business/2016-11/18/content_27421312_9.htm (accessed September 14, 2019).

Chapter 4

Vision and Determination: The Entrepreneurship of Li Shufu

Abstract

A grassroots billionaire businessman and an enduring symbol of entre-preneurship in the booming Chinese manufacture economy, Li Shufu has demonstrated to China and the world that vision and determination are the key ingredients to his remarkable success in launching and expand-ing Geely Auto, China's first private car company and a top-selling brand in the country, as well as a rising player in the global automotive market. Since 1997, Li has leveraged his manufacturing experience and entrepreneurial savvy to overcome multiple difficulties in a highly com-petitive field and risen to the challenge by putting together his dream of designing, manufacturing, and selling automobiles in China and other parts of the world.

This chapter will first explore the basic theoretical framework of Chinese entrepreneurship and then thoroughly examine the endeavors of Li Shufu as a leading entrepreneur in the fast-growing Chinese automobile sector.

Keywords: Li Shufu; Chinese entrepreneurship; Geely Auto; automobile manufacturing; private enterprises; grassroots entrepreneur.

4.1. Theoretical Foundation of Chinese Entrepreneurship

Joseph A. Schumpeter was one the first intellectuals to theorize about entrepreneurship and defined an entrepreneur as someone who is willing and able to convert a new idea or invention into a successful innovation (Schumpeter, 1934, 1976). Although entrepreneurship has been regarded as a very important factor for economic growth, business scholars have struggled with the development of a modern, systematic theory on the role of entrepreneurship. As noted by William J. Baumol, despite attempts by various academics, the economic theory has failed to provide a satisfactory analysis of either the role of the entrepreneurship or its supply (Eliasson and Henrekson, 2004). Recognizing that entrepreneurship study is a multidisciplinary field governed by human factors living in an ever-changing society pursuing simultaneously economic, social, and psychological objectives, many scholars have endeavored to develop different theories of entrepreneurship. In the following paragraphs, we will briefly review some of the most popular theories in the field and examine how they are related to our study of Chinese entrepreneurship.

Despite the fact that there is no generally accepted theory of entrepreneurship, two notions are often cited in entrepreneurial studies: the Discovery Theory and the Creation Theory (Alvarez, 2005). Also known as the Individual/Opportunity (I/O) nexus view, the Discovery Theory centers on the existence, identification, and exploitation of opportunities and the influence of individuals (*Ibid.*, pp. 3–5). While the individuals and the opportunities have influences on each other, the Discovery Theory states that opportunities are objectives, individuals are unique, and entrepreneurs are risk-bearers. In the case of Geely, for example, an opportunity comes into existence only when Li Shufu identifies it. With his experience in and understanding of the Chinese manufacturing industry, Li as a unique individual was able to recognize market opportunities, take up entrepreneurial actions, and bear risks when launching Geely Auto.

Unlike the Discovery Theory, the Creation Theory focuses on entrepreneurs and the creation of enterprises, which suggests that opportunities are subjective, individuals are ordinary, and entrepreneurs are uncertainty-bearers. Despite their different emphases, these two theories are highly complementary in nature and can be used to analyze entrepreneurial behaviors from diverse aspects of opportunities, the nature of entrepreneurs, and the nature of decision-making framework. For instance, as an early-stage enterprise and under the conditions of uncertainty, Geely led by Li was able to exploit new market opportunities by building affordable vehicles for ordinary citizens in the budding Chinese automobile market.

As an evolving subject of study, and along with the rapid development of science and technology, the field of entrepreneurship has undergone some significant transformations and emerged as a critical input for socio-economic development. Within the arena, other notable theories include Economic Entrepreneurship Theory, Psychological Entrepreneurship Theory, Sociological and Anthropological Entrepreneurship Theories, Resource-based Entrepreneurship Theory, and Opportunity-based Entrepreneurship Theory (Simpeh, 2011). Built from those broad frameworks, various models have developed in recent years, which include schemes such as the Innovation Theory; Locus of Control; Need for Achievement Theory; Status Withdrawal Theory; Theory of Social Change; Theory of Social Behavior; Theory of Leadership; Theory of Model Personality; Financial Capital/Liquidity Theory; Social Capital or Social Network Theory; Human Capital Entrepreneurship Theory; and Theory of Systematic Innovation. With different focuses, each of these theories has its strength and weakness and can be applied independently or together for some comprehensive examinations on the intricate development of modern entrepreneurship. A case in point, the Opportunity-based Theory contends that entrepreneurs excel at seeing and taking advantage of possibilities created by social, technological, and cultural changes, which can be used to explain Li Shufu's underlining motivations for acquiring Volvo Cars during the global economic recession. As the founder of Geely Auto, Li has the initiative and necessary skills for innovation and ideas, and as a leading entrepreneur, he looks for high achievements and assumes significant accountability for risks taken and their outcomes.

The entrepreneurial orientation of an effective business leader has been regarded as a crucial ingredient for a firm's success. Referring to "the processes, practices, and decision-making activities that lead to new entry" (Lumpkin and Dess, 1996), entrepreneurial orientation is a strategic response to a complex set of institutional environment and firm factors. Furthermore, a few key entrepreneurial traits have been recognized as good indicators of successful entrepreneurship (Baum and Locke, 2004). Also known as entrepreneurial competencies, entrepreneurial traits denote a combination of knowledge, skills, and personal characteristics required to successfully run a business enterprise. Among recent studies,

Forbes has identified some of the most essential traits possessed by effective entrepreneurs, including passion, resilience, keen sense of self, flexibility, and vision (Rampton, 2014). In the founding and growth of his automobile enterprise, Li Shufu has certainly demonstrated his business vision, strong passion, and personal resilience. His triumph symbolizes the rise of the Chinese entrepreneurs in the 21st century, and the development of Geely as an emerging multinational corporation also signifies the thriving Chinese manufacturing economy on the global stage.

Although the Chinese have been conducting business for thousands of years, the study of Chinese entrepreneurship is a fairly recent phenomenon. In a 2016 essay, *Forbes* reports the rise of entrepreneurship in China (Tse, 216). Zhang, Alon, and Wang research the lives of some prominent Chinese entrepreneurs and contemporary business leaders (Zhang and Alon, 2009; Zhang *et al.*, 2011; Wang, 2012). While Zapalska and Edwards (2001) examine the Chinese entrepreneurship from cultural and economic perspectives, Wong (2008) and a group of scholars also examine the new Chinese entrepreneurship in the global era. Other notable recent researches include works by Chan and Chan (2011), Fernandez and Underwood (2009), Grove (2006), Huang (2008), Huang (2016), Lee (2011), Li (2006), Pérez-Cerezo (2013), Yang (2016), Yu (2015), and Zhang and Stough (2013). Of course, the large economic and sociopolitical environment factors should be carefully considered for any study of Chinese entrepreneurship. For example, at the beginning of the reform era, China's pro-business policies and the changing social altitudes not only contributed significantly to the country's economic development but also led to the rise of private and township entrepreneurship in China, among which Li is a good example. With this understanding, in the following sections, we will closely examine the business career of Li Shufu as a leading entrepreneur in the Chinese manufacturing economy.

4.2. Early Dreams and Endeavors of Li Shufu

Li Shufu was born on June 25, 1963, in the Luqiao District of Taizhou, Zhejiang Province, the third son of five siblings in an ordinary Chinese family. Growing up in a farming village during the Cultural Revolution, Li had an impoverished childhood like million others of that era. Still he had big dreams for his life and once crafted his first cars from sand as a boy, modeled after the Chinese luxury limousine Red Flag from the nearby military airport. He later reflected: "We couldn't afford any toys.

I couldn't imagine making a real car" (Flannery, 2014). Poverty became a great driving force for him to change the path of his life. While in middle school, he began to offer bicycle rides to locals for a small fee, demonstrating his business prodigy at a young age. After graduating from high school in the early 1980s, Li chose to get in to business instead of pursuing a traditional college education, inspired largely by the entrepreneurial spirit prevalent in Zhejiang when China first launched the economic reform.

Li's first business endeavor was photography, and the idea came to his mind while he was standing in line for his high school picture. Despite the initial refusal by the shop owner, Li prevailed by becoming an apprentice with free labor to master the basic skills of photography in two months. At age 19, with a small investment of 120 RMB borrowed from his father, Li purchased a camera and began to ride bicycle around the town, taking pictures of people visiting parks and local attractions. Within six months, he made a net profit of 1,000 RMB and soon set up his own photo studio in town. Along the way he realized more money could be made by recycling precious metals from chemicals used in photo processing. A year later, he closed his profitable photo store to focus on extracting silver from chemical wastes for sale in Hangzhou. By 1984, after learning how to salvage metals from discarded appliances, Li shifted his attention to refrigerator manufacturing, at a time when the country with a rising middle-class population experienced strong demands for modern appliances. He first worked as a factory director of a township enterprise in Huangyan County, which was a market-oriented collective firm under the purview of local government. But he soon launched his own factory manufacturing Arctic Flower refrigerator without official approval, which quickly became a top-selling brand in China, making him one of the few millionaires of the early reform era.

However, a few years later, when the government decided to consolidate the appliance industry in the country, his factory as a private enterprise could not secure proper license from the authority for continual operation; as a result, Li encountered a major setback in his life. Forced out of the appliance business, he tried his luck in real estate investment in Hainan in 1992, only suffering losses in tens of millions when the bubble burst two years later. From this painful experience, Li realized that his strength lay in industrial manufacturing, not speculative investment. Returning to Taizhou, Li launched a firm for manufacturing construction materials and aluminum panels with his brothers that turned out to be a very profitable family undertaking.

While searching for his next adventures, he noticed the great appetite from increasingly affluent Chinese consumers for expensive, imported motorcycles. Here again Li demonstrated his keen business sense and sharp entrepreneurial skills. Realizing the need for mobility services would be the next major growth opportunity, he decided to launch a motorcycle manufacturing business in China. At that time, the production license issued by the Ministry of Machine-Building Industry (MMBI) was reserved for state-owned enterprises (SOE). Learned from his lesson in the refrigerator business fiasco, Li first acquired a state motorcycle plant on the verge of bankruptcy in Zhejiang to secure proper permit for his new enterprise. This important purchase was the first acquisition in Li's career, which significantly influenced the founding and growth of Geely in the ensuing years. Established in 1994, Li's business experienced tremendous growth, and within a few years, it became one of the biggest motorcycle production bases in the country. His *Jiaji* brand motorcycle, sold at less than half the cost of Japanese models, was not only one of the best-known domestic brands in China but was also exported to 22 countries around the world (Flannery, 2014). Consequently, as a private entrepreneur, Li raked in huge profits for his investment.

4.3. Founding of Geely Auto

By the late 1990s, Li Shufu has developed Geely into a multi-structured enterprise that encompassed materials for decoration, trading, real estate, hotels, tourism, and even higher education (Wang, 2008). Although his motorcycle business was doing quite well in China, Li was very concerned with its low barrier of entry and low profit margin in the increasingly competitive market. Reminiscing his childhood dream, he was determined to build affordable vehicles for ordinary Chinese households. At that time, the Chinese automotive industry was dominated by large SOEs and a few joint ventures (JVs). Even though the State Council had issued policy directives to encourage the rapid development of passenger vehicles for the Chinese market, the industry in the 1990s was still tightly controlled by the government, and no private enterprises had ever been granted permission for automobile manufacturing. Facing doubts and daunting challenges, Li boldly claimed: "What is so complicated? It is just a matter of putting two sofas on four wheels" (Young, 2010; Gong and Li, 2016).

Since the global automotive industry has been well developed with mature technologies, Li was confident that he could invest, learn, and build cars himself. He first bought several models of Mercedes, Red Flag, and other best-selling cars in China to be taken apart by his engineers, so that they could have a better understanding of their components and start the process of reverse engineering and integrative imitation. Then, under the pretense of expanding his motorcycle manufacturing base, he began to build production facilities in Linhai, Zhejiang. However, in the tightly controlled market for automobile manufacturing, since no private enterprises could receive governmental approval for passenger vehicles, the production license emerged again a major roadblock. This time Li went around the issue by seeking a partnership with an SOE in Deyang, Sichuan Province, that had permit for minivans and compact vehicles, which was different from passenger cars according to the state classification by the Chinese bureaucracy. Incidentally, Li named his joint venture Geely Boeing Auto, after the book he was reading about the rise of the American airplane manufacturer. Such a beguiling name not only provoked the formal protest by the US aerospace giant but also prompted Ford Motor Company to ponder about Boeing's new strategic move in China (Moss and Boston, 2018).

In 1997, after securing the proper permit, Geely Auto was formally established in Zhejiang, and Li began to focus his attention on the design and manufacture of his new vehicle. Originally, he planned to build a crossover between Benz and Red Flag, but soon toned down his ambition after realizing the difficulties he had to overcome. At that time, the high-end market was dominated by large SOEs and JVs, while the market for economy vehicles was still wide open in China. Under Li's leadership, *building affordable cars for ordinary people* become the first mission of the company, and this strategy contributed significantly to the initial growth of Geely Auto. Nevertheless, the road to success was by no means easy or straightforward. Geely Model I was largely handiworks assembled by his mechanics, and HQ (*Haoqing*), the first production model by Geely in 1998, was a total disaster with numerous problems. Even though the car was named Ambition in Chinese, suitably reflecting his sentiment for automobile manufacturing, there were not much to be proud of, and Li had to use a road roller to crush over 100 of his vehicles. This became a very important moment in Geely's history: by doing so, Li drove home a clear message to his employees on the utmost importance of production quality in automotive manufacturing.

Although Li began to make automobiles in the late 1990s, the license he obtained was only for compact vehicles and minivans, no upgrades could be granted, and the Chinese government still gave preferable treatment to large SOEs and JVs in land acquisitions, bank loans, import/ export supports, and other business measures. In December 1999, when a high-ranking official visited his production base in Zhejiang, Li passionately pleaded for his case: "Please let me try. It is my dream. I'll pay for everything and take all risks. Just give me an opportunity to win or lose on my own" (*China Daily*, 2006). Two years later, Li had his chance. In November 2001, right before China entered the World Trade Organization (WTO), the State Economic and Trade Commission (later incorporated in the Ministry of Commerce) issued a policy document, and Geely finally became one of the nationally authorized production bases for passenger cars.

4.4. Geely's Growth under Li Shufu

Li knew very well he would need production scale in order to survive in the competitive Chinese automotive industry. After the much-improved HQ model was well received in the market, he began to build the second assembly line in Ningbo, Zhejiang, that went in production in 2000. China's entrance into WTO lifted the final bureaucratic policy restrictions and provided the necessary platform for Geely's tremendous growth in the new century. Li's second model was named *Merrie* (MR), which means happy days in Chinese; the phrase also suggests America and Japan, implying the top quality represented by automobiles from the two countries. To build the most affordable vehicles for ordinary Chinese, Li launched *Operation Three-Fives* in Geely: his car would carry five people, run 100 km on 5 liters of gas, and sell at 50,000 RMB (Wang and Liang, 2017). When his new car finally reached the market, it was priced at 65,800 RMB (US$7,950 in 2003), the lowest for the economic vehicles in China and well below the benchmark price of the industry, which led to a wave of price reductions that greatly benefited consumers and contributed to increased ownership among Chinese households. Along the way, Li became one of the richest people in the country, and as a private entrepreneur, he was not only labeled a "spoiler" for the Chinese automobile industry but also praised as China's Henry Ford, who built affordable cars for the mass market (McKenna, 2006; Young, 2010).

Since automobile manufacturing is a very capital-intensive industry and the state-controlled banks typically would not loan to private enterprises, initially Li had to rely on the support from family relatives, friends, and other rich entrepreneurs from Zhejiang for investment in his production lines. As this grassroots financial arrangement was based largely on personal connections, quite a few of his factories for automotive parts were actually owned by others, even though all were listed under Geely Auto. Due to this variance in ownership structure, multiple conflicts emerged when there were diverse interests in corporate profits and different understandings on the future direction of the company. After Geely found its foothold in the Chinese auto market, Li shifted his focus to corporate ownership structure by gradually buying back shares owned by his brothers and others. Within few years, Li became the sole owner of Geely while his brothers concentrated on the other non-auto business of the family. Related to this initiative, in 2004, Li also purchased a shell company listed on the Hong Kong Stock Exchange, and the following year Geely became a fully traded public company with Li as the largest shareholder, raising much needed funding for the sustained development of his automobile operation.

Whereas Li strived to convert his family business, he also made great efforts to transform Geely into a modern enterprise. Shortly after the restructuring of Geely Auto in 2002, Li made a surprising announcement that he decided to step down and turn over corporate operation to management professionals. Instead, he would be responsible for market research and future direction of Geely Group while serving as corporate ambassador in charge of governmental affairs. Within Geely, he also pushed for a strategic re-examination on how business was conducted and encouraged all employees to raise questions and make suggestions for improvement. As a result, over 400 problem areas ranging from corporate culture to budget management were pointed out, which led to redesigned organizational structure, clearly defined responsibilities, more comprehensive company policies and operation procedures, and improved production efficiency. In hindsight, all these measures have demonstrated Li's vision as a modern entrepreneur and contributed greatly to Geely's growth in the new century.

During the early years of its operation, even though Geely was able to make cars that were well received by consumers, Li had to rely on purchased engines and transmissions controlled by other manufacturers. These bottlenecks made him realize Geely must develop its own core technology to have a bright future in the automotive market. He once professed: "Core technology can't be bought. The more you use others' technology, the more reliant you become. We have to innovate on our own. The journey will be tough but the prospects are promising" (Archer, 2018). With such a conviction, he invested heavily in his team of engineers, not only providing necessary funding but also his strong support and trust. Accordingly, within a few years, Geely achieved breakthroughs in both areas with its own core technologies, and the launch of its next major model, Free Cruiser (CK), which marked the rise of Geely as a new automobile manufacturer with modern facilities and a full range of self-development and self-innovation capabilities.

As Geely matured and shifted to a fast lane of growth, Li was also keenly aware that he must continually invest in R&D, and Geely should not forever compete in the compact vehicle sector but move up the value chain and have new models for more diverse households in the country. His answer was a newly designed *Yuanjing* (Vision) model that reached the market in 2007. During the news conference, Li passionately delivered his "Ningbo Declaration," which outlined Geely's new strategic commitment for competing on technology, quality, brand, after-sales service, as well as the corporate social responsibility instead of price wars (CGTN, 2018). This statement marks one of the most important transformations in the history of Geely Auto, and the company under Li's leadership has grown from low-cost production to competing for value-added products and making safe, reliable, environmentally friendly, and energy-efficient vehicles for consumers. Instead of a market follower trying to imitate successful models developed by other large manufacturers, Geely now has established a full line of production competing in different sectors. As a visionary entrepreneur, Li has positioned his company to be an innovative leader ready for new challenges in the global automotive industry, and the global economic crisis in the following year provided him such an opportunity.

4.5. Global Expansion for the Future

Li knew very well overseas expansion would be critical if Geely wanted to be an auto company with global influence, and acquisitions would be the most direct and cost-effective strategy for gaining new technologies, know-hows, and international market share. As early as in 2002, shortly after Geely acquired its official approval for car manufacturing, Li set his eyes on global market and expressed a strong interest in Volvo. That same year Li also made bold claims that General Motors and Ford would file for bankruptcy one day, and in the future the center of automotive manufacturing would be in Asia. At that time, no one believed his wild proclaims, and Li was dubbed as "the automobile maniac" of China (Feng, 2018, p. 162). Despite the sensational news coverage, Li in 2003 launched a small-scale export project to the Middle East, and two years later, Geely entered an agreement with the IGC Group for an assembly production in Malaysia, which marked the first time a Chinese auto brand sought to establish an overseas manufacturing base, even though the contract never materialized in the end. In 2005, Geely presented its new Chinese Dragon (CD) at the Frankfurt Auto Show and its Free Cruiser (CK) at the North American International Auto Show in Detroit the following year, the first Chinese automobile ever displayed at an American auto exhibit (Xing and Tian, 2005; Lienert, 2006). Shortly after, Geely also purchased large shares of London Taxi from Manganese Bronze Holdings and formed a JV with the British cab maker to move its production to China. Through all these efforts, Li began to develop a more comprehensive understanding about the international market, and he was ready for his next strategic move.

Meanwhile in the US, a perfect economic storm was fast approaching Detroit. When Alan Mulally was named president and CEO of Ford in 2006, the company had been struggling for some time, and he was charged to bring Ford back to profitability. As an industry outsider, Mulally pushed through *the Way Forward* restructure plan aimed to turn around Ford's massive losses and falling market shares. In 2007, when Li first learned about Mulally's plan to concentrate only on the Ford brand going forward, he immediately formed a project team and made direct inquiry about Volvo. Although the initial proposal went nowhere, Ford, amid mounting losses during the 2008 global recession, began to seriously entertain the idea, and in October 2008, Geely was named as the preferred buyer of Volvo by the American automaker (*Guardian*, 2008). Li was able quickly to recruit a highly competent team led by the investment bank Edmond de Rothschild Group and submitted a formal bid in March 2009. After obtaining official approval from the Chinese government, securing necessary finance, and going through multiple rounds of technically complicated and emotionally charged negotiations, the two parties finally reached an agreement by the end of the year. On March 28, 2010, Li signed a deal to buy Volvo Cars from Ford Motor Company for US$1.8 billion, along with US$900 million of working capital from Geely and a commitment to build a Volvo factory in China (Ford, 2010). This achievement became the largest foreign purchase by a Chinese car manufacturer of the time. Needless to say, this strategic acquisition was critically important for Li and the future development of Geely, since it complemented Geely's lower-price models and provided "entrée into a key new market: premium foreign-brand cars that are poised to lead growth in China in the coming years" (Flannery, 2014).

The track records of international mergers and acquisitions (M&A) in recent decades indicated that most cross-border takeovers of carmakers have fared badly; Ford's purchase of Volvo is an excellent case in point. When Li acquired Volvo, which had revenues five times larger than Geely, industry observers were not very optimistic about the future of the deal. In absorbing and managing Volvo, Li again demonstrated his entrepreneurial genius. First, he showed his personal interest and great respect for the Scandinavian quality culture in manufacturing. To win support from the trade union, he kept his promise of maintaining Volvo's costly plants and workforce, summarizing his sentiment in three simple words — I love you — when meeting with Volvo workers in Europe. Next, after acquiring the premium brand, he chose to keep its independence, publicly declaring "Volvo is Volvo, Geely is Geely" (*China Daily*, 2011). In his eyes, Volvo is "like a tiger in the mountains," it should be roaming freely in the nature, not "in a cage in a zoo" (Flannery, 2014). Instead of micromanagement, Li only provided necessary strategic support. Under his leadership, Volvo began to operate with China as its second home market. Since then, the company has not only returned to profitability but also significantly enlarged its workforce in Europe. Volvo and Geely have also established a joint research hub in Sweden (China Euro Vehicle Technology AB), which focuses on the development of common manufacturing platforms and common technology to enhance and leverage Volvo's strengths in product safety.

Besides acquiring and reviving Volvo, Geely in recent years has been very active in the international auto market. In 2017, Li purchased a 49.9% stake in Malaysia-based PROTON and a 51% stake in the British sports car maker Lotus to further enhance its global competitiveness and internal synergies. In 2018, he bought 9.69% of stake to become the largest shareholder in Daimler, while pledging on a collaborative partnership with the leading German carmaker for the future development of *smart* cars and mobility services (Taylor and Shirouru, 2019). More notably, to realize his dream of making the flying car a reality, Li also acquired the Boston-based start-up Terrafugia, a world leader in flying-car technology (Barclay, 2017). In addition, in September 2019, Geely jointly invested with Daimler on the German startup Volocopter, with a total investment of €50 million (US$55 million). The goal of the JV is to produce and sell Volocopters in China in the coming years.

Moreover, Li has made great efforts to transform Geely into a technology company. He signed an agreement with a Chinese aerospace company to build "hypersonic" trains (Archer, 2018), and formed the forward-looking Geely Technology Group to work toward the development of the smart travel ecology in autonomous driving, connectivity, and energy diversification. In March 2020, Li announced the launch of *Geespace*, Geely's low-orbit satellite program to aid autonomous driving. All these undertakings have clearly revealed Li's striving vision for the future, and his strong drive to transform Geely from a traditional automaker to an innovation leader in the world.

4.6. Entrepreneurship of Li Shufu

Multiple factors have contributed to the success of Li and Geely. Although his first name means fortune in Chinese, and he gave a very auspicious label for his company, Li had a humble beginning, and the growth of Geely is by no means a smooth driving experience. However, in a way, he is very fortunate. As a son of an ordinary Chinese farmer and a grassroots entrepreneur, Li seized the strong pulse of the country and bravely rode large waves of the opening economic reform, China's entrance into WTO, and the ensuing globalization drives to transform Geely from a family business and the first private auto company in China to a modern enterprise with global influence. Growing up in the booming southeast region of China with savvy entrepreneurial culture, it seems that Li, throughout his career, has seized opportunities to develop his business and foster growth in technology and market shares. In reality, opportunities exist only for those with a vision and purpose and who know where to look. To a large degree, his remarkable achievement is due to his broad vision, long-term outlook, and forward-thinking capabilities. In addition to his business intelligence, he also has a strong curiosity and a spirit for innovation and adventure, and these attitudes have enabled him to develop a clear understanding of his business environment, formulate right strategies, and stay ahead of the curve in a highly competitive market. "Li is indeed a man with vision. He is someone that shouldn't be underestimated" (Young, 2010).

Li is not only a bold thinker but also a doer, not only a dreamer but also a pragmatic realist who knows what it will take to reach his goals.

An intelligent, energetic, and thoughtful person, he always listens to diverse opinions and is willing to adopt different approaches when facing difficult choices; however, he is not afraid of making tough decisions, and when he makes up his mind, Li usually never gives up. According to Flannery (2014), "He is extremely stubborn, and mostly it is beneficial to him." He once claimed: "What is innovation? Innovation should be something you insist on, even though all others disagree" (Feng, 2018, p. 167). From his first entrepreneurship with 120 RMB and his early success in making appliances to manufacturing motorcycles and founding Geely Auto years later, Li has faced numerous challenges that seemed insurmountable to most people. Unlike some high-profile businessmen of the time who chased fortune and fame, he is determined to push forward the development of private enterprises in China and aspires to play a significant role in both Chinese and global automobile markets. His perseverance has been evident throughout the multi-year process of Volvo acquisition. From his original interest in the early 2000s, Li stayed focused on his target, and after the initial refusal, he persisted with new offers while demonstrating his sincerity to Ford as well as to Volvo. During the tough negotiation process and faced with the extremely difficult task of raising necessary funding for the purchase, when others were ready to give up, it was Li who served as both the leader and advocate for the team. In the end, his resolution paid off; he was able to sell his idea to others and turned a bold dream into a reality. He has stated, "I understand that hard work, determination, and courage in the face of enormous challenges will inevitably bring success" (McKenna, 2006).

Although growing up Li did not receive a traditional college education, he attended technical school and is an engineer by training. As a grassroots entrepreneur, he never considers himself a superman or more special than any others. In his audacious endeavors over years, he is always eager to learn and always respects experts in the field, believing they hold the key to his success. In running his business, he is often open-minded, never tries to be heavy-handed or micromanage but trusts and provides encouragement and support to his employees. He knows well that the most effective way to reach the company goals is through a shared vision and teamwork, and his philosophy in human resource management is based on individual talents rather than favoritism, as he believes that everyone has talents, everyone can be a teacher, but at the same time everyone is also a student (人人是人才, 人人也是老师, 可人人也是学生). In cross-cultural management, Li has a cosmopolitan view following the

16-character philosophy (各美其美，美人之美，美美与共，天下大同): appreciating the culture/values of others as do to one's own, and the world will become a harmonious whole; Everybody cherishes his or her own culture/values, and if we respect and treasure other's culture/values, the world will be a harmonious one (People.com.cn, 2012). This pluralistic belief system has contributed greatly in his dealings with international acquisitions and post-merger management of recent years. Because of his moral principles and his track record in practices, Li has gained a reputation as a respectful entrepreneur in China; and as a result, he is able to recruit a team of talented people who share his bold vision of driving Geely swiftly forward onto the world stage.

Li is by no means an articulate person, but he is very media savvy. He always manages to stay in the news, thereby generating some free publicity for Geely. Once dubbed as the automobile maniac of China, he is not afraid of speaking his mind. When he tried to break through the tightly controlled market, Li strongly criticized the JV system in China, which in his view granted unfair advantage to, and produced large profits for, foreign manufacturers at the expense of innovation, quality, and technology advancement by Chinese domestic firms. He once stated: "To build joint-ventures is like getting addicted to opium. The one who holds the brand and core technologies controls the game. We should make efforts to export Chinese cars to the world, rather than watch cars from all over the world getting into China" (Feng, 2018, p. 177).

In the so-called socialist market economy with Chinese characteristics, Li is also very experienced at navigating China's political waters. Due to the recent impressive feats of Geely in global expansion, there was even a rumor that Li's wife was related to the family of President Xi of China, which turned out to be fabricated (*Bloomberg*, 2018). Still, the reality is that even after he stepped down from the CEO position to focus on the future strategic direction of Geely, Li has stayed on to serve as corporate ambassador in charge of governmental affairs. From the painful experience of the forced closure of his first appliance factory, his struggles of obtaining proper permits for his motorcycle and automobile business, and his difficulties in securing loans from banks for corporate expansions, he knows wholeheartedly that governmental support will be one of the most critical factors for the survival and success of Geely. While he has no political ambitions, Li is the current member of the National People's Congress, and he has served three consecutive terms as a member of the Chinese People's Political Consultative Conference. Though both are largely symbolic and ceremonial political advisory positions, they have provided a necessary platform for Li to rub elbows with high-ranking officials and other powerful people in the Chinese business circles. Named one of the Outstanding Figures in the Chinese Automotive Industry, he is the current vice chairman of the All-China Federation of Industry and Commerce and the Zhejiang Federation of Industry and Commerce, and the vice president of the Chinese Association of Automobile Manufacturers. In addition, Li has received the national honor as a Reform Pioneer from the Chinese State Council. As one of the most influential business leaders in the country, he is listed among the Top 10 Private Entrepreneurs and the Top 10 Philanthropists of China. All these official recognitions have further enhanced Li's prestige as a successful entrepreneur in China.

With a farsighted vision and sheer determination, time and again Li has demonstrated the core entrepreneurial behaviors of being proactive, innovative, and risk taking, which contribute directly to the rapid growth of Geely as a new Chinese automobile maker in the world. By dedicating to what he believes, Li is never disheartened by failures. With a clear understanding of both Chinese and global markets, he gains new ideas through vision, insight, and observation; and he is always on the lookout for business opportunities and is ready to exploit them to gain competitive advantage in the market. He is self-motivated toward achievement and is always keen to devise new methods aimed at promoting efficiency and making work easier, simpler, better, and economical. As an optimistic, creative, and resilient individual, Li possesses the core entrepreneurial traits required for business success, and his achievement symbolizes the growth of Chinese entrepreneurship in the 21st century. Of course, his success should be examined within the context of the rising Chinese economy and other large social-political frameworks. Li has certainly learned and benefited from the rich entrepreneurial culture prevalent in southeastern China, and the region's strong manufacturing base and the Chinese government's pro-growth policy initiatives have all played key roles in the development of Geely.

In 2013, *Hurun Report* ranked Li the 63rd richest person in mainland China, with a net worth of US$2.6 billion; five years later he was listed as #16 with 90 billion RMB (*Hurun*, 2018). *Bloomberg* currently ranks Li #109 on its Billionaire Index with US$12 billion, while *Forbes* lists him #91 in the world (US$12.5 billion) and #9 in China (*Bloomberg*, 2019; *Forbes*, 2019). Calling him a "Disrupter," *Motor Trend* in 2019 has recognized Li among the top 10 players of the global auto industry, rising from #21 a year before (Priddle, 2018, 2019). As summarized by *Automotive News*, "Li has proved to be an effective and visionary leader in the auto industry. He has achieved stunning business success in transforming Geely from a little-known motorcycle manufacturer into the largest and most profitable Chinese carmaker" (Yang, 2018). For his impressive accomplishments, Dunne describes him "part poet, part visionary — at heart a fearless entrepreneur" (Anantharaman, 2017). What does the future hold for Li and Geely? Looking forward, according to Young, "I think he has a big chance to make it because he has the Chinese government and, most of all, the huge China market behind him" (Young, 2010).

References

Alvarez, S. (2005). *Theories of Entrepreneurship: Alternative Assumptions and the Study of Entrepreneurial Actions*. Boston: Now Publishers.

Anantharaman, K. (2017). Geely? Really? China's Quiet Disruptor Is Poised to Tackle Big Challenges. *Automotive News*, November 13, 2017.

Archer, J. (2018). Chinese car billionaire signs deal to build 'supersonic' trains. *The Telegraph*, November 6. Available at: https://www.telegraph.co.uk/technology/2018/11/06/chinese-car-billionaire-signs-deal-build-supersonic-trains/ (accessed September 15, 2019).

Barclay, A. (2017). Geely buys US start-up Terrafugia and promises a flying car by 2019. *South China Morning Post*, November 15. Available at: https://www.scmp.com/business/companies/article/2120084/geely-buys-us-start-terrafugia-and-promises-flying-car-2019 (accessed September 15, 2019).

Bloomberg News (2018). What's in a name? A lot of it links a billionaire to China's Xi. October 18. Available at: https://www.bloomberg.com/news/articles/2018-10-17/what-s-in-a-name-a-lot-if-it-links-a-billionaire-to-china-s-xi (accessed September 15, 2019).

Bloomberg (2019). #107 ($12.3 billion) Bloomberg Billionaires Index. Available at: https://www.bloomberg.com/billionaires/profiles/shu-fu-li/ (accessed September 15, 2019).

Baum, J. R. and E. A. Locke (2004). The relationship of entrepreneurial traits, skill, and motivation to subsequent venture growth. *Journal of Applied Psychology*, **89**:4, 587–598.

CGTN (2018). Faces of reform and opening up: Li Shufu leads China's largest private auto company to go global. December 22. Available at: https://news.cgtn.com/news/3041444d30494464776c6d636a4e6e62684a4856/share_p.html (accessed September 15, 2019).

Chan, K. B. and W.-w. Chan (2011). *Mobile Chinese Entrepreneurs*. New York: Springer.

China Daily (2006). BIZCHINA: Li Shufu. March 27. Available at: http://www.chinadaily.com.cn/business/2006-03/27/content_553392.htm (accessed September 15, 2019).

China Daily (2011). Driving ambition. January 14. Available at: http://usa.chinadaily.com.cn/china/2011-01/14/content_11913295.htm (accessed September 15, 2019).

Eliasson, G. and M. Henrekson (2004). William J. Baumol: An entrepreneurial economist on the economics of entrepreneurship. *Small Business Economics*, **23**:1, 1–7.

Feng, Q. (2018). *Variety of Development: Chinese Automakers in Market Reform*. Cham, Switzerland: Palgrave Macmillan.

Fernandez, J. A. and L. Underwood (2009). *China Entrepreneur: Voices of Experience from 40 International Business Pioneers*. Singapore: John Wiley & Sons.

Flannery, R. (2014). Life after Ford: Volvo turnaround gains speed under Chinese billionaire owner. *Forbes Asia,* November. Available at: https://www.forbes.com/sites/russellflannery/2014/10/27/geely-in-swedish/#18fb61b3999d (accessed September 15, 2019).

Forbes (2019). World Billionaire Index. Available at: https://www.forbes.com/sites/russellflannery/2014/10/27/geely-in-swedish/#18fb61b3999d (accessed September 15, 2019).

Ford Motor Company (2010). Ford reaches agreement to sell Volvo Cars and related assets to Geely. March 28.

Gong, Z. and F. Li (2016). Coming to roads near you: Sofas that think. *China Daily*, June 1. Available at: http://www.chinadaily.com.cn/china/2016-06/01/content_25569452.htm (accessed September 15, 2019).

Grove, L. (2006). *A Chinese Economic Revolution: Rural Entrepreneurship in the Twentieth Century*. Lanham, MD: Rowman & Littlefield.

Guardian (2008). Ford set to offload Volvo to Chinese carmaker Zhejiang Geely. October 28. Available at: https://www.theguardian.com/business/2009/oct/28/volvo-ford-geely-china-car (accessed September 15, 2019).

Huang, X. (2016). *Chinese Entrepreneurship*. New York: Routledge.

Huang, Y. (2008). *Capitalism with Chinese Characteristics: Entrepreneurship and the State*. New York: Cambridge University Press.

Hurun (2018). 2018 LEXUS China Rich List. Available at: https://www.hurun.net/en-US/Info/Detail?num=E406EB5BC439 (accessed September 15, 2019).

Lee, H. (2011). *Chinese Entrepreneurship*. Hong Kong: Anything & Everything.

Li, J. (2006). *Entrepreneurship and Small Business Development in China*. Bradford: Emerald Publishing.

Lienert, D. (2006). Highlights from the Detroit Auto Show 2006. *Forbes*, January 12. Available at: https://www.forbes.com/2006/01/11/detroit-auto-show-cx_dl_0112feat_ls.html#5aaac2081231 (accessed September 15, 2019).

Lumpkin, G. T. and G. G. Dess (1996). Clarifying the entrepreneurial orientation construct and linking it to performance. *Academy of Management Review*, **21**:1, 135–172.

McKenna, J. F. (2006). China's Henry Ford. *Tooling & Production*, **72**:(4), 2006.

Moss, T. and W. Boston (2018). How China's Geely turned a disassembled Mercedes into a global car company. *Wall Street Journal*, March 4. Available at: https://www.wsj.com/articles/how-chinas-geely-turned-a-disassembled-mercedes-into-a-global-car-company-1520188109 (accessed September 15, 2019).

People.com.cn. (2012). Li Shufu. Available at: http://auto.people.com.cn/GB/239017/239575/index.html (accessed September 15, 2019).

Pérez-Cerezo, J. (2013). *The Chinese Entrepreneurship Way: A Case Study Approach*. New York: Business Expert Press.

Priddle, A. (2018). Power list: 49 of the auto industry's top players, plus our person of the year. *Motor Trend*, **70**:1(January).

Priddle, A. (2019). Power List: 49 of the auto industry's top players, plus our person of the year. *Motor Trend*, **71**:1(January).

Rampton, J. (2014). Five personality traits of an entrepreneur. *Forbes*, April 14. Available at: https://www.forbes.com/sites/johnrampton/2014/04/14/5-personality-traits-of-an-entrepreneur/#795259083bf4 (accessed December 18, 2019).

Schumpeter, J. A. (1934). *The Theory of Economic Development: An Inquiry into Profits, Capital, Credit, Interest, and the Business Cycle*. London: Transaction Publishers.

Schumpeter, J. A. (1976). *Capitalism, Socialism and Democracy*. London: Routledge.

Simpeh, K. N. (2011). Entrepreneurship theories and empirical research: A summary review of the literature. *European Journal of Business and Management*, **3**:6, 1–8.

Taylor, E. and N. Shirouzu (2019). Daimler to develop smart brand together with Geely. *Routers Business News*, March 28. Available at: https://www.reuters.com/article/us-daimler-geely-electric/daimler-to-develop-smart-brand-together-with-geely-idUSKCN1R90NG (accessed September 15, 2019).

Tse, E. (2016). The rise of entrepreneurship in China. *Forbes*, April 5. Available at: https://www.forbes.com/sites/tseedward/2016/04/05/the-rise-of-entrepreneurship-in-china/#34fc09673efc (accessed December 14, 2019).

Wang, H. (2008). Innovation in product architecture: A study of the Chinese automobile industry. *Asia Pacific Journal of Management*, **25**: 509–535.

Wang, H. (2012). *Globalizing China: The Influence, Strategies and Successes of Chinese Returnee Entrepreneurs.* Bingley, UK: Emerald Group Publishing.

Wang, Q. and D. Liang (2017). *The New Manufacturing Era.* Beijing: CITIC Press, p. 41 (in Chinese).

Wong, R. S.-K. (ed.) (2008). *Chinese Entrepreneurship in a Global Era.* London: Routledge.

Xing, W. and A. Tian (2005). Chinese-made cars: The talk of the town in Frankfurt. *Chinese Automotive Review*, November 1.

Yang, J. (2018). With new partnerships, ventures, sky's the limit for Geely, Li Shufu. *Automotive News*, **93**:6857, November 26.

Yang, K. (2016). *Entrepreneurship in China.* London: Routledge.

Young, D. (2010). Geely's folksy Li known as China's Henry Ford. *Reuters Business News*, July 22. Available at: https://www.reuters.com/article/us-geely-volvo-newsmaker/geelys-folksy-li-known-as-chinas-henry-ford-idUSTRE66L2ER20100722 (accessed September 15, 2019).

Yu, T. F.-L. (2015). *Chinese Entrepreneurship.* New York: Routledge.

Zapalska, A. M. and W. Edwards (2001). Chinese entrepreneurship in a cultural and economic perspective. *Journal of Small Business Management*, **39**:3, 286–292.

Zhang, T. and R. Stough (2013). *Entrepreneurship and Economic Growth in China.* Singapore: World Scientific.

Zhang, W. and I. Alon (eds). (2009). *Biographical Dictionary of New Chinese Entrepreneurs and Business Leaders.* Cheltenham, UK: Edward Elgar.

Zhang, W., H. Wang and I. Alon (ed.) (2011). *Entrepreneurial and Business Elites of China: The Chinese Returnees Who Have Shaped Modern China.* Bingley, UK: Emerald.

Part II

Take Geely to the World: Geely's Acquisition of Volvo

Chapter 5

Geely and Volvo: Value and Strategic Asset Creation through International Acquisition

Abstract

The acquisition of Volvo Cars was a milestone in Geely's multinational expansion efforts. It was the most significant move in Geely's long-term international asset-seeking strategy and served as the starting point of a new strategy of asset creation, innovation, and global expansion. Extended autonomy and independence were given to Volvo, based on the principle "Volvo is Volvo, Geely is Geely." As a result, Volvo rapidly and successfully expanded in China, while the opening of China Euro Vehicle Technology AB (CEVT) in Gothenburg created a key instrument for technology cooperation in the post-merger integration process. This chapter provides an interpretative analysis of the drivers, features, and results of the crucial acquisition of Volvo.

Keywords: Geely Auto; Volvo; Mergers & Acquisitions; Globalization; China; Sweden.

5.1. Introduction

The acquisition of Volvo Cars, concluded in 2010 after an active search and an extensive bargaining process, represented the most significant stage in Geely's long-term international asset-seeking strategy (targeting technology, knowledge, brands, and capabilities), implemented since 2002. At the same time, it was the first stage of a new strategy of asset creation and global expansion. This complex operation was an extremely important step both in the catching up and innovation process and in the internationalization process of Geely to foster continuous growth (Balcet *et al.*, 2012).

In this chapter, we will first survey some relevant approaches and categories, detailing the strategies of emerging multinational companies, including those from China, and applying them to the specific case of Geely. We will then proceed to analyze the process and the key features of the acquisition of Volvo Cars by Geely, discussing drivers, strategies, and implications. We will discuss the stages of the post-merger integration process, focusing on the expansion of Volvo in China and its performances. Special attention will be devoted to the creation of China Euro Vehicle Technology AB (CEVT) in Gothenburg, as a key instrument for technology cooperation between Geely and Volvo and new asset creation. Finally, we will provide some general conclusions on this important step and its impact.

5.2. Asset-Seeking Foreign Acquisition and Asset Creation: An Overview

Several theoretical approaches have employed the category of "asset-seeking strategies" as a key specific explanation of foreign acquisitions and foreign direct investment (FDI) by emerging multinational companies. Moon and Roehl (2001) pointed out that, contrary to the case of Western multinational companies, a firm based in an emerging country may invest abroad to overcome its own disadvantages, such as the lack of technology or managerial know how, or a limited market share on the domestic market. Luo and Tung (2007) argued that multinational firms from emerging countries use outward investment as a springboard to acquire strategic assets. Moreover, emerging multinational companies, as latecomers, tend to internationalize at an accelerated pace, not gradually through incremental steps, in order to catch up with incumbent multinational corporations (MNCs).

John Mathews developed a popular theory to explain the expansion of "Dragon Multinational Enterprises," known as the "linkage, leverage, and learning" (LLL) theory. He stressed that emerging MNCs are keen on establishing linkages, including alliances and joint ventures with incumbent MNCs, leveraging resources, learning, and imitating (Mathews, 2002, 2006). The emerging multinational companies are characterized by their networking abilities, especially in the case of Chinese *Guanxi* or "bamboo networks" (Tolentino, 2008).

All these approaches reach common conclusions. The importance of asset-seeking motivations, vis-à-vis the standard and traditional market-oriented and natural resource-oriented motivations, is highlighted, as well as the capacity of absorbing, assimilating, and adapting foreign technology, as a pre-requisite for the successful multinational growth of an emerging country corporation.

Moreover, an accelerated pace of international growth and the role of networking and international alliances are confirmed as key features of emerging country, and specifically, Chinese MNCs. In China, the role of domestic institutions and political support from the government seems to be hold special importance.

Finally, as Andreff and Balcet (2013) point out, labor cost advantages, especially skilled labor costs, matter and significantly affect these firms' international competitiveness.

In the case of Volvo acquisition by Geely, we should stress the fact that asset-seeking strategies evolved into asset-augmenting and finally into asset-creating strategies, involving both acquiring and acquired corporations in two-way flows of technology, people, and knowledge, producing synergies in terms of production quality and costs, innovation, and performances (Yakob *et al.*, 2018).

As we have seen in Chapter 3, Geely's catching up was driven by quite different strategies through its different stages of development (Balcet *et al.*, 2012). In a first stage, starting in the 1990s, reverse engineering and product architecture innovation were the main ways to acquire, assimilate, and imitate foreign technology. Although this strategy helped Geely to largely reduce production costs and win a place in the low-end market as well as increase exports to price-sensitive developing countries, the limits of such a strategy, based on mature technology, were clear to Li Shufu and Geely's top management. Therefore, after the first stage of knowledge, technology, and capital accumulation, in the second stage, since 2002, Geely changed its growth model toward strategic asset-seeking and value-creating FDIs, in particular through international mergers and acquisitions.

The 2008 financial and economic crisis offered new opportunities for the implementation of this strategy. The main objectives were to gain access to advanced foreign technologies and premium global brands, as well as organizations with excellent management, so that the Geely Group could gain more advantages to compete in the global market and face future challenges. The strategic asset-seeking FDIs of Geely went parallel with the acceleration of its internationalization trajectory.

From a strategic point of view, the acquisition of Volvo in 2010 represented a third stage in Geely's trajectory, that of strategic asset creation through recombination and intense process and product innovation, both for Geely and for Volvo. The acquisition was a significant challenge from the point of view of organizational integration, as the recent business history gives many examples of failure in post-acquisition coordination and integration.

In the case of Geely and Volvo, *ex ante* static complementarity between markets and products was important as a preliminary condition, but not sufficient to ensure success. However, the post-acquisition process made possible a long-term dynamic complementarity that was crucial in terms of joint projects, industrial cooperation, and technology innovation in the decade between 2010 and 2020, achieving important results.

5.3. Volvo Cars Acquisition: The Milestone of Geely's Internationalization Trajectory

Founded in 1927, the Swedish-based AB Volvo (now Volvo Car Corporation) was struggling in the 1990s to adapt to the new competitive scenario in the global automotive industry. Thinking that it was too small to survive alone, Volvo entered into a complex alliance and industrial agreement with the French carmaker Renault, as well as with Japan's Mitsubishi Motors. However, the challenging alliance with Renault collapsed, due to high cultural distance, diverging strategies, and fears of losing control.

In 1999, AB Volvo decided to sell its car business. It was acquired by the American Ford Motor Corporation for US$6.5 billion. Consequently, Volvo Cars was integrated into the Ford Group for 10 years, but showed poor performances. Sales were flat for years after acquisition, falling during the 2008–2009 recession, and finally showing heavy losses, as economies of scale were not sufficient to reduce production costs. When the global financial and economic crisis erupted, the Ford Group decided to divest from Volvo. After a long bargaining process, in 2010, Geely acquired Volvo Cars at the price of only US$1.8 billion, which represented a very good financial deal for Geely.

The process of negotiation followed a search that began in 2002. Since 2005, Geely mobilized international partners comprising 200 lawyers, consultants, banks, and financial experts. Together with external consulting teams, mainly composed of Rothschild, Freshfield Law Firm, Deloitte Touche Tohmatsu, and supported by Goldman Sachs, Geely conducted impressive due-diligence for four months. Before the acquisition, 6,473 documents were reviewed, and more than 10 expert meetings, 2 site visits, and 3 management presentations by Volvo were organized. At the negotiations, more than 15,000 revisions and remarks were made on the 2,000-page contract with Ford, widely covering all the aspects of important details, including transaction pricing, accountant, taxation, intellectual property rights, component supply, information technology, pension, and car financing, among others.

At the time of acquisition, both partners had their respective strengths and weaknesses. Volvo had global reputation and brand recognition, high technology, and innovation strength, whereas Geely had a mass market, rationalization and cost control, and adaptability to fluctuating markets, as China is a price-sensitive market. However, the two groups also had structural weaknesses. Volvo had limited market shares (producing about a quarter of what BMW or Mercedes Benz produced), and its production range was limited (to S40, S60 and S90 models) and undiversified. Geely was still operating at the low end, strongly constrained by competition on price and quality in a very fragmented market. At first glance, this cooperation seemed to be very risky, also because after spending money on the acquisition, Geely was at a dangerously high debt-asset ratio. However, contrary to expectations, Volvo's global sales, and specifically sales in the China market, showed a large increase in the first six months following the acquisition.

For Geely, the values of Volvo assets, brand, and management were multiple, and the deal could in fact benefit both partners. The acquisition of Volvo, a small-sized, bankrupt Western firm in the premium sector, allowed Geely, a mass-market producer operating in the low end, to enter the premium segment and compete with leading European firms present in the Chinese market via an external growth strategy. It could gain access to a globally prestigious brand and an internationally well-established dealership network. Furthermore, through an intensive learning process, working along with Volvo allowed Geely to develop new models and brands to supply the domestic and world markets with middle- to high-end cars.

For Volvo, the acquisition not only created an opportunity for the Swedish carmaker to expand in the growing Chinese market in the premium sector but also enabled the firm to seek new markets with middle- to high-income customers, thanks to the competitive advantage of Volvo brands combined with the cost-cutting solutions offered by Geely. During the acquisition process, Geely already showed its strong attention to the core value of Volvo assets, especially regarding the intellectual property (IP) rights.

Geely's acquisition of Volvo Cars was considered as a "mouse swallowing elephant" operation. Although Volvo Cars' global sales largely decreased in 2008 and 2009, impacted by the financial crisis and resulting in negative net profits, its business revenues were four to five times those of Geely at that time. However, as Jennifer Yu, Rothschild's top executive in China, and advisor to Geely, pointed out, there was "a dragon behind this mouse," i.e. China (Chan and Simmons, 2010). In the end, Li Shufu succeeded in acquiring all the assets and patents of Volvo Cars with US$1.8 billion, compared to the initial price of US$6.5 billion paid by Ford in 1999.

We should note that three local Chinese governments (Shanghai Municipality and the Provinces of Sichuan and Heilongjiang) contributed about 25% of the deal, while the China Construction Bank contributed 11% (Balcet *et al.*, 2012). In the following years, Volvo invested in the same provinces and municipality, in Chengdu, Daqing, and Shanghai, creating new greenfield factories and an R&D center. This choice by local governments could be interpreted as an instrument of regional and industrial development policy, attracting in their territories a new huge automotive investor, able to create skilled jobs and multiple local linkages promoting growth. It was a sort of a new type of public–private partnership.

5.4. Acquisition and Synergies Without Merger: "Volvo is Volvo, Geely is Geely"

After the acquisition in 2010, the main approach by Geely was to give Volvo extended autonomy and independence, based on the principle "Volvo is Volvo, Geely is Geely." As Chairman Li Shufu pointed out,

"Geely and Volvo are like brothers, not father and son" (Wang, 2014). Therefore, the post-acquisition relations between the two companies were similar to an international partnership, or a peculiar form of alliance, oriented to strategic cooperation between two actors with autonomous decision power, moving at the same time toward a gradual but intense post-acquisition integration.

Geely Holding, as the owner of Volvo, set up a shareholder assembly to raise strategic issues and for decision-making and to coordinate the development of Geely and Volvo. As a consequence, the composition of the Board of Directors, comprising eight persons, fully reflected this wise approach, as only two members (including Chairman Li) were Chinese, the others being independent directors. The same independence characterized the Executive Management Team. This was a crucial step, putting Volvo's governance on a global basis, not dependent on Geely's decisions alone.

The post-acquisition period was a success story for both Geely and Volvo. Volvo witnessed an impressive growth. Annual total sales reached 503,127 vehicles in 2015 from 323,300 units in 2009, an historical high in its 89-year-old history. In 2019, global sales were up at 705,452 units, thanks to brilliant growth performance in China, the revival of sales in the US, and good performance in other areas outside Europe (see Table 5.1 and Figure 5.1). That result was not far from the target of 800,000 vehicles to be sold by 2020, which was announced after the acquisition.

From being a loss-making entity in the decade it existed within the Ford Group, Volvo returned to profitability in 2013, while its total employees increased from 20,000 to 45,000, a third shift was added, and the Gothenburg's historic Torslanda factory was further expanded. Moreover, the engine plant located in Skövde, Sweden, was upgraded, as well as the assembly plant in Ghent, Belgium. The improved performance of Volvo Cars was also showcased by the opening of the new plant in Ridgeville (Charleston), South Carolina, USA, which started production in late 2018. S60 Models, based on the Platform Scalable Product Architecture (SPA), were produced for both the domestic and export markets. Finally, from a financial perspective, Volvo also benefited greatly for being part of Geely Holding, which brought much-needed resources for its business expansion (personal interview with Li Donghui, July 12, 2019).

After the Volvo acquisition, Geely also rapidly expanded its operation, as shown in Chapter 3. Its sales grew from about 400,000 units in

Table 5.1.   Volvo Cars global sales, by region.

Retail sales (units)	2010	2011	2012	2013	2014	2015	2016	2017	2018	2019
Europe	2,29,312	2,52,217	2,27,027	2,18,567	2,43,514	2,69,249	2,76,412	2,98,948	3,18,235	3,40,605
China	30,522	47,140	41,989	61,146	81,221	81,588	90,930	1,14,410	1,30,593	1,54,961
US	53,952	67,273	68,079	61,233	56,371	70,047	82,726	81,504	98,263	1,08,234
Other	59,739	82,625	84,856	86,894	84,760	82,243	84,264	76,715	95,162	1,01,652
Total	3,73,525	4,49,255	4,21,951	4,27,840	4,65,866	5,03,127	5,34,332	5,71,577	6,42,253	7,05,452

Retail sales (%)	2010 (%)	2011 (%)	2012 (%)	2013 (%)	2014 (%)	2015 (%)	2016 (%)	2017 (%)	2018 (%)	2019 (%)
Europe	61	56	54	51	52	54	52	50	50	48
China	8	10	10	14	17	16	17	20	20	22
US	14	15	16	14	12	14	15	16	15	15
Other	16	18	20	20	18	16	16	14	15	14
Total	100	100	100	100	100	100	100	100	100	100

Source: Annual reports and financial results published by Volvo Cars.

Figure 5.1. Volvo Cars global sales, by region.

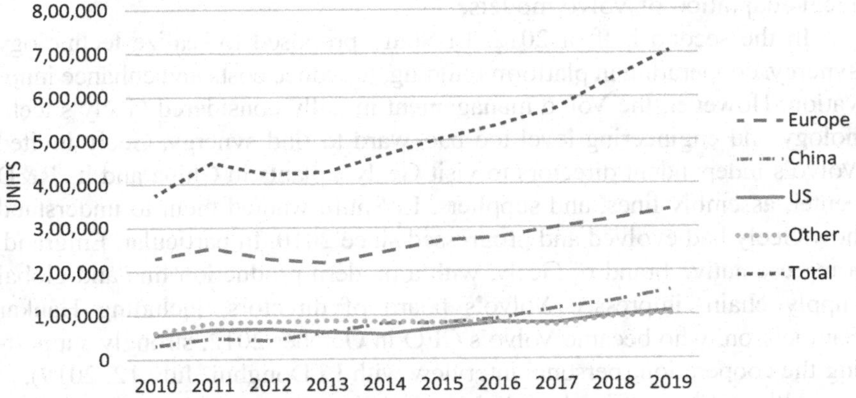

Source: Annual reports and financial results published by Volvo Cars.

2010 to about 1,362,000 units in 2019, emerging as the champion among Chinese brands for the third consecutive year. Profits too increased, from about 2 billion RMB in 2010 to 12.5 billion RMB in 2018, as did productivity. Geely's absorptive capacity was good, but it was substantially improved in relation to Volvo. Its product quality and production standards have also been improved after the Volvo acquisition, and both brands greatly gained in reputation.

In October 2011, Geely, which was originally listed in the Hong Kong stock market a few years earlier, faced strong financial challenges, due to the investment projects of Volvo in China, and raised financial resources at high costs. Synergies were built with Volvo financial team for credit line from China Development Bank, to the tune of €3 billion. This provided the relevant financial resources for the expansion of Volvo in China (personal interview with Li Donghui, CFO of Geely Holding, July 12, 2019).

Notwithstanding the crucial autonomy of the two carmakers, early moves toward future technology convergence and cooperation were made since the immediate after-acquisition stage, shaping the future deep partnership. A Volvo–Geely dialogue and cooperation committee, at top managers' level, was set up after the acquisition, meeting twice a year. As a first step, since 2010, car modification and adaptation for the Chinese market took place at the Gothenburg R&D facilities. As a second step, in 2011, a Chinese R&D Center was created in Jiading (Shanghai) for the local adaptation of Volvo models.

In the second half of 2012, Li Shufu proposed to realize technology synergy, cooperating in platform building, to reduce costs and enhance innovation. However, the Volvo management initially considered Geely's technology and engineering level too backward to find synergy. Geely invited Volvo's independent directors to visit Geely's plants in China and its R&D center, assembly lines, and suppliers. Li Shufu wanted them to understand how Geely had evolved and progressed since 2010. In particular, Emgrand, a representative brand of Geely, with a modern production line and global supply chain, impressed Volvo's board of directors, including Hånkar Samuelsson, who became Volvo's CEO in October 2012, strongly supporting the cooperation (personal interview with Li Donghui, July 12, 2019).

Although no official global engineering cooperation was launched initially, the first moves toward a platform sharing between Volvo and Geely laid the foundation for the next crucial stage of partnership in technology innovation, i.e. the opening of a new joint Volvo and Geely R&D Center in Gothenberg, in late 2013, i.e. CEVT (see Section 5.6).

5.5. Volvo Expansion in China: "Like a Tiger in the Mountains"

Rapid expansion in the fast-growing Chinese market was the first evident consequence of the acquisition of Volvo by the Geely Group (see Table 5.1 and Figure 5.1). In fact, China was seen by Geely as Volvo's potential second home market. According to the metaphor used by Chairman Li Shufu, Volvo was "like a tiger in the mountains," that "shouldn't be in a cage in a zoo" (Flannery, 2014). The message was clear, and the strategy worked, as that vision was confirmed by impressive corporate performances in the following years.

Some scholars (Alvstam *et al.*, 2018) analyzed the transformation of Volvo Cars from a Eurocentric carmaker with a global reach, into a "hybrid" Euro–Chinese actor, reactive to political influence and regional industrial development policies. As mentioned in Section 5.3, the role of Shanghai, Chengdu, and Daqing authorities in supporting the acquisition and the subsequent location of new Volvo investment, production, and R&D facilities was highly significant. The local governments strongly welcomed Volvo's implantation and cooperation with local partners and suppliers, hoping to improve the local companies' competitiveness and build or improve regional industrial clusters.

Two new car assembly plants and a new engine plant started production in China between 2013 and 2014, followed by other new investments during the 2010–2020 decade. The first car plant started production in 2013 in Chengdu (Zhongjia Automobile Manufacturing), with annual capacity of 120,000 units, close to an existing Geely factory. It was a Geely Volvo 50/50 joint venture. Models such as the S60 sedan series (S60L, XC60, and S60) were produced using the Volvo SPA Platform (Alvstam and Ivarsson, 2014). The production was oriented to the domestic Chinese market, with export to the US of the S60 model starting in 2015. In August 2018, the Chengdu plant delivered its 300,000th vehicle.

A second plant started production in 2014 in Daqing (Daqing Volvo Car Manufacturing), again as a Geely Volvo 50/50 joint venture. Also in this case, the SPA Platform was the base for producing the S90 premium sedan series (S90, S90L) and XC90 Classic models. The production was oriented to the domestic Chinese market, with export to Europe of S90 Model starting in May 2017. S90 worldwide production hub should shift from Torslanda to Daqing. In December 2018, the Daqing plant produced the100,000th S90.

A third car plant started production in 2017 in Luqiao, Taizhou, Zhejiang Province (Asia-Europe Automobile Manufacturing Taizhou), under full Geely ownership and industrial cooperation with Volvo. Its annual capacity is 80,000 units. The production of the new brand Lynk & Co started in 2017, and Volvo car production in 2019, based on the new Compact Modular Architecture (CMA) Platform, producing Models 40 series (XC40, also in electric version by 2020), Polestar 2, and Lynk & Co 01/02/03. The production is oriented to the domestic Chinese market (Alvstam *et al.*, 2018).

A fourth car plant started production in June 2018 in Zhangjiakou. Based on CMA Platform, it produces Models Lynk & Co 02 and 03 for the domestic market. Finally, a fifth car plant in Chengdu, dedicated to Polestar brand, started production in August 2019, based on the CMA Platform. It produced the Polestar 1 Model, for Chinese and foreign markets. A new engine plant was also built in Zhangjiakou (Volvo Cars Zhangjiakou Engine Plan), starting engine production in 2013, with an annual capacity of 325,000 units. It is a 50/50 Geely Volvo joint venture.

Table 5.2.   Volvo in China: List of operations.

Start of production	Location	Platform	Annual capacity	Models	Investment	Employees
2010	Shanghai	—	R&D	—	1.7 billion RMB	—
2013	Chengdu	SPA	120,000 units (300,000 potential)	XC60, S60L, S60	5.4 billion RMB	4000
2013	Zhangjiakou (engine)	VEA	325,000 units (1 million potential)	Drive-E (XC60, S60L), engine for S60	3.2 billion RMB	1200
2014	Daqing	SPA	Phase 1 80,000 units + Phase 2 increase to 300,000 units	XC90, S90, S90L	4.57 billion RMB + 20 billion RMB)	—
2016	Luqiao, Taizhou	CMA	80,000 units (200,000 potential)	XC40, Polestar 2, Lynk & Co 01	12.1 billion RMB	—
2018	Zhangjiakou	CMA	200,000 units	Lynk & Co 02/03	12.5 billion RMB	3000
2019	Chengdu	CMA	500	Polestar 1	—	—

Source: Volvo annual reports, Volvo News and various information sources, collected by authors.

Table 5.2 summarizes the rapid expansion of Volvo in China under Geely ownership. It also includes the Shanghai R&D Center, created in 2010, immediately after the acquisition, with the crucial mission to adapt and develop Volvo products for the needs of the domestic market.

Supply chain was a crucial issue in the expansion of Volvo in China. The first problem after the acquisition was to deal with the existing supply chain, built within the Ford–Chang'an Joint Venture, integrating it in the new supply chain, while constructing a new supply system. This was considered in 2011 as a major challenge by Paul Gustavsson, Senior Vice President, Volvo Group. Thanks to the new supplier system, sourcing of local components significantly increased from 40% in 2011 to 80% in 2016 (Balcet *et al.*, 2012).

5.6. Technology Convergence and Asset Creation at Work: CEVT

In September 2012, the decision was taken to create a new C-Segment architecture, based on strict cooperation between Geely and Volvo: a first step toward technological convergence and synergy in innovation processes. The idea was to create a R&D center in Europe, located in Gothenburg Science Park, in the heart of the automotive cluster, close to two prestigious universities, the University of Gothenburg and the private Chalmers University. The decision was made in December 2012 and announced in February 2013 (personal interview with Mats Fagerhag, CEO of CEVT, October 20, 2019).

In the view of Mats Fagerhag, it was a sort of "perfect storm," pooling human resources from Volvo, Geely, and external resources, at the right moment (personal interview, October 20, 2019). Initially, CEVT "borrowed" experienced Volvo engineers for a period of two years. Teamwork and a strong modular approach were crucial for its success, in addition to trust and good reputation.

CEVT was born, marking a strategic upgrade of Geely. CEVT is a wholly owned subsidiary of the Geely Group, established in order to develop a new joint CMA car platform for C-Segment vehicles. In Spring 2013, the new CMA was launched. CMA is a platform designed for smaller vehicles, developing and innovating on the Volvo SPA Platform. Based on modularization, it allows innovative design and the integration of new technology. This applies to the premium cars in the Volvo 40 series but also to other cars produced within the collaboration of Volvo Cars and Geely. Its IP rights are owned by Geely (Yakob *et al.*, 2018).

Initially, the Chinese engineers were more "cost-oriented," while the Swedish engineers more "technology-oriented," with different expectations. Teamwork helped to transform problems into richness and creativity (personal interview with Mats Fagerhag, October 20, 2019). The challenge was to meet quality and performance requirements of Volvo as well as cost performance of Geely. This was achieved by developing modularity, i.e. components and systems with multiple performances serving both brands. This development has progressed rapidly.

In December 2013, Li Shufu visited CEVT and was very impressed by its initial progress — accordingly, more responsibilities were given to the development center. In 2014, Geely sought CEVT's inputs for 11 Models. Since its founding, CEVT has been a fast-growing organization: starting with 200 people in 2013, including engineers, technicians and designers, it grew to 2,400 in 2019, including both employees and onsite consultants. The development missions of CEVT include innovation and technology support for Volvo Cars, Geely Auto, and Lynk & Co, a newly created joint brand since 2017 within the Geely Holding Group (see Chapter 7). CEVT is characterized by its very quick reaction capacity and rapid evolution (personal interview with Gang Wei, CEVT Vice President, October 21, 2019). As an example, the Volvo SPA Platform needed 22 months to be built up, while the CMA Platform was created in just 9 months. In 2019, the company's annual budget was over US$350 million.

In China, CEVT cooperates with the Geely Research Institute (GRI), focusing on testing and launch support, while CEVT in Sweden focuses on architecture, subsystems, and components. CEVT has different development missions for Volvo and Geely. For Volvo, it centers on the modular architecture and components for C-segments cars and shared component development. For Geely, CEVT concentrates on the development of architecture and components, shared component development, complete vehicle design, and advanced engineering and technologies. It provides technical solutions applicable to both brands and customer profiles and completes vehicle design and advanced engineering. For all these reasons, CEVT has been the key and most important result of technological and organizational convergence and synergy between Geely and Volvo in the post-acquisition process.

Challenging intercultural relations occurred at different levels within CEVT, between Swedish, other European and Chinese engineers, designers, and managers. Moreover, the impact of digital innovation implied a not always easy dialogue between traditional automotive engineers and software developers. Chapter 6 will be devoted to analyzing and discussing the crucial features and the impact of cross-culture relations, which were crucial for the success of the cooperation.

In 2017, CEVT entered into a new stage of its young history, with the launch of the Lynk & Co brand in China, based on its innovative work. Challenges, results, and trajectories in terms of new products and technologies will be further analyzed in Chapter 7.

5.7. Concluding Remarks

The acquisition of Volvo Cars and the following process of the post-acquisition integration during the 2010–2020 decade represented a success story and a decisive turning point for Geely. The process accelerated its trajectory as a global player and increased its competitiveness in the Chinese domestic market. Its strategic perspective evolved from a more traditional asset-seeking foreign acquisition toward a global complex asset creation strategy, involving mainly operations in China and Europe. Notwithstanding the initial challenges and risks, both industrial and financial, and the cultural distance between the acquiring and the acquired companies during the 2010–2020 decade, the acquisition gave rise to positive results and performances.

In a first stage, the extensive autonomy given to Volvo Cars ("Geely is Geely, Volvo is Volvo") went along with a strong and rapid expansion of the Swedish company in China, supported by huge investment efforts ("Like a Tiger in the Mountains"). In a second stage, since 2013, with the creation of CEVT in Gothenburg, the process of technology convergence, cooperation, asset creation, and joint innovation speeded up and gave rise to a new shared platform, named CMA.

In the following chapters, we will try to deepen this analysis, focusing on cross-culture relations, management, and cooperation, in the trajectory of the post-acquisition integration (Chapter 6), and then analyze the new brand Lynk & Co from the perspective of innovation and synergies between Geely and Volvo (Chapter 7).

References

Alvstam, C. and I. Ivarsson (2014). The 'Hybrid' Emerging Market Multinational Enterprise. The Ownership Transfer of Volvo Cars to China. In: C. Alvstam,

H. Dolles and P. Ström (eds.), *Asian Inward and Outward FDI: New Challenges in the Global Economy.* London: Palgrave Macmillan, pp. 217–242.

Alvstam, C., I. Ivarsson and B. Petersen (2018). Are multinationals and governments from emerging economies configuring global value chains in new ways? *International Journal of Emerging Markets* **15**:1, 111–130.

Andreff, W. and G. Balcet (2013). Emerging countries' multinational companies investing in developed countries: At odds with the HOS paradigm? *The European Journal of Comparative Economics*, **10**:1, 179–202.

Balcet, G., H. Wang and X. Richet (2012). Geely: A trajectory of catching up and asset-seeking multinational growth. *International Journal of Automotive Technology and Management*, **12**:4, 360–375.

Chan, C. and J. Simmons (2010). Jennifer Yu Leads Rothschild's China Push. *Bloomberg Businessweek.* August. Available at: https://www.bloomberg.com/news/articles/2010-08-05/jennifer-yu-leads-rothschilds-china-push (accessed March 5, 2021).

Flannery, R. (2014). Life After Ford: Volvo Turnaround Gains Speed under Chinese Billionaire Owner. *Forbes Asia*, November. Available at: https://www.forbes.com/sites/russellflannery/2014/10/27/geely-in-swedish/#18fb61b3999d (accessed September 15, 2019).

Luo, Y. and R. Tung (2007). International expansion of emerging market enterprises: A springboard perspective. *Journal of International Business Studies*, **38**:4, 481–498.

Mathews, J. A. (2002). *Dragon Multinational: A New Model for Global Growth.* Oxford: Oxford University Press.

Mathews, J. A. (2006). Dragon multinationals: New players in 21st century globalization. *Asia Pacific Journal of Management*, **23**:1, 5–27.

Moon, H.-C. and T. W. Roehl (2001). Unconventional foreign direct investment and the imbalance theory. *International Business Review*, **10**:2, 197–215.

Tolentino, P. E. (2008). Explaining the competitiveness of multinational companies from developing economies: A critical review of the academic literature. *International Journal of Technology and Globalisation*, **4**:1, 23–38.

Wang, J. (2014). Li Shufu said: Geely and Volvo are like brothers, not father and son. Available at: https://carnewschina.com/2014/05/16/li-shufu-said-geely-and-volvo-are-like-brothers-not-father-and-son/#:~:text=There%20was%20more%3A,different%20brands%20and%20product%20positioning (accessed March 5, 2021).

Yakob, R., H. R. Nakamura and P. Ström (2018). Chinese foreign acquisitions aimed for strategic asset-creation and innovation upgrading: The case of Geely and Volvo Cars. *Technovation*, **70–71**, 59–72.

Chapter 6

Geely's Way of Cross-Culture Management

Abstract

Cross-culture relations and management deeply affect the performances of multinational corporations and the success or failure of post-acquisition integration processes. Cultural differences may cause poor performance and explain failures, but they may also give opportunities for creative sharing of knowledge, innovation, and synergies. This chapter compares Swedish and Chinese corporate cultures, applying an analytical framework to the case of Geely and Volvo, and discussing relevant intercultural issues. It illustrates the gradualist approach adopted by Geely and sheds light on how cross-culture cooperation successfully operated at the China Euro Vehicle Technology AB (CEVT) in Gothenburg, Sweden, creating convergences and synergies. Initial negative coverage by local media and skepticism by civil society, trade unions, and policy-makers eventually evolved toward a positive appreciation when local communities have observed tangible benefits from the presence of Geely in their territories.

Keywords: Geely Auto; cross-cultural management; post-acquisition integration; CEVT; talent management.

6.1. Introduction

In this chapter, we analyze and discuss the issues of cross-culture relations and management, which typically and deeply affect the performances of multinational corporations (MNCs) and the success or failure of post-acquisition integration processes. After reviewing relevant literature, we point out four key bipolar dimensions, especially useful in order to analyze the case of Chinese MNCs investing in Europe, including Geely with the acquisition of Volvo. We then compare Swedish and Chinese corporate cultures and apply this framework to the case of Geely and Volvo. We analyze, in particular, how cross-culture cooperation successfully operated at China Euro Vehicle Technology AB (CEVT) in Gothenburg, Sweden. Finally, we shed light on the relations between Geely and Swedish media and policy-makers, evolving from initial skepticism and concern to a positive attitude and appreciation of the creation of new jobs, activities, and spillovers in the industrial agglomeration of Gothenburg. We conclude with some more general remarks.

6.2. Cross-Culture Distance and Cooperation: Problems and Opportunities

The concept of culture, central in anthropology, covers a complex variety of phenomena. It consists of beliefs, social behavioral patterns, traditions, customs, norms, laws, and shared values, associated with symbolic aspects and economic dimensions. Cultural distance also depends on regulatory regimes governing the economic, social, and political life of a country (Ietto-Gillies, 2019, Chapter 16). It includes expressive forms like arts and music, as well as scientific and technological knowledge. All those elements of culture, specific to countries, communities, and regions, are largely the result of history: they are constantly evolving over time through different ways of cultural change, resulting from the interaction between traditional forces resisting change and innovating forces promoting it. From a historical perspective, since the 16th century, cultural foundations — including institutions, legal frameworks, and science — deeply influenced modern economic growth and the Industrial Revolution (Mokyr, 2017).

Within this framework, organizational and corporate cultures directly affect international mergers and acquisitions (M&As) as well as post-acquisition integration processes and performances. Corporate cultures are, on the one hand, path-dependent, related to the specific history and trajectory of a firm, and on the other hand, embedded in home-country cultures, deeply and constantly interacting with them. In cross-border operations, MNCs manage not only production, supply chains, finance, and technology but also ethical, environmental, and labor issues in different and sometimes distant cultural contexts. Therefore, core values of the firm, embedded in the home-country culture, need to be adapted to local situations in host countries. Hence, two levels of cross-culture relations interact — i.e. country-specific and the firm-specific relations. Looking to this specific dimension, MNCs, considered as key actors of the globalization of industry, may be viewed as "integrators of fragmentation" in global markets (Balcet and Ietto-Gillies, 2020).

Cultural distance is usually associated with higher costs and risks of operating in different countries and regions, as global managers have to adapt to different languages, legal frameworks, and institutions. The concept of cultural distance plays a central role in the pioneering studies of the Scandinavian School, also known as Uppsala School, on the internationalization process of firms. Analyzing the patterns of international growth and geographical spread of several Swedish multinationals, including Volvo, in the post-WWII decades, Johanson and Vahlne (1977; 1990) take into account what they define the "psychic distance" between the home and the host country: it includes several factors limiting the flow of information and is at the origin of specific costs and risks. This concept includes "differences in language, education, business practices, culture and industrial development" (Johanson and Vahlne, 1977, p. 24). Psychic and spatial distance tend to be related each other, but they need to be analyzed as different factors. Both affect the international involvement and international trajectories of firms, via exports, greenfield foreign direct investment (FDI), alliances and M&As, as well as their performances. In a more recent and revised version of their model, Johanson and Vahlne (2009) substituted the notion of cultural, psychic, and spatial distance with that of "liability of outsidership," i.e. the cost of insertion, for a foreign firm, within a production value chain and/or a localized innovation network in the host country. This interesting notion represents an evolution of the idea of "liability of foreignness," originally introduced by Stephan Hymen in his seminal work on FDIs and MNCs (Hymer, 1976). Hymer referred to a set of initial disadvantages faced by the foreign direct investors, as FDI implies additional costs and uncertainties vis-à-vis domestic investments. Both notions are relevant and may be fruitfully applied to the case of Chinese multinationals investing and operating in Western countries, where cultural and institutional distance with China is high.

Organizational culture and identity-building are crucial in post-acquisition processes. Identity refers to the values and routines shared by organization members, both in the acquiring and in the acquired companies. Building of trust typically tends to characterize successful post-acquisition integration, promoting interaction and synergies and avoiding dangerous opportunistic behavior, while distrust tends to be associated with the emergence of conflicts leading to the failure of post-acquisition integration processes (Lander and Kooning, 2013).

Business history and a wide empirical literature on post-acquisition and post-merger integration trajectories provide evidence that cultural differences may cause poor performance and explain failures. Cultural differences are a great challenge and risk, including in the automotive industry, as they may produce frequent clashes and conflicts between partners (Shimizu *et al.*, 2004). It was the case in the huge and promising merger between Chrysler and Daimler-Benz, signed in 1998, one of the most disastrous in history. In that year, Daimler invested US$35 billion in the historic acquisition, but nine years later, in 2007, the German carmaker sold it for just US$7.4 billion to the private equity group Cerberus. Notwithstanding the *ex-ante* complementarities between products and markets and expected scale economies, no fruitful integration took place. On the contrary, cultural clashes between German and American managers and employees produced poor performances and significant losses.

A more recent example, concerning another industry, is that of the acquisition of Motorola smartphone division by China's Lenovo in 2015, for US$2.91 billion. The deal included valuable brands and technology assets, intellectual property (IP), and patents. Because of intercultural dialogue difficulties and diverging administrative heritages of acquiring and acquired firms, market performances have been poor, contrary to the previous case of the successful acquisition by Lenovo of IBM's computer division in 2005. As pointed out in the managerial literature, acquiring companies may face a "liability of foreignness" in the host country and try to overcome it by importing home-country organizational capabilities, while copying the good practices of local firms (Zaheer, 1995). This issue is especially relevant in the case of emerging country multinationals and of Chinese MNCs.

However, cultural differences may also provide opportunities for creative sharing of knowledge, innovation, and synergies, producing potential future advantages. Some scholars found evidence, based on empirical research, of benefits for MNCs operating in different cultures. This is possible if they are able to acquire new knowledge, spreading it to the local economies in which the MNCs operate, via the business linkages with both market and non-market actors, such as customers, suppliers, distributors, universities, research centers, and governmental agencies (Cantwell, 2003; Forsgren, 2017, Ch. 4).

In success stories, a good inter-firm communication between acquiring and acquired companies tends not only to reduce the potentially negative effects of high cultural (or "psychic") distance but also to give rise to potentially positive effects in terms of synergies. Weber *et al.* (2011) consider cultural differences as potential sources of value creation, with a positive impact on post-acquisition performances, creating synergies between complementary capabilities, knowledge, and skills. According to Lasserre (2012, p. 164), the cultural gap may be reduced through mutual understanding, which "is enhanced when the acquiring company staff and executives ... adopt an attitude sensitive to cultural differences." In their important contribution, Shimizu *et al.* (2004) focus on dynamic two-way learning processes deriving from matching different cultures. These processes may give rise to effective and relevant value-creating strategies, increasing the corporate competitiveness.

6.3. Swedish and Chinese Corporate Cultures Compared: Geely and Volvo

As a starting point, drawing from the classic analysis by Geert Hofstede (1984) on international differences in corporate and work-related cultures, we can take into consideration four main bipolar cultural dimensions, which seem relevant to shed light in the case of Geely and Volvo in the post-acquisition process.

Power Distance, between decision-makers and other employees. In the case of high levels of this dimension, lower-ranked personnel will not be involved or will be only marginally involved in decisional processes. On the contrary, a low level of this cultural dimension will correspond to more decentralized and flat organizations, stimulating the participation of employees in decision-making and quality improvement, thereby increasing their responsibilities.

Individualism versus Collectivism, affecting cooperation, internal competition dynamics, and teamwork. Higher levels of individualism create higher competition between employees, oriented to reach mainly personal goals rather than team and corporate goals. On the contrary, collectivism means a strong orientation toward teamwork and cooperative behavior within the company.

Uncertainty Avoidance, affecting risk-taking and the role of corporate routines and standard setting. High values of this cultural dimension imply a strong preference for predictability, giving rise to organizations based on rules and established routines. On the contrary, organizations with low values will be more flexible and oriented to risk taking.

Time Orientation, affecting the links with past traditions and the attitude to implement long-term or short-term strategies. A high score of this dimension is consistent with the orientation to efficiently plan for the future, while a low score corresponds to a strong path-dependency and to high consideration given to past experiences, the preservation of traditions, and the orientation to reach short-term results.

These four basic cultural dimensions are linked to each other. Therefore, an orientation toward collectivism will usually be associated with low power distance, while a low time orientation will probably be associated with a high level of uncertainty avoidance. If we move to apply these basic dimensions to the case of intercultural relations and dynamics to comparing Swedish/Scandinavian organizational cultures with the Chinese one, and applying to the case of Volvo and Geely, we can shed light on the following features, pointing out some differences.

6.3.1. *Power distance at Volvo and Geely*

In Swedish and more generally in Scandinavian organizational cultures, equality is a pervasive cultural and social value and tradition. Therefore, power distance is low and consistent with a tradition of decentralization of power and an organizational structure that is relatively flat. In Chinese organizational culture, on the contrary, a higher power distance may be observed, implying stronger hierarchy, authority, and respect for social ranking in decision-making processes.

6.3.2. *Individualism versus collectivism at Volvo and Geely*

Teamwork is deeply embedded in Scandinavian traditions. This strong orientation does not prevent also giving value to individual responsibility and initiative: personal responsibility is connected to the Protestant religion tradition. Therefore, individualism and collectivism seem to be harmonized in that cultural context. However, the younger generations tend to be more individualistic than older ones, following a cultural change and shoving a generational gap in that respect.

A high degree of collectivism is rooted in the Chinese culture and tradition, as opposed to individualism. At the same time, organizational and corporate behavior is also affected by the *Guangxi* tradition of informal relational networks.

6.3.3. *Uncertainty avoidance at Volvo and Geely*

Uncertainty avoidance is usually considered low in Scandinavian culture, because of a long history of entrepreneurial initiative and propensity to innovate. However, routines, industrial traditions, and path dependency play a role in the decision-making of consolidated big corporations, including historical and multinational groups such as Volvo Cars.

In the Chinese corporate culture, a strong risk-taking attitude, rooted in history, goes along with a pragmatic behavior, able to quickly adapt to specific situations, context, and policy constraints. Therefore, a great operational and strategic agility represents a key competitive advantage for Chinese corporations, as it is well shown by the case of Geely.

6.3.4. *Time orientation at Volvo and Geely*

Long-term planning capabilities traditionally characterize large and consolidated Swedish industrial corporations, representative of a model of managerial capitalism, sensible to stakeholder interests, as opposed to short-term orientation on producing immediate financial results.

A long-term orientation in strategic decision and implementation is also a significant feature of the Chinese organizational culture. However, it is coupled with fast, pragmatic, and short decision-making processes, especially in the case of new dynamic start-ups and fast-growing global actors, such as Geely.

From this comparative overview, initial cultural differences emerged with respect to the power distance (lower for Volvo), organizational structures (more hierarchical in China), timing of decision-making (shorter for Geely) and risk-taking attitude (higher for Geely).

6.4. Swedish *Jantelagen* and Chinese Luxury: Social Norms Affecting Corporate Culture

In this context, due attention should be given to a peculiar Swedish and Scandinavian cultural feature, affecting corporate and market behavior: the role of *Jantelagen* (the Law of *Jante*). This term refers to a code of conduct that emphasizes adherence to the collective values and propensity to harmonize individual behavior with the shared values of the community, avoiding individualism and any socially diverging attitude. This cultural tradition, deeply rooted in Swedish tradition and religious Protestant values, promotes a frugal style of life and suggests avoiding or limiting the exhibition of luxury by rich people because it would not be socially approved. As a consequence, luxury cars are not (or were not, till recently) socially welcome in the Scandinavian tradition; on the contrary, premium vehicles are well accepted and appreciated, especially with respect to safety, energy-saving, and solidity (personal interview with Peter Horbury, Geely Design VP, October 21, 2019). This specific cultural feature, related to the cultural values shared by Scandinavian middle classes, traditionally shaped the domestic demand in Sweden, affecting design and manufacturing. It therefore created asymmetries with the Chinese and the American markets, where on the contrary luxury models are highly appreciated by high-income buyers and emerging social groups. These asymmetries affected in particular the design process of new models produced for global markets. This was a concrete challenge and opportunity in the cooperation between Geely and Volvo.

6.5. Culture Difference between Geely and Volvo in Early Stages of Cooperation

From evidence discussed in Sections 6.2 and 6.3, we can see how *ex-ante* the cultural distance between Geely and Volvo was striking when the acquisition took place. The major cultural challenge was partly derived from the fact that Volvo Cars was recognized as a typical Swedish and Scandinavian "National Champion," and as a symbol of the national successful economic and social model, deeply rooted in the history and embedded in the institutions of that country.

A relevant difference derived from the dominant product-driven orientation of European and Swedish engineers, looking primarily to optimize their results in terms of best technology and product quality, while Chinese engineers tend to be more user-driven, oriented toward business and cost reduction. Senior Volvo engineers and managers had a corporate culture linked to strong traditions and consolidated routines. Initially, this dichotomy created diverse expectations, but it evolved toward shared views, thanks to teamwork experience (personal interview with Mats Fägerhag, CEO CEVT, October 20, 2019).

Looking at vertical integration issues and value chain management, Volvo culture was focused on industrial cooperation and co-design with first-tier suppliers, while the Geely tradition was more oriented to put pressure on suppliers in order to reduce costs. Again, a positive evolution took place, as in teamwork experience these two approaches converged toward an integration (personal interview with Per Ferdell, VP CEVT, October 23, 2019).

The focus on safety is a good example of Corporate Social Responsibility (CSR) as an intercultural issue. CSR is highly valued in Scandinavian countries and in Volvo tradition, and high standards are achieved on social, environmental, and safety issues, while CSR in China tends to be lower compared to the Scandinavian case, in relation to the same standards. In particular, safety issues are crucial in Volvo culture. The high priority attributed to safety is shown, *inter alia*, by the invention of the three-point seatbelt in 1959 by a Volvo engineer, Nils Bohlin.

Another intercultural issue between Geely and Volvo was the internal competition, frequent (within tacit but well-defined rules) in the experience of Chinese corporations, and much less usually in Europe and in Sweden, where cooperative behavior was considered to prevail. It was the case for new projects of R&D and product development.

6.6. Cultural Convergence in the Cooperation between Geely and Volvo

In the case of the acquisition of Volvo by Geely, socially embedded cultural differences represented not only major challenges, as we have seen in Section 6.4, but also a source of potential advantages from new synergies and innovation processes. Some interesting factors of potential synergies emerged over time during the post-acquisition process (Yacob *et al.*, 2018).

As we pointed out in Chapter 4, Geely's philosophy of cross-culture management and cooperation was well represented by some statements by

Chairman Li Shufu — appreciating culture and values of others as do to one's own would make the world harmonious. This approach substantially contributed to create synergies.

We should note that this acquisition was not followed by a merger in the following decade but gave rise to an original form of partnership between acquiring and acquired companies, producing innovation and creating new assets. After the 2010 acquisition, Geely decided to deal with corporate culture differences between Volvo and Geely with a gradualist approach and in different ways. It was decided to revive the Volvo brand as a global independent premium brand, keeping independent the management of Volvo and providing continuity. As a consequence, the specific corporate culture of Volvo was recognized and accepted. Communication and exchanges between Chinese and Scandinavian staff were promoted through internal training programs. New supervision and incentive systems on performance and sales were established.

This strategy was summarized in the slogan "Volvo is Volvo, Geely is Geely," frequently reaffirmed in the early years after acquisition, while a parallel process of cultural integration was launched. According to the well-informed and valuable assessment by Mats Fägerhag, CETV CEO, within few years the advantages deriving from interculture synergies exceeded the costs. Finally, it was good for both companies to have such a cultural diversity, stimulating creativity and innovation (personal interview, 20 October 2019).

Long-term orientation became a common cultural attitude, as well as the propensity for teamwork. Pervasive Swedish orientation toward teamwork may fit well with the Chinese culture of collective work. To this respect, the Scandinavian capitalism and the Chinese economic model look less distant from each other than the American and the Chinese ones.

Both in Sweden and China, a generational shift was underway, given the more individualistic attitude of younger generations. In the case of Volvo, a specific problem of the post-acquisition period was the separation from the previous dominating highly individualistic American business culture, a heritage of the Ford period (1999–2010): the cooperation with Geely opened a new perspective in this field.

As a tool for communication between partners and within teams, English was chosen as the common language. Using a third international language, and not a native one of any of the partners, created good conditions for mutual understanding and joint teamwork. Moreover, mathematics served as a second common language of European and Chinese engineers and managers.

Two-way intense staff mobility between China and Sweden was a key instrument for cross-culture management. The imagination of younger Chinese designers, cooperating with their Scandinavian colleagues, contributed to overcome cultural gaps in this field (as highlighted in Section 6.4). The concept of "Scandinavian luxury," proposed by Chairman Li Shufu, and reflected in new-generation global models such as the XC90, may be seen as a sort of cross-cultural paradox, or as the outcome of a dynamic interaction and cultural cross-fertilization (Fang and Chimenson, 2017).

Due to different cultural features and tastes of buyers in Sweden and in China, safety has traditionally been a major general objective for Volvo while comfort took precedence for Geely. The integration of these two aspects was one of the keys to the success of new global models in the post-acquisition era. In the case of new Volvo factories built in China, higher safety standards were introduced, showing an evolving strategy and a significant convergence process, which was also a crucial CSR issue.

The general conclusion we can reach is that the cooperation between Geely and Volvo had to face great challenges but finally resulted in it being more an opportunity than an obstacle, in terms of teamwork, creativity, and innovation.

6.7. Cross-Cultural Cooperation at Work: The Case of CEVT

Employing people from 35 different countries, CEVT, located in Gothenburg, has been a living laboratory of intercultural cooperation, clearly showing its challenges and opportunities. From a strategic point of view, the launch of CEVT in 2013 represented a new stage in the process of integration and technological convergence between Geely and Volvo (see Chapter 5, Section 5.6).

Although owned by the Geely Group, CEVT has neither been perceived as a fully Chinese institution nor a Swedish one, but as a truly global center of advanced research and engineering, where "open-minded people" interact in a bilateral learning process (personal interview with Mats Fägerhag, CEO CEVT, October 20, 2019). CEVT emphasized its own specific culture, where teamwork is crucial. It created its own identity of high-level engineering culture and competences, as well as problem-solving and operational organization. Free from short-term, day-to-day management problems, CEVT could devote itself to build a long-term vision.

Intercultural talent management was a key instrument of success at CEVT. According to Mats Fägerhag, CEO CEVT, "As a foundation we had a lot of good people from Volvo Cars and Geely to support us. I also knew many people from around the world because of my twenty-year experience in the industry. During spring 2013, we managed to get very talented people that were from other OEMs: BMW, Volkswagen, Japanese companies, Korean companies, in addition to Ford and General Motors. Being able to do something from a blank sheet of paper and doing something totally new without any baggage from the past was very interesting for many folks" (Geely Media Center, 2019). CEVT was able to attract highly skilled young researchers, engineers, and software developers from Sweden, Scandinavian and Baltic countries, as well as from China and other European and Asian countries.

An important mission for CEVT has been to facilitate interaction and knowledge transfer between its employees, in cooperation with Geely Research Institute (GRI), located in Hangzhou Bay, Ningbo. Geely and GRI people provided crucial knowledge and understanding of their home auto market's features, policies, and consumer tastes. Intensive collaboration between Scandinavian and Chinese engineers, designers, and researchers greatly benefited from two-way staff mobility, seen as an important facilitator and supported by a specific instrument, the International Service Exchange (ISA).

Intense staff mobility was a crucial and effective instrument for cross-culture knowledge, cooperation, and management at CEVT. Mobility to Sweden for Chinese staff — including engineers, managers, software programmers, and designers — lasted from three months to two years, according to the different needs of learning, exchange of competences, and coordination.

Tacit knowledge exchanges too played a significant role, also through forms of informal relationship building, socialization, and interaction. Social events, such as Christmas party or "*Fica* Time" (weekly informal meeting) contributed to ease intercultural communication at CEVT (personal interview with Gang Wei, VP CEVT, October 21, 2019). Engineers and researchers benefited from working together in a stimulating multicultural environment, while the learning experience became stronger in a global environment (personal interview with Mats Fägerhag, CETV CEO, October 20, 2019).

The acquisition of tacit knowledge is also related to the access to localized innovation clusters (Antonelli, 1995), where contextualized learning and regional innovation dynamics spread technological and organizational knowledge. That is why the choice of locating CEVT in Gothenburg Science Park, close to universities and research institutions, played a crucial role. That choice of proximity facilitated the flow of knowledge and specifically the implementation of the strategic partnership agreement with the Gothenburg Engineering University (personal interview with Gang Wei, VP CEVT, October 21, 2019).

Design has been especially relevant for intercultural relations, as the interaction between experienced European designers and an increasing number of young Chinese designers produced intense synergies and original results. It was the case of emotional design of the face of new models or of internal panels specially shaped for Chinese customers, giving attention to the Chinese culture and traditions (personal interview with Peter Horbury, Geely Design VP, October 21, 2019). For example, internal panels of Lynk & Co models have been inspired by the shape of the famous Hangzhou Bridge. At the same time, Geely invested in young international design talents both in Sweden and in China, in order to "take Geely to the world," developing new really global models (Geely Global Media Center, 2019).

Beside the cultural distance between Europe and China, a second divide overlapped with the first one, between automakers' traditions as represented by car industry engineers on the one hand, and digital innovation as represented by software developers on the other hand. This second divide became increasingly important as software content of new generation vehicles was fast growing, seeking dialogue between these different groups of competencies. To overcome this key challenge, close collaboration with Geely and GRI was promoted in the field of connectivity, autonomous drive, electric architecture, and software development capability.

6.8. The Evolving Relations with Media, Policy-makers, and Civil Society in Sweden

At the beginning of the acquisition process, Chairman Li Shufu made several commitments to the Swedish government and Volvo and Ford management: the headquarters in Gothenburg, Sweden, would remain unchanged; the capacity and production facilities in Europe (Gothenburg, Sweden, and Ghent, Belgium) would not be reduced; the status and role of R&D centers in Sweden would remain unchanged; and all agreements with dealers will remain unchanged. In addition, he also promised that Volvo's intellectual property and production system, marketing network, management team, and brand operations would remain independent from Geely. These commitments were consistent with the repeated slogan that "Volvo is Volvo, Geely is Geely."

However, immediately prior to the 2010 acquisition, concerns, skeptical opinions, and lack of confidence were expressed by most trade unions, as they were afraid of possible upcoming job losses, and of massive technology transfer to China, followed by relocation of production activities to low-wage locations. Fears were also expressed about the closure of the historic Torslanda factory in the area of Gothenburg (Fang and Chimerson, 2017). On the contrary, the acquisition of Volvo Cars by Ford in 1999 was applauded at the beginning but ended in a fiasco 10 years later. One must note that, in Gothenburg, there has been traditionally a close connection between Volvo (and the other historical companies, such as SKF) on one hand and local political mileu on the other, within the context of a strong working-class tradition, expressed by the governing Social Democratic Party.

Within Volvo Cars, middle-ranked management, and older employees with several years of average work experience expressed similar distrust, fears, and concerns. When first visiting Geely plants in China, a number of Volvo engineers and managers held negative impressions, comparing them to European standards. A widespread opinion in those times was that Volvo, as a typical national champion, was "too Scandinavian," i.e. too deeply embedded in that society and culture, to start fruitful cooperation with a Chinese owner and expand in the Chinese market.

Moreover, in 2010, Swedish Industry Associations as well as the European Association of Automobile Suppliers (CLEPA) suggested Swedish suppliers to limit technology transfer to Volvo, as far as frontier new technologies were concerned, in order to prevent "technology theft" by the new Chinese partners. Some local entrepreneurs and policy-makers acted to promote a Swedish consortium to bid for Volvo Cars, before the deal was closed.

Analyzing 366 newspaper articles, Fang and Chimenson (2017) found that the Swedish media mainly had negative coverage of the Volvo–Geely deal during five years, since 2008 till 2013, i.e. during the last two years of the negotiation process before the 2010 acquisition, and during the following three years. Notwithstanding some positive voices, the Swedish media expressed negative views associated with dangerous scenarios for the country. The "Chinese offensive" was in general considered a threat to European industry. Moreover, the argument of lacking reciprocity for European companies investing in China was pointed out. Some media were suspicious about the role of the Chinese government in the acquisition, arguing that "Geely is not a private company in Western sense" (Fang and Chimenson, 2017, p. 5).

The negative coverage by the Swedish media during the bargaining and establishment stages reflected a deteriorating image of China in Western countries in general, and in particular, fears and concerns about the international growth of Chinese firms at unprecedented speeds. They ignored or underevaluated the fast catching up by Chinese firms, while the image of Chinese multinationals was on the average more favorable in developing countries. Western public opinion was not ready to understand and accept the rise of Chinese companies as global leaders in key industrial sectors and frontier technologies. This stereotyped view was also related to an increasing anti-globalization move of public opinions in Western countries, supporting nationalist and populist movements.

This context of distrust was related to ineffective soft power campaigns and to new forms of "liability of foreignness" or disadvantage specific to Chinese MNCs. It was the case, among others, of the rapid expansion of Huawei in the US: in that case, concern was expressed about the possible role and strategic interests of the Chinese government behind foreign acquisitions.

However, such negative attitudes evolved rapidly and changed substantially after the initial transitional period, when Swedish trade unions, media, and policy-makers developed a new attitude. Indeed, 2013 represented a turning point toward a more positive approach and appreciation of the role of Geely in Swedish economy and society.

The main factor was the success story of Geely–Volvo cooperation in the following years. The clear mission given to Volvo, along with consistent financial resources, greatly facilitated improving relations with policy-makers, central and local governments, trade unions, and public opinions. The rapid growth of Volvo in the Chinese market and the positive impact of this growth on production and employment in Sweden, with 4,500 new jobs created in Gothenburg, a third shift introduced and new models launched, positively impressed stakeholders and social actors in Sweden, as well as the public sentiments toward the Chinese automaker.

In this evolving perception, a single relevant role was played by Mr. Goran Johansson, a charismatic political leader in Gothenburg, former trade-unionist at SKF, with deep relations with Volvo, where he was member of the board for Volvo's Research and Educational Foundation. He was considered to represent the Gothenburg labor movement at large, during the negotiations and the Geely takeover of Volvo. When he supported the deal, with a pragmatic and realist attitude, understanding that the alternatives would be a disaster for the city, his view deeply influenced local public opinion.

6.9. Concluding Remarks

Is it possible to combine Western and Chinese corporate cultures? Cross-culture relations between Geely and Volvo since 2010 suggest that the answer to this question may be positive. In this chapter, we compared the Swedish/Scandinavian and Chinese corporate and organizational cultures in the specific case of Volvo and Geely, reaching some significant conclusions.

The initial hard challenge of integrating deeply different approaches finally gave rise to great synergies producing new resources. Cross-culture relations have been characterized by a gradualist approach to the post-acquisition process, and to an attitude that could be defined as "sensitive to cultural differences" (Lasserre, 2012), producing creative dynamics and innovation.

The decision of keeping Geely and Volvo management separate, with Geely only taking two seats on Volvo's global board, was wise, turning out to be crucial for the two companies' future growth and cooperation. Therefore, both Chinese-owned Volvo and CEVT were able to attract international young talents from Scandinavian countries, Europe, China, and other countries of origin.

In Sweden, initial negative coverage by the local media and skepticism of civil society, trade unions, and policy-makers were mainly due to a misleading perception of Geely's long-term strategies, associated with negative expectations. More in general, the dynamics of global industry and the multinational growth of Chinese corporations were not fully appreciated. However, this initial attitude did not affect Volvo's performance after the acquisition, as Geely developed its strategy of expansion of Volvo in China. When this strategy produced positive feedback in Sweden in terms of growth, production, technology, finance, and job creation, the situation changed, overcoming the initial difficulties. As a consequence of evident positive results, the approach of Swedish media, trade unions, and policy-makers gradually evolved toward a positive appreciation of Geely's role in the country.

The absence of domination by the acquiring company (as observed in other cases in Western countries) has produced positive effects in terms of a real long-term alliance between Volvo and Geely. Local communities have observed tangible benefits from the presence of Geely in their territories. The improvement of the CSR issue presents potential for further developments in the field of interculture management.

The traditional Chinese *yin-yang* thinking, both holistic and dynamic, coupled with a pragmatic attitude has helped to build up a cultural flexibility and interculture constructive relations (Fang, 2012), finally reaching a win-win situation for both Geely and Volvo.

References

Antonelli, C. (1995). *The Economics of Localized Technological Change and Industrial Dynamics*. Berlin: Springer.

Balcet, G. and G. Ietto-Gillies (2020). Internationalization, Outsourcing and Labour Fragmentation: The Case of FIAT. *Cambridge Journal of Economics*, **44**:1, 105–128.

Cantwell, J. (2003). Innovation and Information Technology in the MNE. In Alan Rugman and T.L. Brewer (eds.), *The Oxford Handbook of International Business*. Oxford: Oxford University Press, pp. 431–456.

Fang, T. (2012). Yin Yang: A new perspective on culture. *Management and Organization Review*, **8**, 59–72.

Fang, T. and D. Chimerson. (2017). The internationalization of Chinese firms and negative media coverage: The case of Geely's acquisition of Volvo Cars. *Thunderbird International Business Review*, **59**:4 (July/August), 483–502. https://doi.org/10.1002/tie.21905.

Forsgren, M. (2017). *Theories of the Multinational Firm: A Multidimensional Creature in the Global Economy*. 3rd edition, Cheltenham, UK and Northampton, USA: Edward Elgar.

Geely Global Media Center (2019). A designer journey to the East. April 12. Available at: http://global.geely.com/media-center/story/a-designer-journey to-the-east/ (accessed June 22, 2020).

Geely Media Center (2019). The foundation of a global enterprise, creating a global architecture: An interview with Mats Fägerhag. November 29. Available at: http://zgh.com/media-center/story/the-foundation-of-a-global-enterprise-creating-a-global-architecture/ (accessed March 5, 2021).

Hofstede, G. (1984). *Culture's Consequences: International Differences in Work Related Values*. London: Sage.

Hymer, S. H. (1976). *The International Operations of National Firms: A Study of Direct Foreign Investment*. Cambridge, MA: MIT Press.

Ietto-Gillies, G. (2019). *Transnational Corporations and International Production: Concepts, Theories and Effects*. 3d Edition. Cheltenham, UK and Northampton, USA: Edward Elgar.

Johanson, J. and J.-E. Vahlne (1977). The internationalization process of the firm — A model of knowledge development and increasing foreign market commitment. *Journal of International Business Studies*, **8**, 93–98.

Johanson, J. and J.-E. Vahlne (1990). The mechanism of internationalization. *International Marketing Review*, **7**, 11–24.

Johanson, J. and J.-E. Vahlne (2009). The Uppsala Internationalization Process model revisited: From liability of foreignness to liability of outsidership. *Journal of International Business Studies*, **40**:4, 1411–1431.

Lander, M. W. and L. Kooning (2013). Boarding the aircraft: Trust development amongst negotiators of a complex merger. *Journal of Management Studies*, **50**:1, 1–30.

Lasserre, P. (2012). *Global Strategic Management*. 3rd Edition. Hampshire: Palgrave McMillan.

Mokyr, J. (2017). *A Culture of Growth: The Origins of the Modern Economy*. Princeton and Oxford: Princeton University Press.

Shimizu, K., M. Hitt, D. Vaidyanath and V. Pisano (2004). Theoretical foundations of cross-border mergers and acquisitions: A review of current research and recommendations for the future. *Journal of International Management*, **10**:3, 307–353.

Weber, Y., T. Shlomo Yedidia and B. Ziva Rozen (2011). Mergers and acquisitions performance paradox: The mediating role of integration approach. *European Journal of International Management*, **5**:4, 373–393.

Yakob, R., H. R. Nakamura and P. Ström (2018). Chinese foreign acquisitions aimed for strategic asset-creation and innovation upgrading: The case of Geely and Volvo Cars. *Technovation*, **70–71**, 59–72.

Zaheer, S. (1995). Overcoming the liability of foreignness. *The Academy of Management Journal*, **38**:2, 341–363, April.

Chapter 7

CEVT, Lynk & Co, and Technology Catching Up: From Learning and Following to Innovation

Abstract

Cooperation needs to be supported and implemented by appropriate insti-tutions. Since its establishment in 2013, China Euro Vehicle Technology AB (CEVT) represented the most impressive and fruitful instrument for the cooperation process between Geely and Volvo. Evolving from the previous "asset-seeking" strategy stage, based on imitation, learning, and technological catching up, CEVT opened a new stage that we can define as "asset augmenting" and "strategic asset creation," speeding up innovation in products and processes. This chapter focus on the evolv-ing strategies of CEVT and its original trajectory: from the founding of CEVT to the launch of the new Compact Modular Architecture (CMA) platform and finally to the new brand Lynk & Co in 2017, a globally focused car brand and a turning point of Geely's integration with Volvo.

Keywords: Geely Auto; CEVT; Lynk & Co; asset-seeking strategy; asset creation strategy.

7.1. Introduction

In Chapter 5, Section 5.6, the origins and early developments of China Euro Vehicle Technology AB (CEVT) have been described and analyzed, in terms of a "perfect storm," focusing on its mission, location, features, responsibilities, performance, and quality. We analyzed how it opened the way to a fast-growing trajectory and to the building of a new modular platform, the Compact Modular Architecture (CMA).

In Chapter 6, Section 6.6, the understanding of the CEVT experience was further developed from a different point of view, that of its specific and original corporate and organizational culture. Its experience was indeed at the core of cross-culture cooperation between Geely and Volvo, highlighting challenges, cultural distance, risks, and potential opportunities. CEVT has attracted international talents from more than 30 countries, enhancing teamwork and generating flows of new knowledge and innovation as well as positive externalities. Cultural distances became a key resource instead of a limit.

In this chapter, in order to complete the analysis of the previous chapters, we will focus on the evolutionary side, i.e. the evolving strategies of CEVT and the associated corporate dynamics, to shed light on its original trajectory: from CEVT to the CMA platform and to the new brand Lynk & Co with its related models.

7.2. CEVT as a Synergic and a Dynamic Asset-Creating Corporation

As Yakob *et al.* (2018) pointed out, foreign direct investments (FDIs) oriented to "strategic asset creation" may be interpreted as a new and different stage of the previous "asset-seeking" strategy that has been considered for a long time to be the main driver of FDIs operated by emerging country multinationals (Mathews, 2006; Buckley *et al.*, 2007; Buckley *et al.*, 2016). In Chapter 5, Section 5.2, we reviewed and discussed the relevant literature on asset-seeking versus asset-creating strategies by emerging country multinationals, which is also relevant to this chapter.

We may also refer to other relevant contributions for interpreting our case study. Contractor and Lorange (1988) paved the way for important research streams on technology-oriented partnership, alliances, and cooperative strategies in international business, as a means to create new assets and knowledge. The seminal research work by John Cantwell shed light on the dynamics of technological globalization, when multinational corporations (MNCs) interact with innovative clusters in the host countries where they operate (Cantwell and Janne, 1999). These two pioneering contributions seem complementary to each other, while the management-oriented approach of David Teece (2007) deeply analyzed the implications of technology transfers and technology sharing on intellectual property (IP) and licensing issues.

In the case of CEVT, localized in a crucial Swedish innovation cluster, the interesting research question is how it was able to couple Volvo's quality standards with Geely's cost management, in a sort of dynamic synergy. That synergy allowed it to produce new technology and knowledge, a new joint platform, and finally new components, process technologies, and vehicles.

CEVT may be analyzed as a deeper integration stage between Geely and Volvo, following the financial integration, crucial since 2011, and the technology cooperation and synergy, launched by Chairman Li Shufu since the second half of 2012 (personal interview with Li Donghui, CFO of Geely Holding, July 12, 2019). It is significant that, as we pointed out in Chapter 5, the decision to create CEVT was taken in September 2012, immediately after that strategic move, in order to make it operational. The trajectory of CEVT represents a success story that has been highly beneficial to both partners. It has served as the converging point between the two companies, exerting profound influences on both corporations as a major instrument for developing their cooperation and affecting their growth trajectories. Thanks to CEVT, Geely and Volvo built up a deep-rooted alliance, well beyond a usual relationship between acquiring and acquired company.

CEVT's business operations consist of research, development, and design of components, systems, architectures, and other solutions for the automotive industry. CEVT also executes assignments in these areas for stakeholders within the Geely Holding Group, primarily working on projects for the car brands Volvo Cars and Geely, and in a second stage for Lynk & Co.

The original mission given to CEVT included five main pillars (Yakob *et al.*, 2018):

(1) Developing a new, common modular architecture for next-generation compact cars;
(2) Creating complete, customer-focused vehicles based on the new architecture;
(3) Developing shared components for C-segments cars: creating technical solutions applicable to different brands and customer profiles, both for Volvo and for Geely;

(4) Completing vehicle design;
(5) Finally, promoting advanced engineering and new technologies solutions.

Moreover, if we look at the diversity of missions of CEVT with respect to Volvo and Geely, we can point out the following: creating new architecture and shared modular components was the key mission for Volvo, whereas for Geely, along with creating new architecture and shared modular components, providing complete vehicle design, product development, and advanced engineering and technology services was part of the mission. Interestingly enough, we can note that the mission appears to be more extended in the second case. This means that Geely was expected to intensively benefit from R&D activities of CEVT for its growth process.

For Geely, the creation of CEVT represented both a reactive and a proactive strategy. It was, on the one hand, a reactive move in the face of potential obstacles on intellectual property issues, as in the early stages of cooperation with Volvo, also related to the use of scalable product architecture (SPA) platform. On the other hand, it was a proactive strategy, oriented to create a new high-volume and high-tech platform, complementary with SPA. This strategy aimed to overcome differences between Geely and Volvo, in terms of R&D activities, absorptive capacities, and managerial skills, combining their competences (Yakob *et al.*, 2018). It was therefore a typical case of strategic asset creation strategy.

Over time, CEVT expanded its scope, stimulating innovation for the whole Geely Group while also hosting the Swedish headquarters of Geely Design. Most of CEVT's employees are located in Lindholmen Science Park, Gothenburg, and in Trollhättan, Sweden, while a small number is based in Hangzhou, China. In the early stages of activity, including the origin of CMA platform, Volvo mainly provided personnel and its valuable platform development experience, while Geely provided most of the financial resources.

CEVT has been a very dynamic organization, with around 2,000 staff members in 2020, considered as its appropriate standard, after peaking at 2,400, including both employees and onsite consultants (personal interview with Mats Fägerhag, CEO CEVT, October 20, 2019). It has been one of the fastest growing companies in Sweden. The company's budget was over US$350 million in 2019.

Since the early stages of new projects, great efforts were made to involve first-tier suppliers in the co-design and development process of key components. This approach, termed "design for profitability," allowed the simplification and rationalization of components, reaching important technical and economic (cost-reducing) results. The process was facilitated by the fact that CEVT was a greenfield newcomer, without previous contracts and cooperation agreements with a well-established supplier network. In 2017, CEVT completed the basic development of the new CMA architecture, at a cost of US$1.7 million. Volvo invested about a quarter of the total, while the rest was mainly supported by Geely (personal interview with Mats Fägerhag, CEO CEVT, October 20, 2019).

Table 7.1 provides a summary of the key features, mission, and objectives of CEVT.

7.3. The CMA Platform: Asset Creation for Geely and Volvo

The modular platform strategy in the automotive industry may lead to improved coordination of manufacturing plants within a global network and better economies of scale and scope, enhancing performance (Lampón *et al.*, 2015). The CMA platform is a completely new modular architecture, designed for B- and C-segment vehicles. It represents a major original goal of CEVT and was created at a very rapid pace, with a focus on performance, quality, and cost reduction. CMA allowed new design and the integration of new technology solutions, supported by continuous and integrated quality control.

At the beginning of the CMA development, Volvo and Geely expressed their respective needs. Volvo needed a modular architecture for smaller cars instead of the existing SPA platform. At the same time, Geely also needed a completely new basic platform in order to produce high-tech and high-quality cars in the same segment. Therefore, the CMA applied not only to the premium cars in the Volvo 40 series but also to the development of other new C-segment vehicles within the Geely Group (Yakob *et al.*, 2018).

At the beginning, Volvo was crucial to the development of CMA. In a first stage, this platform benefited from the huge development

Table 7.1.   Strategic summary of CEVT.

Location	Located in Lindholmen Science Park, within the automotive cluster of Gothenburg, Sweden. Close to Volvo. Positive externalities generated from this location for engineering and industrial experience.
Ownership	Wholly foreign owned by the Geely Holding Group, with high autonomy.
Entities and responsibility	CEVT, Gothenburg; Geely Design, Gothenburg. Complete responsibility for Geely Auto, cooperation with Volvo for top hats.
Organization structure	<u>Eight departments</u>: R&D, CMA Product Strategy & Vehicle Line Management, Quality, Finance, HR, Purchasing, Geely Design Gothenburg, Business Office. <u>Eight R&D functions</u>: Architecture, Powertrain Integration, Chassis & Safety Electronics, Interior, Exterior & Body, Vehicle Integration, Transmission, Manufacturing Engineering.
Operational objectives	Planning, development, and maintenance of a cross-brand, interorganizational automotive platform for C-segment cars. Creating scale economies and scope economies, including procurement synergies. Division of labor among CEVT Gothenburg, Geely Design, and GRI China. Accelerating learning curve on technology and project development process. Developing human resources and skills.
Strategic values to Geely Group	Promoting competitiveness, coupling the technology strengths of Volvo and the cost advantages of Geely. Developing a world-class vehicle architecture. Improving product quality and brand image. Optimizing cost synergies and resource utilization. Implementing shared platform strategy inside the group. Contributing to sustainable mobility.

Source: Developed from Yakob *et al.* (2018), p. 65.

experience at Volvo Cars. In the initial stages of the development process, CEVT engineers had frequent meetings with Volvo and Geely personnel in order to agree on a joint requirement setting. In total, 35 different projects had been developed at CEVT in 2019 (personal interview with Per Ferdell, VP — CEVT, October 23, 2019). A cost-sharing agreement took place between Geely and Volvo; moreover, the partner companies own 50-50 of the patents and intellectual properties of CMA.

Modularization and flexibility have been the key CMA concepts and operational tools, as pointed out to us by Mats Fägerhag, CEO of CEVT. "Based on the platform, Volvo Cars created the 'top hat' — the visual design and the interior — of their cars. We, in the case of Geely, also won the contract for the complete design of the Geely cars. In all, we have orders for more than ten complete Geely models" (personal interview with Mats Fägerhag, CEO of CEVT, October 21, 2019). CMA benefited from huge investments: Geely and Volvo have invested US$2.4 billion in research and development to jointly develop this basic modular architecture.

Within CMA, the general process starts with thorough market research, then moves from marketing to engineering, and back to marketing, thus balancing technology, quality, consumer needs, and cost requirements. Adapting to changing conditions and promoting continuous learning are the rules and represent the key elements of success. Five cross-functional module teams have been set up at CMA, comprising Volvo and Geely representatives, for engineering, purchasing, quality, product design, manufacturing, and testing, in different areas of powertrain, body, interiors, chassis, and electrical/electronic items.

In the CMA platform, engineers and virtual test teams have been working together, adopting sophisticated simulation tools and Computer Aided Engineering (CAE). It was developed with Geely's investment and involvement, with huge expenditure of funds and human resources. Born under the Global Industry 4.0 framework, it covers the development needs of different car models. It can also provide shared R&D solutions based on many factors and variables, such as brand definition, user tastes, and market positioning. CMA may support several vehicle and body variants, including sedan, hatchback, SUV, and cross-country, and it is compatible with 3-cylinder and 4-cylinder gasoline and diesel engines, as well as with hybrid powertrain (personal interview with Per Ferdell, VP — CEVT, October 23, 2019).

The safety engineering at CMA highly benefited from the Swedish and Volvo tradition. It introduced active safety features, such as 360-degree surround view, forward collision warning, autonomous emergency brakes, and pedestrian detection. It also introduced some passive safety features, such as strategic use of special steel, innovative front and rear crumple zones, and energy-absorbing features.

CMA-based engines reached high performances in energy saving and fuel consumption levels, allowing to meet the Euro 7 standards, introduced in 2019. Hybrid development took place through a version of the Dual Clutch Transmission, 7DCT, also prepared for full electrification. The architecture engineers and managers worked to combine a sporty driving feeling with high comfort, through adapted technical solutions, including wheel steering and pedal braking.

For all these reasons, CMA is considered one of the best of global auto architectural infrastructures. Compared to benchmark platforms, it is more advanced than Toyota's TNGA platform and Volkswagen's MQB platform. CMA has advanced electronic architecture, including high-performance car chips, high computing power intelligent driving chips, technology sensors, Laser Imaging Detection (LIDAR), high-definition cameras, and high-speed network connections.

In summary, the CMA platform could achieve three essential results: to speed up the development process of new cars and components, shortening time; to reach high quality standards; and to reduce development costs, creating economies of scale as well as economies of scope. By 2017, the basic development of the CMA architecture was completed, paving the way for the ambitious launch of a new brand within the Geely Group: Lynk & Co. Table 7.2 provides key information on the models

Table 7.2.   Vehicles based on CMA platform.

Vehicle/Model	Type	Start of production	2018 Sales volume	2019 Sales volume
Volvo XC40	Compact SUV	2017	75,828	139,847
Volvo V40	Compact	2017	60,461	39,561
Volvo V40 cross country	Compact	2017	17,126	11,981
Polestar 2	BEV	2020	—	—
Lynk & Co 01	Compact SUV	2017	89,405	51,636
Lynk & Co 02	Subcompact SUV	2018	21,751	23,543
Lynk & Co 03	Compact sedan	2018	9,258	52,887
Lynk & Co 04	Subcompact hatchback	2020	—	—
Lynk & Co 05	Compact SUV	2020	—	—
Lynk & Co 06	Subcompact SUV	2020	—	—
Geely *Xingyue*	Compact SUV	2019	—	23,944
Total	—	—	**273,829**	**343,399**

Source: Volvo website; Geely website; CarSalesBase.

based on CMA Platform, produced in the 2017–2020 period, for the brands Volvo, Geely, Lynk & Co, and Polestar.

The products derived from this system include traditional fuel vehicles (Volvo XC40, Lynk & Co 01, Lynk & Co 02, Lynk & Co 03, Lynk & Co 05, and Geely *Xingyue*), hybrid models (Lynk & Co 01 PHEV, Lynk & Co 01 HEV, Lynk & Co 02 PHEV, and Lynk & Co 03 PHEV, Geely *Xingyue* PHEV), a pure electric model (Polestar 2), and high-performance models (Lynk & Co 03+ and Lynk & Co 03 TCR cars, Geely *Xingyue* 350T AWD).

Polestar 2 is a premium five-door fastback based on CMA and features two electric motors and a 78 kWh battery capacity that enable a targeted range of 500 km (European WLTP cycle), with all-wheel-drive electric powertrain. On the contrary, the previous model, Polestar 1 PHEV (Plug-in Hybrid Electric Vehicle), used the Volvo Scalable Platform Architecture.

CEVT and CMA architecture may be considered the bridge connecting Geely and Volvo's R&D systems, covering multiple brand ranges and products. Before the birth of the modular architecture, it was difficult to imagine a great variety of models with such a differentiated positioning under one same platform. CMA as a new-generation architecture allowed Geely Holdings to truly establish a comprehensive product system, generating a crucial competitive advantage in global markets.

7.4. Lynk & Co Brand — A Turning Point for a New Stage of Growth

As a globally focused car brand, Lynk & Co is an excellent case study on Geely's motivation for new brand development. The launch of Lynk & Co in 2017 represented a turning point in the process of technological convergence between Geely and Volvo, which marks the strategic asset creation and global integration of production by the Geely Group, thereby opening a new chapter in its corporate history. Lynk & Co models, based on CMA architecture, are the direct result of product and process innovation within CEVT, only four years after its creation. In the words of Mats Fägerhag, CEO of CEVT, the launch of Lynk & Co 01 was "a very demanding experience" (personal interview, October 20, 2019).

The launch of Lynk & Co represented a huge change in the attitude of Volvo (with a shareholding of 30%) toward deeper strategic synergy with Geely (personal interview with Li Donghui, CFO of Geely Holding,

July 12, 2019). The focus of the new brand is on Internet connectivity and innovative models, targeting mostly young professionals as potential clients (Savov, 2016).

The project started in 2013, under the name "V" given by Geely, which did not want to unveil the plan before 2017. Lynk & Co's ownership was shared between Geely Holding at 50%, Volvo Cars at 30%, and Geely Auto at 20%, while IP ownership was shared 50-50 between Geely Holding and Volvo. Overcoming initial doubts, after 2016 Volvo engineers have been increasingly confident in Lynk & Co as a successful product, and the strategic partnership with Geely has been therefore significantly enhanced (personal interview to Li Donghui, July 12, 2019).

Lynk & Co 01 as a PHEV was first introduced to the Chinese domestic market in July 2018, while Lynk & Co 02 PHEV and Lynk & Co 03 PHEV were marketed from September 2019. Based on P2.5 technology, the Lynk & Co PHEV models are all equipped with the Drive-E 1.5TD+7DCT-H powertrain shared with Volvo, in order to achieve a comprehensive maximum output power of 262Ps (see Table 7.2).

On production side, the first model was Lynk & Co 01 (both ICE and PHEV), produced at Luqiao Taizhou factory, using the same plant that produces Volvo 40 series and some of Geely's mid- to high-end new models. This location choice allowed the company to reach economies of scale, in terms of volumes of production, as well as economies of scope, in terms of variety and synergies between different products.

The second and third models, Lynk & Co 02 and Lynk & Co 03, have been produced at Zhangjiakou Industrial Complex, as it will be the case for the future planned models of Lynk & Co. This represented a new investment for further expansion, after the case of the Volvo engine plant, built in 2012–2013 and strongly supported by the local government (providing 1.7 billion RMB industrial funding). The new Lynk & Co plant, a greenfield project, started construction in 2014 and went into production in 2018. These two new plants have been built according to Volvo's high-quality standards, and with strong financial support from Geely Holding. Industry 4.0 system and high levels of automation have been introduced in the production systems. Again, the synergy between Volvo's technological excellence and Geely's financial and organizational strength was a decisive asset to success.

In terms of design, Lynk & Co has a high-end trend, mainly carried out by the international team in Gothenburg. More than 200 designers from more than 20 different countries around the world cooperated in the team. In terms of quality, Lynk & Co benchmarks high-end brands and shares high-standard manufacturing and components, as well as supply chain management, with Volvo Cars.

In 2019, a sport version of the Lynk & Co 03, the TCR Touring Car, based on the Lynk & Co 03 mass-produced model, won the international auto race WTCR. This represented a relevant breakthrough for Chinese auto brands in the world's top competitions, opening a new page for the development of Chinese auto sports. While Lynk & Co products cover traditional fuel vehicles and hybrid vehicles in 2020, Lynk & Co's pure electric vehicles are under development, in a dedicated pure electric factory in Hangzhou Bay.

Based on the CMA platform, all Lynk & Co models are positioned between those of the Geely and Volvo brands. In branding terms, Volvo wanted to keep its distance and Geely stressed that this is a wholly independent brand. However, many human resources and technology know-how are internally shared through closely related offices. Geely CEO An Conghui acknowledges this, saying that "along this journey, we can't go without the help of Volvo as a good mentor," and Volvo also confirms that "a strong Lynk will also be good for Volvo" (Savov, 2016).

In terms of performance, Lynk & Co shares with Volvo the Drive-E powertrain: it integrates advanced technologies in the engine field, obtaining more power, reducing fuel consumption, and producing less emissions. Moreover, advanced gear shifting, transmission, braking, and other devices derives from a network of the world's top suppliers (Auto Research Institute, 2020).

From a service perspective, Lynk & Co relies on the structure of the entire Geely Automobile Group. For some remote areas, the conditions of Geely brand services are borrowed and remote technical support is provided. Relying on Geely Group's large resources, Lynk & Co can guarantee its user services in areas where channels are not yet established.

In China, Lynk & Co models are usually sold through traditional marketing channels. In Europe, on the contrary, the proposed concept is more of a subscribed membership, which should allow clients the right to lease new or used Lynk & Co cars instead of buying them. This project builds on an innovative shared ownership, with a central user experience orientation. The Lynk & Co brand was supposed to sell its first vehicles in Europe in the fourth quarter of 2020, offering electric and plug-in hybrid models, when the pandemic crisis broke out. The production was planned to be located in China, instead of the Volvo plant in Ghent, Belgium, as originally planned.

7.5. Concluding Remarks

The creation of CEVT in 2013 opened the way to the development of a new world-class modular architecture, CMA platform, in 2017, and the subsequent launch of the first model of the new Lynk & Co brand in the same year. In this chapter, we show how these three steps represented three stages in the same trajectory of technology convergence between Geely and Volvo, followed by a new asset-creation strategy, producing rapid innovation.

Also thanks to this new trajectory, Geely Holding Group has created nearly 20 high-performance models in the 2017–2020 period, including Volvo, Lynk & Co, and Polestar brands, covering different vehicles.

Geely has been moving from early stages of technology catching up, imitation, and asset-seeking international acquisitions, toward significant learning processes and finally creative technological and organizational innovation and systemic integration in a completely new product architecture.

The result has been a success story not only in pure productive and technological terms but also in cross-culture cooperation between companies with profoundly different corporate history and traditions, rooted in Europe and China, that initially represented a major challenge. It is worth to note that CEVT benefited from crucial externalities and spatial dynamics within the production and innovation cluster where it is located in Gothenburg.

This win-win cooperation has achieved important productive and economic results, opening new perspectives of technology innovation, product development and global expansion for the Geely Group as well as Volvo Cars.

References

Auto Research Institute (2020). *Lin Jie & Chen Siying — Our View on Lynk: Lynk & Co's Mission Is to Participate in Global Competition.* January 7. Available at: https://www.yidianzixun.com/article/0OLTwWut (accessed September 8, 2020).

Buckley, P. J., L. J. Clegg, A. R. Cross, X. Liu, H. Voss and P. Zheng (2007). The determinants of Chinese outward foreign direct investment. *Journal of International Business Studies*, **38**:4, 499–518.

Buckley, P. J., S. Munjal, P. Enderwick and N. Forsans (2016). Cross-border acquisitions by Indian multinationals: Asset exploitation or asset augmentation? *International Business Review*, **25**:4, 986–996.

Cantwell, J. and O. Janne (1999). Technological globalization and innovative centres: The role of corporate technological leadership and locational hierarchy. *Research Policy*, **28**:2, 119–144.

Contractor, F. and P. Lorange (1988). *Cooperative Strategies in International Business*. Lexington, MA: Lexington. Books.

Lampón, J., P. Cabanelas and J. Benito (2015). The impact of implementation of a modular platform strategy in automobile manufacturing networks. *GEN Working Paper B 2015-2*. Available at: https://ideas.repec.org/p/gov/wpregi/1502.html (accessed August 29, 2020).

Mathews, J. A. (2006). Dragon multinationals: New players in 21st century globalization. *Asia Pacific Journal of Management*, **23**:1, 5–27.

Savov, V. (2016). Lynk & Co is a new car brand that was 'born digital. *The Verge*, October 19. Available at: https://www.theverge.com/2016/10/19/13328674/lynk-and-co-geely-connected-car-volvo-launch-official (accessed September 8, 2020).

Teece, D. (2007). *The Transfer and Licensing of Know-How and Intellectual Property: Understanding the Multinational Enterprise in the Modern World*. Singapore: World Scientific Publishing.

Yakob, R., H. R. Nakamura and P. Ström (2018). Chinese foreign acquisitions aimed for strategic asset-creation and innovation upgrading: The case of Geely and Volvo Cars. *Technovation*, **70–72**, 59–72.

Part III

Geely's Further Expansion on the Global Stage

Chapter 8

Geely Takes Stake in Daimler: A New Chapter in Globalization

Abstract

This chapter examines the motivation and key process of Geely's indirect acquisition of Daimler's stake. With a focus on the complex financial operation by Geely, this chapter outlines the sophistication of acquisition by Geely, including its deep understanding on the regulations of host country (Germany in this case). After surveying the cases of two joint ventures, one on the premium ride-hailing and another one on the smart car, the chapter further reviews Geely's strategy upgrading, expanding from the traditional car toward intelligent electric vehicles and mobility services. In addition, the chapter also highlights the phenomenon of reverse technology transfer, a platform developed by Geely to be used by Diamler's smart car and provides a comprehensive review on Daimler's multiple presence in China.

Keywords: Geely Auto; Daimler; equity investment; *smart*; ride-hailing business; reverse technology transfer.

8.1. Introduction

For Geely, the ambition of becoming a globalized company does not stop at the Volvo deal. Geely is continually seeking sustainable growth by acquiring high-quality global assets. Employing indirect acquisition to become the largest shareholder of Daimler opened a new chapter of

Geely's globalization drive. In the short run, Geely started with two significant operations with Daimler: one is the creation of a joint venture (JV) in the premium ride-hailing business for the China market; another one is the JV on *smart*, for the building and sales of electric and intelligent smart cars with richer portfolio both for China and global market.

8.2. Why Geely Needs Daimler After the Acquisition of Volvo?

There is no doubt that Geely's acquisition of Volvo, based on the business results of 10 years between 2010 and 2020, is one of the very few successful cases of cross-border acquisitions by Chinese automobile companies. As the vision of Li Shufu is to seek new opportunities for sustainable growth continually, it is natural to see new acquisitions to be made after the case of Volvo. The acquisition of PROTON and Lotus in 2017 did not satisfy the appetite of Li Shufu, who is seeking a new target of global significance.

In the global automobile market, the top three luxury carmakers — namely ABB (Audi, Benz, BMW) — have been recognized for their constant growth and steady profit levels. ABB's global sales volume is at around 2 million units in 2019, with that of Volvo less than one-third of Benz or BMW. China is the most important strategic market for all the luxury carmakers. In parallel with Volvo's remarkable growth in China, ABB's aggressive sales reveal their significant localization efforts for the adaptation of Chinese customer tastes. After years of operations, China's market shares in the global sales for ABB all exceed 30%, while Volvo only reached 23%. This benchmarking signifies ABB's excellent performance and extra efforts to be made by Volvo, both in the global and China markets (Table 8.1).

Their volumes of R&D investments also exhibit the sustainability of carmakers. Between 2010 and 2015, Volvo invested US$11 billion in R&D to cover a wide range of projects, including new car models, new platforms, new powertrain, new energy cars, and autonomous driving. In 2018, Volvo Group (including trucks, buses, construction equipment, etc.) spent US$1.7 billion in R&D, while Audi, BMW, and Daimler invested $3.8, $8.6 and €9.1 billion, respectively, in the same year (Volvo, 2020; Daimler, 2018; Reid, 2018). This gap in R&D, jointly with the gap in sales, may forecast the future landscape of the global (and China) luxury

Table 8.1. Global and China sales of luxury car brands 2015–2019.

	2015	2016	2017	2018	2019
Global					
Mercedes-Benz	1,871,511	2,083,888	2,289,344	2,310,185	2,339,562
BMW/Rolls-Royce	1,905,234	2,003,359	2,088,283	2,125,026	2,168,516
Audi	1,803,200	1,871,300	1,878,100	1,812,485	1,845,550
Volvo	503,127	534,332	571,577	642,253	705,452
China					
Mercedes-Benz	373,459	472,844	587,868	652,996	693,443
BMW	463,736	516,355	594,388	639,953	723,680
Audi	570,889	591,554	597,866	663,049	690,083
Volvo	81,588	90,930	114,410	130,593	161,436
China/Global					
Mercedes-Benz	20%	23%	26%	28%	30%
BMW	24%	26%	28%	30%	33%
Audi	32%	32%	32%	37%	37%
Volvo	16%	17%	20%	20%	23%

Source: https://www.best-selling-cars.com/.

car market. Even from the point of pure investment, having a stake in ABB will be a safe bet.

Behind the aggressive investment in R&D, Daimler also takes the leadership position in pure electric vehicles and autonomous driving, among the others. Electrification is the strategic shift for the future auto-mobile industry, either proactively chosen by carmakers, or reactively as a response to government regulation on the reduction of CO_2 emission. Daimler has invested more than €10 billion for its EQ series alone. By 2022, the company aims to bring more than 10 models of electric vehicles (EVs) and offer one electric alternative in each Mercedes-Benz model series (Daimler, 2019). In comparison, Geely's five-year plan "Blue Geely Initiative," initiated in 2015, aims to reach an ambitious objective of 90% cars sold by Geely Group to be new energy vehicles, among which 65% are plug-in hybrid electric vehicles/hybrid electric vehicles (PHEVs/ HEVs) and 35% are pure EVs (*Geely Annual Report* 2016, p. 17). However, by 2020, the sales of new energy vehicles (including Volvo) was less than 10%, significantly lower than the plan. Under that context, the solid technology sets on electrification are vital for Geely's sustainable strategic development in the long term.

Another important asset of ABB is branding. These three brands enjoy luxury brand positions and substantial sales volumes, a rare asset in the automobile industry. In the early stage of Volvo's acquisition, Li Shufu had ambition to further upgrade Volvo to a luxury brand, via new design and technology upgrading. However, Volvo people are rooted in the Scandinavian culture of *Jantelagen* (Law of *Jante*, or "let us better not have a much bigger house or boat than our neighbors"). Rooted in this regional culture, Volvo is always identified as a "premium" car. Using the word "luxury" is even considered a negative remark and not complimentary. Instead, the compromising word used for the international market is "modern Swedish luxury." Under such context, Volvo's brand positioning vis-à-vis ABB will not be easily changed in the coming decade. For Li Shufu, the quickest way to acquire a luxury brand asset is via acquisition.

Regarding ABB's potential targets, the challenge of stake acquisition is significantly different among those three big players, and Daimler is probably the "easiest" in relative terms. Audi belongs to the Volkswagen group, and the Porsche family holds over 30% of the stocks. The biggest shareholder of the BMW group, the Quandt family, controls around 46% of the shares. Mr. Stefan Quandt alone controls 25.83% of the grand total and can exercise the right to block any potential takeover (Nica, 2018). As for Daimler, as we will elaborate in detail in the coming section, before Geely's stake acquisition, the biggest shareholder was Kuwait's sovereign wealth fund, holding a 6.8% stake (Table 8.2).

Table 8.2.　Largest shareholder of Volkswagen, BMW, and Daimler AG by 2017.

	Stock code	2017.01.01 share value	2018.01.01 share value	Largest shareholder by 2017	Largest shareholder stake
Volkswagen	VOWG	136.75	168.70	Porsche	53.1%
BMW	BMWG	88.79	87.19	The Quandt	46.7%
Daimler AG	DAIGn	70.72	70.80	Kuwait investment authority	6.8%

Source: Investing.com

8.3. Why Is China Market Important to Daimler?

After years of investment, China has become the largest single market for Daimler. In 2018, China's sales doubled that of the US and were more significant than the consolidated European markets (excluding Germany). The importance of the China market to Daimler is outlined in Table 8.3.

For Daimler, there is a clear evolution from import substitution by localized production in China. Between 2014 and 2019, the company experienced a structural change. The importation rate over the total sales dropped from 50% to 18% (Table 8.4). Daimler is making a massive investment in different vehicle types by creating JVs in different provinces in China. The most important partner is the BAIC Group (Beijing Automotive Industry Holding Co.), a state-owned company (SOE), supervised by the Beijing branch of the State-owned Assets Supervision and Administration Commission.

Table 8.3.   Mercedes-Benz cars unit sales by regions 2017–2019.

Year	2017	%	2018	%	2019	%
China	619	26	678	28	694	29
United States	338	14	327	14	313	13
Germany	320	13	324	14	335	14
Europe excl. Germany	694	29	659	28	657	28
Rest of world	403	17	395	17	386	16
Total	2374	100	2383	100	2385	100

Note: Units in thousands.
Source: Daimler (2020a, p. 47).

Table 8.4.   Mercedes-Benz cars unit sales in China 2014–2019.

Year	2014	2015	2016	2017	2018	2019
Locally produced	146	250	317	423	485	567
Imported	147	150	171	196	193	127
Total	293	400	488	619	678	694
Locally produced%	50%	63%	65%	68%	72%	82%
Imported%	50%	38%	35%	32%	28%	18%
Total	100%	100%	100%	100%	100%	100%

Note: Units in thousands.
Source: Daimler (2020a, p. 48).

By the 2010s, Daimler has five JVs and three affiliates in China:

- Two JVs were created with BAIC Group: Beijing Benz Automotive Co., Ltd. (BBAC), and Beijing Mercedes-Benz Sales Service Co. (BMBS). These two JVs are the most important ones for the mass production and sales of passenger cars.
- Fujian Benz Automotive Corporation (FBAC) is a three-party JV created in June 2007 by Daimler Vans Hong Kong Limited, BAIC Motor Corporation Limited, and Fujian Motor Industry Group Co., on the production of commercial vans (V-Class models).
- Shenzhen BYD Daimler New Technology Co. Ltd. is a JV created in 2011 in partnership with BYD, for the production of DENZA, a new brand dedicated to New Energy Vehicles (NEVs) in China.
- The JV established in 2012 with Foton Motor is in the mid-to-heavy truck business, Beijing Foton Daimler Automotive Co., Ltd. (BFDA).

Other smaller operations in Asia include sales companies in the Hong Kong area, South Korea, and Taiwan. Affiliates of Daimler include Mercedes-Benz (China) Ltd., Mercedes-Benz Auto Finance Ltd., and Daimler Northeast Asia Parts Trading & Services Co., Ltd.

The first JV, BBAC, was founded in 2005. With a 50-50 share and a total registered capital of US$401 million, BBAC integrates R&D, engine and vehicle production, sales, and after-sale services. Eight main Mercedes-Benz models were produced locally, including SUV (EQC, GLC, GLB, GLA), AMG, A-Class, C-Class, and E-Class. Benz-branded passenger cars' annual sales in China were 567,000 units in 2019, as illustrated by Table 8.4.

In December 2012, two companies established another 50-50 JV, named BMBS. The main objective is to merge two previously separated channels, one for imported cars, and another for locally produced Mercedes-Benz cars, into one. This JV integrates the functions of sales & marketing, after-sales, expansion of dealer network, used-car and fleet-car sales, and dealer and workshop training into one system.

During 2013–2019, Daimler and BAIC formed a cross-holding between them. In February 2013, Daimler and BAIC further deepened their partnership. Daimler AG claimed to take a 12% stake of BAIC Motor, the passenger car unit of BAIC Group, and took two seats on the Board of Directors. Thus, Daimler becomes the first non-Chinese automotive company to take a stake in Chinese state-owned original equipment manufacturer (OEM). To facilitate the initial public offering (IPO) of BAIC, the share of BAIC in the production JV BBAC was increased from 50% to 51%; and in return, Daimler increased its share of BMBS to 51%. This operation enabled BAIC to move forward with its IPO. By 2019, Daimler's actual stake in BAIC Motor (Hong Kong-listed, code 1958) was 9.55% (BAIC, 2019). To further deepen the strategic cooperation, in March 2018, Daimler took a 3.93% stake in Beijing Electric Vehicle Co., Ltd. (BJEV), an affiliate of BAIC Group. Thereafter, BJEV was listed in China and also named as BAIC Data (BAICDT), with the actual stake of Daimler being 3.01%. In July 2019, BAIC bought a 5% take at Daimler AG and thus become the third-largest shareholder, right after Geely (9.7%) and Kuwait's sovereign wealth fund (6.8%). This 5% holding has a market value of around €2.5 billion (US$2.8 billion) (Figure 8.1).

Chinese media expressed that Daimler is becoming more Chinese, as the Chinese ownership by Geely and BAIC emerged the largest at Daimler. This fact worried some investors outside of China. As expressed by Ingo Speich, Head of Sustainability & Corporate Governance, from Deka Investment GmbH, which represents some 9 million Daimler shares, during Daimler's annual meeting in May 2019: "Despite all joy about long-term anchor shareholders: we still want to see the Mercedes star and not the Chinese dragon on the hood" (Sims, 2019).

Figure 8.1.   Daimler and BAIC cross-shareholding and JVs.

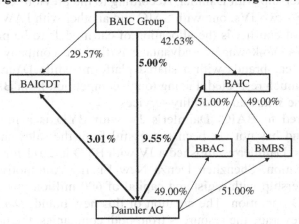

Source: Official website of BAIC, Daimler, and their JVs. Compiled by the author.

In December 2019, it was reported that BAIC has set in motion a plan to increase its stake to around 10% and to win a seat on Daimler's supervisory board. While the deal has not yet been made, HSBC played a vital role in the deal of 5% stake purchase and may continue to do so for the future possible increase in stake. As HSBC holds 5.23% in Daimler's voting rights directly, it is not surprising to see the future investment move by BAIC, via equity swaps for example. If this can be realized, BAIC's decision-making power will be much stronger than Geely, as Geely does not have a seat on the supervisory board yet (Sun *et al.*, 2019).

BAIC's increase in stake at Daimler is vital for both partners. For BAIC, the JV with Hyundai Motor Co. has seen low performance, and BAIC's indigenous brands are still at the investment stage. Daimler is a secured investment for BAIC. As for Daimler, BAIC has become China's biggest producer of electric cars. The partnership with BAIC can secure the China market's compliance issue regarding the quota on clean vehicles. Second, as illustrated above, Daimler's expansion in the China market depends heavily on the localized production base. Reinforcing the partnership with a state-owned company in Beijing is also a safe choice. The financial market delivered a positive signal. In July 2019, Daimler shares rose by as much as 5.2% in Frankfurt trading after BAIC's investment announcement. It is the first time Daimler rebounded in the stock market, after declining 15% in the past 12 months.

Interestingly, there is a competition between two Chinese carmakers on the partnership with Daimler. According to the previous experience of Volkswagen's two JVs, one with SAIC and another with FAW, one of the core topics of conflict is the allocation of car models to be produced by different JVs. Volkswagen's advantage is that the company has a rich portfolio of car brands with a shared platform, while Daimler's brand portfolio is much restricted. Facing tough competition from BAIC, Geely has to choose *smart* and mobility services.

Compared to BAIC, Daimler's JV with BYD is a much smaller operation and has not yet been successful from the sales and financial perspectives. Daimler established a JV with BYD in 2011 for its strategy of electrification. Shenzhen Denza New Energy Automotive Co. is a 50-50 partnership with registered capital of 600 million yuan, including a joint R&D operation. The creation of this new brand, *Denza*, has the strategy to leverage the resources from both companies, the battery technology from BYD in particular, while protecting Benz's brand image in China.

However, the commercial operation of *Denza* has encountered challenges. The company launched batch sales in 2014. Due to the limited number of models available and relatively higher prices, sales were limited in recent years. In 2017, the JV only sold 4,713 EVs, and sales further dropped to 1,974 and 2,089 units in the coming two years (Carsales, 2020). *Denza* is losing money. In May 2017, the two partners further invested 500 million yuan (US$72.6 million) each into the JV, then another 400 million yuan (US$62.5 million) each in 2018. The total capitalization is 4.16 billion yuan. There is still a long way for both partners to make this project successful.

8.4. Geely's Indirect Acquisition of Daimler via Sophisticated Financial Operations

Eight years after Volvo's acquisition, Geely acquired 9.69% of Mercedes-Benz owner Daimler, becoming its largest shareholder in February 2018. The total investment was at around US$9 billion, through an investment company. Before Geely, Kuwait's sovereign wealth fund was the largest stakeholder for decades, with a 6.8% holding.

Geely approached Daimler in November 2017 to propose the acquisition of a stake or reach a technology-sharing deal but was rejected by Daimler. Several months later, Geely Group employed a complex financial structure to make this indirect acquisition happen while avoiding the request of disclosure according to German regulation (Jourdan and Shirouzu, 2018). This acquisition seems sudden, but it is a project that lasted for at least more than one year, under Li Yifan, with a small task force.

Geely deployed at least two Hong Kong shell companies. The company used derivatives, bank financing, and carefully structured share options to make this deal happen. One shell company, Tenaciou3 Prospect Investment Ltd., had the purpose of amassing the stake. The company had just one ordinary share, worth HK$1 (12.8 US cents) and a single director: Li Yifan. This shell company is owned by another Hong Kong–registered company, Fujikiro Ltd., which lists a third company, Miroku Ltd., and an individual who is the senior partner at global law firm King & Wood Mallesons as a director. Investment via the use of shell companies as investment vehicles and lawyers acting as directors is common. In brief, this is a complex financial structure featured as shells within shells. Thus, from the legal perspective, Li Shufu is not named in any official documents, while Geely's official communication indicated Geely is the owner of the stake held by Tenaciou3. Tenaciou3 Investment Holdings used its share capital in Tenaciou3 Prospect Investment as collateral for the loan. Morgan Stanley made the structure of investment in the secondary market and a part of this project's financing. To speed up the project, Geely recruited two former executives of Morgan Stanley.

One important part of the operation is the direct purchase via the Hong Kong branch of Industrial Bank Co. Ltd. The Industrial Bank lent €1.67 billion (US$2.04 billion) to Tenaciou3 Investment Holdings Ltd., which then purchased some shares of Daimler on its own, but to a level that is not enough to require disclosure.

Another important part of the operation is to use equity collar by Bank of America Merrill Lynch (BAML), also at a level of no need of disclosure, only when those shares are to be sold to Tenaciou3 (Heller, 2018). Equity collar is an options strategy. It consists of simultaneous buying an equity put option (with a strike price below the price of the equity) and selling an equity call option (with a strike price above the price of the equity). The objective is to protect profits and hedge against possible losses. The official disclosure from Geely side to the public on equity collar is vague. Based on limited information disclosure, Jun Lu, Professor of Finance from Emlyon Business School, made the following hypothesis:

BAML and Geely signed an agreement to purchase and hold Daimler shares for Geely. The two parties agreed to perform share delivery at a certain time in the future (similar to a forward contract). Then, BAML purchased Daimler shares in the market (assuming an average cost of €70 per share). In order to avoid market risks, BAML conducted equity collar operations in the options market

Buying Daimler's put option (assuming strike price is €60) and selling call options (assuming strike price is €80), BAML used the options market's net short position to hedge the long position in the stock market. For BAML, this approach has the following advantages: (1) The funds needed to buy put can be solved by the funds obtained from selling calls, and there is no need to have additional funds to pay; and (2) Even if the worst happens, that is, Daimler's stock price plummets and Geely defaults, BAML can still sell its shares for €60 per share, thus ensuring controllable losses.

The core content of the agreement between Geely and BAML may include the following information:

(1) On the delivery day, if Daimler's stock price is less than €80, it will be delivered at €80 per share (the €80 here are only assumptions, but this price must be higher than the purchase price of BAML, as interest and commission service fee). If it is higher than €80, it will be delivered at the actual market price;

(2) The parties agree on who owns Daimler's dividends during the holding period;

(3) The contract uses Daimler shares held by BAML as collateral. When Daimler's share price falls, the value of this collateral declines. Therefore, in this case, BAML has the right to request Geely to replenish the collateral (cash or cash equivalent).

The deal's above structure is a sophisticated practice that skirted disclosure rules requiring investors to notify German authorities if the investor's share of voting rights in a company passed 3%, and then 5%. This structure also makes the source of financing opaque.

After this strategic operation, Li Shufu expressed his main reason to acquire Daimler: the technology leadership Daimler in electrification, smart car, driverless car, and shared mobility. The advantage of Daimler is complementary to Geely and Volvo. Li Shufu further explained his motivation and his vision on the future automobile industry:

> In the 21st century, the global automotive industry faces huge opportunities for innovation and challenges from non-automotive companies. It is difficult for individual auto companies to fight alone. In order to take the initiative to seize opportunities, we must refresh our way of thinking, unite with friends and partners, and take the leadership of technology through collaboration and sharing. The investment in Daimler is based on this strategic thinking (Fang and Li, 2018).

Having previous experience in Volvo's acquisition, Li Shufu also tried to ease the concern on Geely's influence over Daimler's strategy and management: "I respect the values and culture of Daimler. I have never asked for a seat on the supervisory board, and that does not have any priority for me" (Heller, 2018).

This acquisition aroused the German government's concern about protecting the domestic industry and its existing rules on foreign takeovers. After the acquisition, one report of the Economy Ministry for the

Economics Committee of the German parliament stated: "Against the backdrop of the current case, the federal government will examine whether the existing rules are sufficient to provide an adequate level of transparency, or if further guidelines are necessary" (Heller, 2018).

Although the German government's related rules have not been updated right after Geely–Daimler deal, several cases on further tightening the control on investment from China and intervention by the German government have occurred. In July 2018, five months after Geely's deal, the German government tried to prevent the acquisition of a 20% stake by the State Grid Corporation of China (SGCC) in the German grid operator 50 Hertz. The German government first tried to search for private investors in the European Union and in the end requested KfW, a German state-owned development bank, to invest on behalf of the German federal government to block this acquisition. In the same year, China's Yantai Taihai Group had planned to purchase Leifeld Metal Spinning AG, a German company specialized in the aerospace and nuclear industries. After receiving Berlin's signal on the blocking of the deal, the Chinese company pulled its bid in early 2018. However, the German government still officially vetoed this potential takeover in August. It is a signal to the market on the widening power to restrict investments from China.

During COVID-19, the German government's toughened its stance toward foreign investments by requesting information to be made public if investments in Artificial Intelligence (AI), robotics, semiconductors, biotech, and quantum are over 10%, much lower than the average threshold of 25%.

8.5. JV on Premium Ride-Hailing

In October 2018, the signing of a Memorandum of Understanding on the creation of a premium ride-hailing JV was held at Daimler Headquarters in Stuttgart, with the participation of An Conghui, Geely Holding President, and Liu Jinliang, President of Geely Technology Group, as well as by Klaus Entenmann, CEO Daimler Financial Services AG, and Jörg Lamparter, Head of Mobility Services at Daimler Financial Services AG.

In May 2019, the JV, named *StarRides* Technology, was created. Geely is represented by Geely Technology Group, a subsidiary of Zhejiang Geely Holding Group. Daimler Mobility Services GmbH represents Daimler. The 50-50 JV has a registered capital of RMB1.7 billion (US$250 million), located in Hangzhou, Zhejiang Province, China.

Li Jinliang, Chairman of Geely-backed ride-hailing platform *Cao Cao Zhuanche*, acts as its legal representative.

Both parent companies have already had experience in mobility solutions in different geographic regions. Geely Technology Group focuses on the strategic investment of clean energy, innovative technology, and creative business models in the automobile ecosystem. The Group has the ambition to become the leading investor and operating entity in Mobility as a Service (MaaS) ecosystem in China. Daimler Mobility Services GmbH is the financial holding company for Daimler mobility services. The business scope mainly includes *car2go, moovel*, and *Ride4Hire*.

In December 2019, the ride-hailing service by *StarRides* was officially launched in Hangzhou. The *Yao Chuxing* service team initially consisted of 100 vehicles, including Mercedes-Benz S-class, E-class, and V-class models. According to the initial plans, the service will expand to other cities in China in the coming years. The car type will also further expand to Geely and other car brands at the segment of premium and luxury pure electric vehicles, including EVs of Volvo, Lotus, and Polestar.

As discussed in the chapter on Geely's mobility innovation, China's ride-hailing business is the biggest globally and is expected to have double-digit growth in the coming years. Both companies have the strategy to expand from being car manufacturers to providers of car services, engage the change in the business model, and pursue customers' evolving needs. Geely and Daimler have complementary interests in the China ride-hailing business.

Geely's affiliate *Cao Cao* has expanded to over 50 cities in China, including Hangzhou, Beijing, Shanghai, Guangzhou, and Shenzhen, by 2020. The deployed EVs expanded from 32,000 units to over 42,000 vehicles from 2018 to 2019, serving a cumulative of 31 million registered users across China, while the missing part of the business is the luxury car segment (*Automotive World*, 2019).

In China, Daimler does not operate the ride-hailing business but the car-sharing business, *Car2Go*. This business experienced a temporary failure. Launched in April 2016 in Chongqing, *Car2Go* stopped its operations in June 2019. Despite the promising initial stage, with registered users of 255,000 in the highest season, the business declined for various reasons, including lack of parking space, less competitive rental price than competitors using cheaper cars, and small scale of operation by employing only 800 vehicles for Chongqing city with a population of over 30 million (Gasgoo, 2019). This mediocre commercial endeavor illustrates the weak point of Daimler in this segment, which is in sharp contrast with Daimler's global operation with 3.6 million members of the free-floating car-sharing business. The result is less impressive because China is the biggest single overseas market for Daimler.

Daimler's absence in the ride-hailing business in China is also in contrast with its global operation and its global partnership with BMW. The joint operation of smart urban mobility by Daimler and BMW, named *FreeNow*, is expected to reach revenues of €2.4 billion (US$2.7 billion) in 2019 (Nica, 2019). The business model of *FreeNow* has been expanded from ride-hailing to private-hire services, car sharing, micro-mobility options like e-scooters, and even public transport indications in some cities. *FreeNow* has successfully expanded to 130 cities in Europe and Latin America, except China.

We can observe that BMW is taking several independent initiatives in the field of mobility services. In December 2018, the BMW Group announced its *ReachNow* service in Chengdu, Sichuan Province. The service is operated by its wholly owned subsidiary, BMW Travel Service Co., registered in Chengdu in April 2018. In the first stage, 200 BMW 5 Series cars with full-time drivers were invested to ensure its quality. This ride-hailing business is the extension of the high-end, car-sharing business of BMW, launched in December 2017 in Chengdu, in partnership with EVCard, the affiliate of SAIC, by using 100 EVs of BMW i3s.

It is worth to mention that Audi, another luxury brand, is also expanding in this field. The *OnDemand* by FAW-Audi started its operation from September 2017 in Beijing. It is the first luxury car brand to launch the ride-hailing operation in China. The zone of service first focuses on the Beijing airport, then expands to the airport located at Hainan Island, with a service range of 300 square kilometers. The entire service was outsourced to a digital & mobility service provider company named FutureMove.

Based on the above analysis, this JV between Geely and Daimler should be both the proactive strategic choice and reactive tactics of both companies. This JV aims to jointly develop the software infrastructure required to support the business in China.

8.6. JV on *Smart*

In January 2020, Zhejiang Geely Holding Group and Daimler AG announced the 50-50 JV, with an equal investment of 2.7 billion yuan

(US$388.8 million) each, to build "premium and intelligent electrified" vehicles under the *smart* brand. This JV will own, operate, and further develop the *smart* brand established in 1998 (Li, 2019). Daimler's global design department will be in charge of the overall design, and Geely's global research center is mainly in charge of the engineering, R&D, and manufacturing. Both sides will share the work on the supply chain.

The Board of Directors of the new *smart* JV will comprise six executives with equal representation from both parties. Daimler AG board representatives include Hubertus Troska, member of the Board of Management of Daimler AG, responsible for Greater China; Britta Seeger, member of the Board of Management of Daimler AG and Mercedes-Benz AG, responsible for Marketing & Sales; and Markus Schäfer, member of the Board of Management of Daimler AG and Mercedes-Benz AG, responsible for Group Research and Mercedes-Benz Cars Development. Geely board representatives include Geely Holding Chairman Li Shufu; Geely Holding President, Geely Auto Group President, and CEO An Conghui; and Geely Holding Executive Vice President and CFO Daniel Donghui Li.

Tong Xiangbei has been appointed the new global CEO of the *smart* JV, overseeing all operations relating to the brand, including sales, marketing, R&D, production, and after-sales. Tong has more than two decades of experience in the automotive industry. Before joining the *smart* JV, he has worked for global automotive OEMs both in the US and China.

Ola Källenius, Chairman of the Board of Management of Daimler AG and Mercedes-Benz AG, noted on occasion: "Having received all necessary regulatory approvals, we are now ready to start the JV with our partner Geely that has been in preparation for the past several months. The JV will bring the next generation of zero-emission *smart* electric cars to the Chinese and global markets. We look forward to continuing our collaboration to bring desirable products and services to customers around the world" (Daimler, 2020b).

Li Shufu, Geely Holding Chairman, remarked: "The *smart* brand has a unique value and global influence, it has grown to be a leader in urban mobility. Geely Holding will fully support the *smart* brand with its full advantages in R&D, manufacturing, supply chain, and other fields into the JV and support its development in China and globally. We will work together with Mercedes-Benz to transform the *smart* brand into a leading player in urban premium, electric, and connected vehicles to successfully develop its global potential" (Daimler, 2020b).

The manufacturing plant of *smart* is located in Xi'an, Shaanxi Province. The total production capacity is planned to be 600,000 vehicles per year, being implemented in several phases. Interestingly, the Phase One project's construction started in November 2017, more than two years before the official announcement of this JV, with a planned annual capacity of 300,000 vehicles, and the actual production objective of 150,000 vehicles per year. The plant includes four conventional functions: stamping, welding, painting, and assembly, as well as supporting management center, logistics center, living and supporting area for staff, and other facilities. The manufacturing site will integrate the technology of digitization, automation, intelligence, and flexibility.

The site's construction part is planned to be completed in 2020, then moved to the subsequent testing and trial production and other engineering inspection stages. This timing can be in line to put electric *smart* cars on the market by 2022. One of the main reasons to choose Xi'an as the manufacturing site is its geographic location. Xi'an is the starting point of China–Europe international freight trains, connecting Kazakhstan, Russia, Belarus, Poland, Germany, Netherlands, Holland, Uzbekistan, Kyrgyzstan, and Turkmenistan.

Daimler started the production of the all-electric version from 2006. Since then, four generations of electric models have been sold in small volumes. Key models are *smart* Fortwo and Forfour. This JV will enable further portfolio expansion to the A+ and B-segments, a fast-growing market in China. It is expected that the new electric *smart* car will be based on the Pure electric Modular Architecture (PMA) platform, more precisely PMA2 platform provided by Geely, aiming for mass production and sales. The PMA2 platform signifies Geely's reverse technology transfer, while based on Geely and Volvo's asset co-creation. It is worth exploring in the future the mechanism of this transaction and the intellectual property rights issues among the three companies. Despite having no voting seat on Daimler's supervisory board, Geely demonstrated its capacity to implement its electric vehicles platform strategy across different brands, especially Volvo and Daimler.

Dieter Zetsche, Daimler's Chairman, expressed his confidence in the new JV: "It is the beginning of a new chapter in the history of *smart* brand–a chapter that includes new models, entry into new segments, and the start of a new period of growth" (Li, 2019). Behind the statement, there is a crucial situation of *smart*, since its establishment in 1998 in partnership with Swatch Group. Since then, *smart* has never been profitable.

By 2013, the cumulated loss over its lifetime was around US$4.6 billion, or about US$6,100 per car (Edelstein, 2013). Daimler does not release a separate report for *smart*, but different analyses estimate the annual loss is between €500–700 million (US$560–785 million). By 2019, *smart* stopped its sales of Fortwo in the US, and the incoming CEO Ola Kallenius in that year remarked that he has "no scruples about killing the brand if necessary," in a quote to the German newspaper *Handelsblatt* (Reid, 2019).

Geely's new partnership can benefit from its outstanding cost-controlling abilities, the shared platform of PMA, and its marketing capacity in China. From the Daimler investors' perspective, this JV helped Daimler reduce *smart*'s loss in half. Introducing new *smart* cars with a richer portfolio and increased price competitiveness, even by reaching the breakeven situation, means a saving of €500–700 million (US$560–785 million) per year, a significant improvement over the status quo of *smart* in the past decades.

In July 2020, *smart* Europe GmbH, a wholly owned subsidiary by *smart* Automobile Co. (*smart*) in Hangzhou Bay, was established in Leinfelden-Echterdingen, Stuttgart. The objective is to supply, sell, and service pure electric *smart* vehicles in the European market. Among the six core management positions, two are from China, taking the function of CEO and Vice President Research & Development. Four functions, including Vice President of Sales, Marketing and After Sales, Vice President Finance and Chief Financial Officer, the CEO, and CFO of *smart* Europe GmbH are from Daimler side, either with experience on *smart*, or Daimler, or Daimler's China market.

For Geely, the *smart* car's brand assets at the global level, supported by Daimler, are valuable for enriching its multi-brand strategy in the electric vehicle segment. Compared to its newly built brand such as *Geometry*, the pricing power is much more robust, thus ensuring profitability, not only for the China market but also for the global market access.

Soon, there could be the possibility of the electric *smart* car being used by the mobility service business unit of Geely: *Cao Cao*. In February 2019, *Cao Cao* announced its upgrading from "*Cao Cao* Ride Hailing" (*Zhuanche*) to *Cao CaoTravel* (*Chuxing*). After the upgrade, in addition to the ride-hailing service, the business will expand to car-sharing, same city delivery, tourism travel, and corporate travel.

The ambition of *Cao Cao* is to build a travel and related consumption ecosystem. After the partnership with Daimler, Geely might have access to and benefit from the experience of *Car2go* in China, including its rental platform. The electric *smart*, being served as a fleet, is also in line with the positioning of *Cao Cao* on the new energy vehicle. It will be a win-win solution for Geely and Daimler, both in boosting *smart* cars' sales and the development of mobility services for the two companies.

8.7. Conclusion

This chapter illustrates a higher level of sophistication of Geely's globalization efforts, not only as a carmaker but also as a multinational group. Its acquisition of Daimler's stake demonstrates its new competency in the financial operation and its more in-depth understanding of local regulations. Geely's motivation to obtain a stake in Daimler is not a simple financial operation but part of a continuous asset-seeking and asset creation strategy, leading to a JV on premium ride-hailing and *smart* car. These two JVs also illustrate Geely's dynamic strategic upgrading, expanding from the traditional car toward intelligent electric vehicles and mobility services. This chapter also provides more information on Daimler's complex presence in China, which offers a broader context analysis on the Geely–Daimler case.

Interestingly, it seems that the media reports on skeptical reactions from Daimler's stakeholders are much less than that of the Geely–Volvo deal in 2010. It is a positive sign to illustrate the progressive improvement of the corporate image of Geely, rooted in its recent commercial success of various domestic and global operations, especially the Volvo acquisition.

The significant finding in this chapter is the new asset augmentation, a phenomenon of reverse technology transfer, Geely's PMA2 platform to be used by *smart* car of Daimler, then the creation of electrified *smart* car, a new vehicle type that Daimler has not yet managed before the operation by Geely. Despite having no voting seat on Daimler's supervisory board, Geely has demonstrated its capacity to implement the platform strategy across different brands, especially Volvo and Daimler. It is also a clear indication of the dynamic capabilities of emerging multinational corporations.

References

Automotive World (2019). Cao Cao leads Chinese growth in ride-hailing active users. November 7. Available at: https://www.automotiveworld.com/news-releases/cao-cao-leads-chinese-growth-in-ride-hailing-active-user/ (accessed October 19, 2020).

BAIC (2019). BAIC Motor 2019 Annual Report. Available at: http://www. baicmotor.com/Uploads/file/20200421/20200421100619_52237.pdf (accessed October 19, 2020).

Carsales (2020). Denza sales data & trends for the Chinese automotive market. Available at: https://carsalesbase.com/china-denza/ (accessed October 19, 2020).

Daimler (2018). Research & Development. *Annual Report 2018*. Available at: https://annualreport.daimler.com/ar2018/combined-management-report/ sustainability-and-integrity/research-and-development-# (accessed October 19, 2020).

Daimler (2019). Plans for more than ten different all-electric vehicles by 2022: All systems are go. Global Media Site. Available at: https://media.daimler. com/marsMediaSite/ko/en/29779739 (accessed October 19, 2020).

Daimler (2020a). Daimler AG Corporate Presentation February 2020. Available at: https://www.daimler.com/dokumente/investoren/praesentationen/200212-daimler-corporate-presentation-feb-2020.pdf (accessed October 19, 2020).

Daimler (2020b). Mercedes-Benz and Geely. Global Joint Venture Formally Established. Available at: https://www.daimler.com/company/news/joint-venture-with-geely.html (accessed October 19, 2020).

Edelstein, S. (2013). Tiny *smart* cars lose 5 billion for Mercedes Benz: Report. *Green Car Reports*, October 13. Available at: https://www.greencarreports. com/news/1087568_tiny-smart-cars-lose-5-billion-for-mercedes-benz-report (accessed October 19, 2020).

Fang, Q. and X. Li (2018). Li Shufu on the Daimler acquisition: Where the $9 billion came from and why such a purchase. *Pengbai News*, February 24 (in Chinese).

Gasgoo (2019). The up and down of Daimler's Car2Go. June 2. Available at: https://auto.gasgoo.com/News/2019/06/020826372637170108501C302.shtml (in Chinese, accessed October 19, 2020).

Geely Automobile Holdings (2020). *Annul Report 2016*. Available at: http://www. geelyauto.com.hk/core/files/financial/en/2016-02.pdf (accessed October 23, 2020).

Heller, G. (2018). Germany could tighten rules after Geely takes Daimler stake. *Reuters*, February 28. Available at: https://www.reuters.com/article/us-daimler-geely-regulation/germany-could-tighten-rules-after-geely-takes-daimler-stake-idUSKCN1GC0QA (accessed October 19, 2020).

Jourdan, A. and N. Shirouzu (2018). How Geely's Li Shufu spent months stealthily building a $9 billion stake in Daimler. *Reuters*, March 1. Available at: https:// www.reuters.com/article/us-daimler-geely-shell-insight/how-geelys-li-shufu-spent-months-stealthily-building-a-9-billion-stake-in-daimler-idUSKCN1GD5ST (accessed October 19, 2020).

Li, F. (2019). Geely, Daimler announce plans for joint venture. *China Daily*, March 29. Available at: http://www.chinadaily.com.cn/global/2019-03/29/ content_37453065.htm (accessed October 19, 2020).

Nica, G. (2018). Stefan Quandt becomes most powerful BMW shareholder. *BMW Blog*, February 22. Available at: https://www.bmwblog.com/2018/02/22/ stefan-quandt-becomes-powerful-bmw-shareholder/ (accessed October 19, 2020).

Nica, G. (2019). FreeNow, BMW and Daimler's ride-sharing app, to double revenue in 2020. *BMW Blog*, December 19. Available at: https://www. bmwblog.com/2019/12/16/freenow-bmw-and-daimlers-ride-sharing-app-to-double-revenue-in-2020/ (accessed October 19, 2020).

Reid, D. (2018). BMW research and development spend to hit record as the firm looks to electric future. *CNBC*, March 21. Available at: https://www.cnbc. com/2018/03/21/bmw-research-and-development-spend-to-hit-record-as-the-firm-looks-to-electric-future.html#:~:text=Menu-,BMW%20research%20 and%20development%20spend%20to%20hit%20record,firm%20looks%20 to%20electric%20future&text=BMW%20group%20is%20to%20 spend,investigation%20into%20emissions%2Dcheating%20software. (accessed October 19, 2020).

Reid, A. (2019). The *smart* brand could be dead by 2020: Report. *Driving*, March 26. Available at: https://driving.ca/smart/auto-news/news/the-smart-brand-could-be-dead-by-2020-report (accessed October 19, 2020).

Sun, Y., J. Zhu and E. Taylor (2019). Exclusive: China's BAIC raising Daimler stake to unseat Geely as top shareholder. *Reuters*, December 15. Available at: https://www.reuters.com/article/us-daimler-baic-investment-exclusive/ exclusive-chinas-baic-raising-daimler-stake-to-unseat-geely-as-top-shareholder-sources-idUSKBN1YJ08H (accessed October 19, 2020).

Sims, T. (2019). China's BAIC buys 5% stake in Daimler. *Automotive News Europe*, July 23. Available at: https://europe.autonews.com/automakers/ chinas-baic-buys-5-stake-daimler (accessed October 19, 2020).

Volvo (2020). Innovation. Available at: https://www.volvogroup.com/en-en/ innovation.html (accessed October 19, 2020).

Chapter 9

Geely and London Electric Vehicle Company: The New Energy Vehicle for Modern Metropolis

Abstract

The progressive acquisition by Geely of London Taxi Company was a part of an evolving strategy of asset-creation foreign direct investment (FDI), developed in different stages. A first step in this trajectory took place in 2006, with the acquisition of shares from Manganese Bronze Holding (MBH), owner of London Taxi. This investment, Geely's first acquisition in Europe, aimed at acquiring a highly valuable and globally recognized niche brand, improving the international exposure of Geely. Following the establishment of a joint venture, in 2008, the taxicab production started in Shanghai. After the full acquisition took place in 2013, it evolved into an asset-augmentation strategy, oriented to new electric vehicle technologies and products. Significantly, London Taxi was renamed London Electric Vehicle Company (LEVC). This evolutionary trajectory showed a remarkable capacity by Geely to absorb, integrate, and augment foreign assets within its international network, creating synergies with its firm-specific resources. Moreover, it was able to leverage from international partners to acquire new organizational capabilities.

Keywords: Geely Auto; London Taxi; LEVC; asset augmentation.

9.1. Introduction

The progressive acquisition by Geely of London Taxi Company, renamed London Electric Vehicle Company (LEVC), was part of a process of international growth, and of an evolving strategy of asset-creating foreign direct investments (FDIs), developed in different stages. An initial asset-seeking investment, aiming at acquiring a globally recognized, highly valuable niche brand, evolved over time into an asset-augmentation strategy, oriented to new electric vehicle technologies and products. This strategic initiative may be analyzed and interpreted as a significant development of the "twin trajectories" of the catching up process and of the internationalization trajectory of Geely, as described in Chapter 1 (see Figure 1.1). A quite clear long-term strategic vision supported this development toward a global configuration of R&D and production.

In 2006, this initiative by Geely represented a first investment in Europe, building the bases for growing international experience and managerial expertise. It evolved in parallel with, and was complementary to, other strategic moves, including the major one, the acquisition of Volvo in 2010, followed by a post-acquisition convergence and integration process (see Chapter 5).

After shortly reviewing some relevant theoretical categories, in this chapter we will follow the main steps of this strategic initiative, from the initial minority equity participation till the full ownership control and the creation of assets and knowledge in new energy technology, including electric vehicles. Finally, we will draw some more general conclusions.

9.2. A Theoretical Framework

As pointed out by Yakob *et al.* (2018), the literature on emerging country multinational enterprises (EMNEs) highlighted several key drivers in their strategies of international growth. The overseas production locations, through mergers and acquisitions (M&As), provide access to country-specific and location-specific advantages, not available at home in emerging economies, such as knowledge, industrial skills, design, technologies, and brands (Narula, 2006).

Therefore, a large literature flow concludes that asset-seeking motivations are a key driver to explain EMNEs' behavior (Buckley *et al.*, 2007).

These new international investors look for country-specific and location-specific advantages abroad, deriving from positive externalities in industrial and technology clusters, generating skills, knowledge, and innovation. In other words, FDIs are not driven by *ex-ante* competitive and oligopolistic advantages, as was supposed by standard international business theories in the case of Western and Japanese multinational investors (Dunning, 2000); on the contrary, these FDIs are driven by competitive disadvantages of the acquiring firms, based in emerging economies. Global brand-seeking FDIs are a specific and interesting case of asset-seeking strategies (Narula and Zanfei, 2006).

As stated by Li *et al.* (2016, p. 474), "when exploiting existing resources, acquirers are teachers; when seeking strategic assets abroad, they are students." Spatial dynamics may result in specific clusters and regions, where cross-border M&As take place, reshaping international production and innovation networks and global value chains (Bathelt and Glückler, 2003). The accumulation of location-bound knowledge may result in new location-specific advantages, attracting further domestic and foreign investments and creating new agglomerations and clusters, in a sort of virtuous circle.

However, asset-seeking FDIs and M&A may represent only a first stage within a trajectory of international growth. A second stage may be represented by an "asset-augmentation strategy," where foreign assets and resources are integrated with home-country and firm-specific assets (Buckley *et al.*, 2016, p. 2). Knowledge absorption and recombination capabilities are needed to fruitfully combine home-country and host-country resources. As pointed out by Mathews (2006), the ability to create linkages and leverages abroad, extending production and R&D networks, is crucial for the success of such international strategies. As a result, M&As in most developed markets may represent the premise for successful leapfrogging or a "springboard" for technological innovation and global expansion by EMNEs (Luo and Tung, 2007).

We can define the final result of these two stages as "strategic asset creation" and "creative innovation" (Yakob *et al.*, 2018). In the case of Chinese emerging multinationals, a crucial country-specific advantage is represented by the size and rapid growth of the domestic market, while firm-specific advantages of investing companies may be initially poor in terms of technology, international experience, skills and brands, but later see a rapid increase.

The story of Geely is a good example of the capacity to combine firm-specific resources and domestic Chinese country-specific advantages with host-country advantages, as in the case of Sweden after the acquisition of Volvo, in order to build up new corporate advantages and capabilities, increasing competitiveness.

The case of the acquisition of the London Taxi Company may be viewed as a starting hypothesis, as a case of asset-augmenting strategy, based on the first stage of a global asset-seeking and brand-seeking niche acquisition. We will move now to some empirical evidence, looking at the main stages of this strategic move.

9.3.   First Step: An Asset and Brand-Seeking Investment

The London Taxi Company was officially founded in 1948. However, the history of the iconic London black cabs goes back to the horse-drawn carriages of the 17th–19th centuries. Its unique design, standardized in 1906, derives from some initial requirements: enough headroom for a passenger wearing a bowler hat, and a vehicle turning circle of 25 feet (8 meters), to navigate the Savoy Hotel's entrance roundabout.

In October 2006, Geely Automobile, a Hong Kong–listed company, part of Geely Group, acquired 30% of new shares (valued £14.25 million) from Manganese Bronze Holding (MBH). One month later, the two companies established a joint venture in Shanghai, LTI Automobile Components Company Limited ("Shanghai LTI"), with a 52% and 48% share split between Geely and MBH, in order to create a joint taxicab manufacturing in China. The objective was to produce the new London taxi in Shanghai (Monaghan, 2013; Geely 2012 *Annual Report*, pp. 10–11). After these two transactions, Geely became the biggest single shareholder of MBH, holding 23% of its equity. Production in Shanghai started in 2008: for the first time, an icon of the British capital since World War II was built outside England.

It must be noted that the agreement followed two failed efforts by the British company to find a partner in China, in order to access the promising Chinese market, and to meet the fast-growing demand for urban mobility. In 2002, MBH had reached an agreement with Brilliance China Automotive Holdings. Two years later, it agreed to make the cabs in Lanzhou, Western China, with National Bluestar (Blackden, 2006).

From the point of view of Geely, the acquisition of a niche player and London taxi brand was a first move in Europe. The creation of the joint venture in Shanghai, and future manufacturing of the car by Shanghai Maple, a subsidiary of Geely, intended to absorb a significant technology transfer, lowering the cost of manufacturing. Targeting this niche player corresponded to the capacity of Geely at that moment. Taking a pragmatic approach, it wished to access the potential value of the iconic London Taxi brand and its overseas marketing and sales network, focusing on the Chinese and Asian markets, while acquiring valuable foreign technology and good image. The cost advantages in China were considered a source of synergy with British technology and brand, when the joint venture started production of London Taxis in Shanghai in 2008.

The relocation of production to Shanghai Maple, was consistent with the objective of learning new product and process technology. In terms of sales, the joint venture agreement made Geely responsible for the Asian region, while MBH had the right to sell in the rest of the world, in order to avoid competition between the JV partners (Blackden, 2006).

However, in the early years of the cooperation, the production and sales of London taxi in China were poor, due to various reasons. The technology of London Taxi was considered obsolete, and because of the nature of stand-alone product architecture and therefore low economies of scale, further technology upgrading was costly. The global financial crisis too negatively impacted the business of London Taxi. The net loss of MBH in 2009 was £6.9 million, selling only 1,724 units of cars, a decrease compared to the sales of 1,951 units in 2008.

This niche but relevant initiative evolved in parallel with the bargaining process for the acquisition of Volvo. In August 2010, while closing the Volvo deal, Geely declined the offer of purchasing 20 million new ordinary shares of MBH, due to bad performances of MBH, and consequently it diluted its share to 19.97% (Geely Annual Report 2009, p. 35).

At the same time, a new generation of London Taxi was designed and developed, in order to increase fuel efficiency and to better adapt to different market conditions, with the objective of increasing sales in the booming Chinese market.

Table 9.1 shows the main steps in the strategic initiative of Geely with London Taxi, the later LEVC.

Table 9.1.　Geely and London Taxi: Main steps in evolving strategies (2002–2020).

2002	Manganese Bronze Holding (MBH) reached an agreement with Brilliance China Automotive Holdings to make its cabs in China. The cooperation failed later.
2004	MBH reached an agreement with National Bluestar to make its cabs in Lanzhou. The cooperation failed again.
2006	– Geely made an initial investment in MBH in return for a 19.97% equity stake. – Geely and MBH established a joint venture in China, Shanghai Yinglun Dihua Automobiles, with Geely holding 52% share.
2008	Geely started to produce taxicab in Shanghai, under the agreement with MBH.
2009	Geely bought further shares in MBH.
2013	– Geely fully acquired the business of London Taxi from MBH for £11.4 million (US$14.6 million). – London Taxi Corporation Limited became a subsidiary of Geely New Energy Commercial Vehicle Group (GCV). – Shanghai Yinglun Dihua Automobiles became a wholly owned subsidiary of Geely Holding Group and placed under the management of GCV.
2017	– London Taxi Company was renamed London Electric Vehicle Company (LEVC). – Geely invested £325 million for the new plant of LEVC in Ansty Park near Coventry, with a capacity of 36,000 vehicles per year. – Production of new TX electric taxi started in March and its official launch in London was on August 1.
2018	– The new LEVC TX electric plug-in hybrid taxi went on sales in January 2018. – Geely built a new taxicab factory in Yiwu, Zhejiang, with the capacity for 100,000 electric vehicles a year. The Yiwu model, a variant of the black taxi, will serve a niche segment of premium ride-hailing service in China. – Shanghai Yinglun Dihua and Asia Cab signed a cooperative agreement on the production and sale of the TX4 in Thailand.
2019	– The electric van TX Shuttle was revealed by LEVC on June 17, 2019, planned to come to market in the early 2020. – LEVC has seen major demand for the TX model across the UK and Europe, with more than 3,000 units sold by the end of 2019 since its launch.
2020	– In January, Geely's subsidiary Cao Cao Mobility started to operate the first LEVC TX fleet in Paris central city. – In January, LEVC TX eCity has also been launched in Japan, with Fleetway and Service Company selected as the official importer and retailer. – In July, LEVC launched the first model in a line of new commercial electric vehicles, its taxi-based VN5 hybrid van, with delivery starting at the end of 2020.

9.4. Asset Creation, New Investment, and Innovation: LEVC

A turning point took place in 2012, when MBH went through a deep financial crisis and entered administration due to lack of funding. London Taxi in Coventry went into administration in October that year, with 99 out of its 176 workers losing their jobs. Geely was the biggest single creditor when it went into administration: this opened the way to the full acquisition of the London Taxi Company. In 2013, Geely acquired the remaining 80% of assets of MBH and became the full owner of MBH for £11.4 million (US$14.6 million).

The deal, which intended to safeguard production in the UK, was agreed with administrators PricewaterhouseCoopers. This acquisition was made by Geely UK Limited, a subsidiary of the Zhejiang Geely Holding Group. The agreement included retaining the London Taxi Company head office production, the Mann & Overton dealership in London, including its property, and all related dealership assets, plus those in Manchester and Edinburgh. The acquisition also included plant, equipment and property, intellectual property rights, trademarks and the "goodwill of the business" of MBH, as well as the stock of unsold vehicles. In addition, the agreement included MBH's 48% stake in the joint venture manufacturing company in Shanghai. Therefore, Shanghai LIT became a wholly owned equity affiliate of Geely, which promised to safeguard the current workforce as much as possible (BBC, 2013).

The iconic brand was renamed to LEVC to reflect its new focus on developing and producing electric taxis and commercial vehicles with zero-emission for the modern metropolis in the global market. This move was integrated into a wider strategy by Geely to transform urban transport. At the same time, Geely also announced its intentions to start production of electric commercial vehicles in addition to taxicabs.

This strategic initiative was also taken in view of the incoming deadline of January 1, 2018, when London's new clean air regulations required newly licensed taxis to be able to drive for 30 miles without releasing pollution. Moreover, more than 200 cities across Europe created low-emission zones, imposing charges on heavily polluting vehicles, including ban of diesel cars; this opened market perspectives for electric and clean vehicles, including new demand for electric taxis in Europe and globally. However, competition is strong from Toyota and other carmakers.

Chairman Li Shufu made an announcement on the deal, revealing a long-term commitment that Geely could bring to the new London Taxi business:

> We are a long-term and committed investor and we believe the illustrious past of the London Black Cab can be matched by a successful and healthy future. Despite its recent difficulties, we have long believed that the company and the Black Cab have huge potential. We have ambitious plans for the business and, despite it being clear that there are a number of challenges to be overcome, we are committed to working with all stakeholders to build a solid future for the Black Cab business that will enable it to return to profitability in the short term and grow substantially in the longer term. We intend to use Geely's knowledge and expertise to improve the MBH business but we also believe that the brand, technology and design knowhow of MBH will create synergies that will benefit Geely and our own model range (BBC, 2013).

In 2015, Geely announced plans to build a new plant for the London Taxi Company in Ansty Park near Coventry, in the British Midlands, with a huge £325 million investment, with the aim of safeguarding the assembly of the TX4 model of London Taxi. Geely was in talks with UK government officials over the possibility of converting London's black cabs into electric-powered vehicles. In the mid-term, Geely promised to inject new technologies and supply chain expertise, to upgrade the model of TX4, and to improve the fuel efficiency. It also announced the production of an electric taxi, which represented a truly radical innovation.

Production of new taxis started in March 2017, with an annual capacity to assemble 36,000 vehicles a year. With 30,000 square meters, the plant is a relatively small production unit, dedicated to a niche vehicle. However, it represented the Britain's first car factory to start production in more than a decade, and the first in the UK to be solely dedicated to electric vehicles. Moreover, £30 million were invested by LEVC to develop an electric commercial van, announced in June 2019, and put on the market by 2020.

On the financial side, an offshore US$400 million Green Bond was issued by Zhejiang Geely Holding Group through LEVC, with the support of French Société Generale, in order to finance R&D, design, industrial development, and production of zero-emission TX5 electric taxis. The

Green Bond benefited from a standby letter of credit issued by Bank of China's London Branch (Société Générale, 2016). After the acquisition, Geely said that its priority will be to re-establish the manufacture, sale, and service of new and current vehicles "on broadly the same basis" as before the administration, including the continued assembly of London Taxis at the Coventry plant and retaining its 107 staff.

The mission to design the New London Taxi was given to the Barcelona Geely Design Center. Design was initially deliberately fresh and contemporary, but with the average working life of a taxi being 15–20 years, something a little more traditional and "timeless" was proposed by the Design Team headed by David Ancona, to try and "capture that same feeling of comfort" (Reynolds, 2018). The distinctive humped bonnet and bumpy rear make the new black cabs instantly recognizable, with a touch more luxurious, while the seat arrangement has been tweaked to fit an extra passenger, up to six people in total.

This importance of the cooperation between LEVC and Barcelona Geely Design Center must be stressed, as an interesting result of growing global integration of the facilities and corporate functions within the Geely Group, as a growing and mature multinational actor. In the same direction of integrating resources within Geely Group, we can note that since 2016 synergies took place between Volvo's Scalable Product Architecture (SPA) Platform and a new-generation taxi produced by LEVC in Coventry (personal interview with Li Li, Vice President, Geely R&D, July 11, 2019). Moreover, the new London Taxi also influenced the development of new-generation commercial vehicle models by Geely Group.

As a result of this investment, and intense work on R&D, design, and product development, LEVC launched the all-new hybrid electric London taxi, named TX in 2017. Unlike early models, which had steel frames, the TX was built of aluminum, in order to compensate for the weight of its bulky lithium-ion battery, but at 2.2 tons the entire vehicle still was 250 kilograms heavier than the previous model, also because of the strict regulations that traditionally determine the size and shape of the vehicle. The Coventry factory would be supplying vehicles for the UK while others will be made in the sister factory in Shanghai for the left-hand drive market.

Since its launch in London on August 1, 2017, the number of TX eCity on the streets of Great Britain's capital climbed to almost 600 by the end of 2018. The TX took full advantage of the 2018 Transport for London rules that allowed only zero-emission capable vehicles to be added to the city's existent taxi fleet; it was the only taxi capable of meeting these rules at that time.

Commenting on the difficulty and future direction of LEVC, Chairman Li Shufu remarked: "We have ambitious plans for the business and, despite there being a number of challenges to overcome, we are committed to working with all stakeholders to build a solid future for the black cab business that will enable it to return to profitability and grow substantially" (BBC, 2013). Moreover Li Shufu indicated in an interview with the *South China Morning Post* that Geely wanted to "bring the product to the new world and into the new generation" (Ng, 2018).

Sharing an optimistic viewpoint from the British perspective, LEVC CEO Chris Gubbey noted: "If you take this quintessentially London product and turn it into a zero emission, purpose-designed taxi, it can become a transport solution and a contributor to improving air quality in every major city across the world" (Ng, 2018).

It is interesting to note, in this official declaration, the strong determination to combine host-country advantages, i.e. the British specific tradition in urban mobility, with other firm-specific key assets and resources existing within the Geely Group, including those of the "sister company" Volvo and the Barcelona Design Center. Mr. Gubbey added that London was leading the way in improving air quality and the new TX London electric taxi would help achieve that goal, while creating huge opportunities for global expansion.

Moreover, local trade unions in Coventry welcomed the news, hoping that new investments would preserve employment levels, while the company signed a deal to export the new TX model to the Netherlands, with an initial order of 225 vehicles, delivered in 2018.

In 2018, Geely built a new factory in Yiwu, Zhejiang, Eastern China, with the capacity for 100,000 electric vehicles a year. The Yiwu model, a variant of the black taxi, is intended to serve a segment of premium ride-hailing service in China.

9.5. Concluding Remarks

The progressive acquisition of London Taxi and its transformation into a new energy vehicle producer showed a remarkable capacity by Geely to absorb, integrate, and augment foreign assets within its international network, creating synergies with its firm-specific resources. Moreover, it was able to leverage from international partners to acquire new organizational capabilities.

Based on the theoretical framework referred in Section 9.2, we can interpret the first stage of this trajectory as a minority-owned asset-seeking FDI, and more precisely as a global brand-seeking and image-building investment, followed in a second stage by full acquisition and control, within an asset-augmenting and asset-creating long-term strategic vision. Geely Group operated to integrate the assets and capabilities acquired in the UK within its rapidly expanding multinational network, including Volvo engineering and Barcelona Design Center, combining different resources and country-specific and firm-specific advantages.

Finally, the evolution from London taxi to LEVC was a highly significant test for Geely's ambition to take the leadership in electric vehicles industry.

References

Bathelt, H. and J. Glückler (2003). Toward a relational economic geography. *Journal of Economic Geography*, **3**:2, 117–144.

BBC (2013). Coventry taxi maker LTI sold to Chinese firm Geely for £11.4m. February 1. Available at: https://www.bbc.com/news/uk-england-coventry-warwickshire-21290935#:~:text=The%20black%20taxi%20manufacturer%20LTI,manufacturer%20of%20the%20London%20cabs (accessed March 5, 2021).

Blackden, R. (2006). Black cab, U.K. transport icon, to be made in China — Business — International Herald Tribune. *The New York Times*, October. Available at: https://www.nytimes.com/2006/10/04/business/worldbusiness/04iht-taxi.3031990.html (accessed September 5, 2020).

Buckley, P., J. Clegg, A. R. Cross, X. Liu, H. Voss and P. Zheng (2007). The determinants of Chinese outward foreign direct investment. *Journal of International Business Studies*, **38**:4, 499–518.

Buckley, P. J., S. Munjal, P. Enderwick and N. Forsans (2016). Cross-border acquisitions by Indian multinationals: Asset exploitation or asset augmentation? *International Business Review*, **25**:4, 986–996.

Dunning, J. H. (2000). The eclectic paradigm as an envelope for economic and business theories of MNE activity. *International Business Review*, **9**:2, 163–190.

Geely Annual Report (2009). Various issues.

Li, J., P. Li and B. Wang (2016). Do cross-border acquisitions create value? Evidence from overseas acquisitions by Chinese firms. *International Business Review*, **25**:2, 471–483.

Luo, Y. and R. Tung (2007). International expansion of emerging market enterprises: A springboard perspective. *Journal of International Business Studies*, **38**:4, 481–498.

Mathews, J. A. (2006). Dragon multinationals: New players in 21st century globalization. *Asia Pacific Journal of Management*, **23**:1, 5–27.

Monaghan, A. (2013). China's Geely saves London cab maker Manganese Bronze. *The Telegraph*, February 1.

Narula, R. (2006). Globalization, new ecologies, new zoologies, and the purported death of the eclectic paradigm. *Asia Pacific Journal of Management*, **23**:2, 143–151.

Narula, R. and A. Zanfei (2006). Globalization of Innovation: The Role of Multinational Enterprises. In Fagerberg, J. and Mowery, D. C. (eds.), *The Oxford Handbook of Innovation*. Oxford: Oxford University Press, pp. 318–345.

Ng, E. (2018). Li Shufu has a US$15 million dream for Geely's London black taxis to ply the world's city streets. *South China Morning Post*, June 23. Available at: https://www.scmp.com/business/companies/article/2152000/li-shufu-has-us15-billion-dream-geelys-london-black-taxis-ply (accessed September 9, 2020).

Reynolds, M. (2018). An obscure Chinese firm has taken over London's black cabs. Its next target? Beat Uber at its own game. *Wired*, May 29. Available at: https://www.wired.co.uk/article/levc-geely-london-electric-black-taxis-cabs (accessed March 5, 2021).

Société Générale (2016). When London black cabs go green. Available at: https://www.societegenerale.asia/en/newsroom/success-stories/success-stories-details/news/societe-generale-supports-zhejiang-geely-the-first-offshore-green-bond-issuance-chinese-auto-industr/ (accessed March 5, 2021).

Yakob, R., H. R. Nakamura and P. Ström (2018). Chinese foreign acquisitions aimed for strategic asset-creation and innovation upgrading: The case of Geely and Volvo Cars. *Technovation*, **70–71**, 59–72.

Chapter 10

Asian Market and More: Geely's Strategic Investment in PROTON and Lotus

Abstract

The globalization of new multinationals from emerging economies has been a relatively new phenomenon. In 2017, Geely Auto entered into a strategic partnership to bring Malaysia's first national carmaker PROTON and the iconic British sports car brand Lotus under its corporate wings. Due to intense domestic competition and market stagnation in recent years, Geely regards internationalization as a key growth strategy and an opportunity to expand its operations overseas. While its expansion in Malaysia is seen as mainly market-seeking, its acquisition of Lotus is largely a strategic-asset–seeking move. As an example of the so-called dragon enterprises rising from China, Geely has become a globalized enterprise today, with business covering the entire automotive industrial chain.

Keywords: Geely Auto; PROTON; Lotus; mergers & acquisitions; globalization; China; Malaysia; UK.

10.1. The Rationales of Geely's Strategic Drive in Southeast Asia

10.1.1. *The theoretical context of Geely's global expansion*

Before diving into Geely's corporate strategies in Southeast Asia, we will briefly examine the underlying academic framework of its recent global expansion drives. As noted in early chapters, multiple theories in international business can be used to explain the rise of emerging multinational corporations (EMNCs) in recent decades. Specifically, the growth of Geely fits very well the definition of "Dragon Multinational Enterprises," due to its origin from Asia-Pacific, its initial lack of resources, and its success as a latecomer in the global market. Also known as the "Linkage, Leverage, and Learning" (LLL) Theory, John Mathews developed this popular notion to describe the expansion of those EMNCs that are keen at establishing linkages, including alliances and joint ventures with incumbent MNCs, leveraging resources, learning, and imitating (Mathews, 2002). Dragon MNCs are seen as aggressive and at the forefront with regard to shaping their own future rather than being "passive observers" (Mathews, 2006). After decades of rapid development, although China is already the largest auto market in the world, the country is experiencing a flattened demand and oversupply of products in its domestic market. Therefore, it is easy to comprehend the underling rationale for Chinese firms such as Geely to aggressively grow abroad.

Moreover, the Uppsala Model is also useful in describing Geely's expansions in the Southeast Asian market. Also known as the "Scandinavian School," the Uppsala Theory describes internationalization as a learning process when a firm gradually intensifies its foreign market commitments to acquire market knowledge and promote international development (Johanson and Vahlne, 1977). Some examples of such incremental activities in foreign markets are: firms first gain experience from the domestic market before they move to foreign markets; firms start their foreign operations from culturally and/or geographically close countries and move gradually to culturally and geographically more distant countries; and firms start their foreign operations by using traditional exports and gradually move to using more intensive and demanding operation modes, both at the company and target country levels (Blomstermo and Sharma, 2003). As a private enterprise, Geely is known for its visionary entrepreneurship and culture of innovation. In its ambitious drive to become an effective EMNC, the company has taken concrete steps to gradually expand its global footprints, and these measures have become a source of sustained competitive advantage and growth strategies for shaping its own future in the worldwide market.

10.1.2. *Dynamic evolution of industrial policies and host country's institutional environment*

Although numerous differences exist between the neoclassical and national development schools on how an economy should develop, it is a known fact that the dynamic evolution of industrial policies from developing countries has a profound impact on economic development. In his research for the Asian Development Bank, Felipe (2018) reviews the role of Asia's developmental states in consciously accelerating industrial development and learning, as well as the region's mixed experiences with industrial policies. He argues that the single most important factor that explains Asia's development success was its swift structural transformation toward industrialization. In particular, since manufacturing activities are subject to increasing returns to scale, and many manufacturing goods have high income elasticities of demand, as workers move out of agriculture into manufacturing, the sector diversifies and upgrades its structure, thus becoming the "engine of growth" for the region (Felipe, 2018).

Facing powerful multinationals from advanced economies, it is very common for a developing country to protect its infant industry and build national champions via protective measures such as high import tax, mandatory technology transfers, and local production. While the ultimate goal of such industrial policies is to build up local competitive capabilities, frequently those policy initiatives lead to continuing operation of low-efficiency companies and hinder the long-term growth of the domestic industries. Therefore, for an emerging economy to achieve sustainable development, further deregulations and foreign direct investments (FDIs) are often required to encourage growth and innovations from local competitions and neutralize the so-called "national industry" and "national champions."

Should the state actively interfere in the market using state resources and cultivate certain industries to achieve specific developmental goals? The development of the Malaysia automobile industry is an excellent case in point. In their study on the interactions between the state and industry,

Tai and Ku (2013) find that although industries in developing countries need government assistance, the specific political and economic contexts affect the policies adopted and their effectiveness. In the case of Malaysia, the "autonomous development" policies and politics have deterred its automotive industry from adopting a "market following" position. Therefore, they conclude that the choice of strategy and political interference are the two primary reasons for the low competitiveness of the automobile industry in Malaysia (Tai and Ku, 2013). In his study on the growth trajectory of the country's automobile business, Athukorala (2014) further examines its national car project PROTON, which was envisioned to lead the development of an internationally competitive national automotive manufacturing in Malaysia. Designed primarily with an intrinsic import-substitution bias and without successful export strategies, for years PROTON remained a high-cost producer whose survival depended crucially on government support through tariff protection, tax concessions, and other preferential treatments, including periodic capital injections on concessionary terms (Athukorala, 2014).

10.1.3. *Geely's motivations in strategic market-seeking and asset-seeking*

FDI is generally regarded as a high-risk market entry strategy, since it typically requires significant capital, research, marketing teams, and market knowledge. The decision-making process is also largely influenced by both push and pull factors, since business leaders often seek new market opportunities as a result of unfavorable developments in their home markets and more attractive opportunities abroad. As China's manufacturing economy is known globally for its low-cost production and relentless competition, we can argue that Geely's acquisition of PROTON is primarily market-seeking for its overseas operation in the Southeast Asia. To take advantage of the fact that Southeast Asia has become one of the fastest growing regions of the global economy, Geely's acquisition of PROTON is to gain strategic access to a new market and explore new business opportunities. For Geely, PROTON and Malaysia also mean the important right-side driving sector of the global automobile market, which the company lacks in its current lineups. By establishing a local presence through FDI, Geely hopes it can deepen its understanding of the new sector of its target market. By establishing local operations and following key customers abroad, the firm seeks to better understand customer needs and improve customer services while reducing both the production and transportation costs. In addition, judging from the large institutional perspective, the acquisition of PROTON also makes good economic sense, since the measure takes the full advantage of the recent "going global" initiative promoted by China while reducing the trade barriers established by the Malaysian government.

Furthermore, we can say with confidence that Geely's recent investment in Lotus Cars is largely based on a motivation for seeking strategic assets. In this case, the goal is to gain the technological knowledge and managerial know-hows of the well-respected racecar maker and the luxury British brand. As an upcoming automobile manufacturer on the global stage, Geely has been making great efforts in recent years to move up the industry value chain; however, up to that point the company still has no upscale models. The acquisition of Volvo is certainly a strategic move in the right direction, even though Volvo is still widely regarded as a premium model, not a luxury brand. Therefore, the Lotus purchase has enriched Geely's vehicle lineups and put the company in a good position to fully compete in the global auto market. Instead of a wholly owned FDI, Geely has chosen to collaborate with a well-established partner in order to reduce the risks of entry and gain expertise before launching its own undertakings in the market. Since this operation is based in the culturally rich Europe, a key industrial cluster for luxury vehicles, the company can also benefit from other like-minded firms in its drive to innovate and advance. In a nutshell, through its investment in Lotus Cars, Geely has secured key assets in its bold global expansion drive; and by learning from Lotus operations, Geely hopes to gain better access to advanced knowledge, customers, and distribution systems in the highly competitive global automobile market.

In the following sections, we will first review the historical backgrounds of the Malaysia automobile manufacturer and the luxury British sports carmaker, then study Geely's strategic partnership with and equity investment in both PROTON and Lotus, and finally examine the new growth dynamics of both firms under Geely.

10.2. Brief History of PROTON and Lotus Cars

Headquartered in Shah Alam, Selangor, PROTON Holdings Berhad is the second largest Malaysian automotive corporation that actively engages in automobile design, production, distribution, and sales. Established as the national automobile company in 1983, PROTON is a Bahasa Malaysia acronym for Perusahaan Otomobil Nasional. It was first envisioned by Tun Mahathir Mohamad, the long-term serving prime minister of Malaysia, who held a strong personal belief that a national automotive manufacturing and assembling plant would greatly speed up Malaysia's industrialization process and reduce the technology gap between Malaysia and the developed countries (Wain, 2010). Under his leadership, the Malaysian government established a partnership with Mitsubishi Motors, with a total investment of £140 million, and the joint venture was 70% owned by the state-holding company, the Heavy Industries Corporation of Malaysia (DRB-HICOM), with the Japanese automaker holding the remaining 30% (Tank, 1986). Its first production model, PROTON *Saga*, which was based on the design of Mitsubishi Lancer Fiore 4-door sedan with Japanese engine, rolled off the assembly line in Shah Alam in 1985, a moment of great pride for Mahathir and all Malays. Since its inception, PROTON has become a key driver of national development as it paves the way forward with technology transfer, strategic partnerships, and technical collaborations. With the support of protective tariffs, PROTON quickly captured a large share of the domestic market. By the end of the decade, it became a profitable enterprise and the largest carmaker in Southeast Asia, and began to export to Bangladesh, Brunei, Hong Kong, Pakistan, Sri Lanka, New Zealand, and the UK.

Inspired by the initial success of PROTON, the Malaysian government in 1992 established Perodua, its second national automobile manufacturing company, which began to take away market shares and eventually grew to be the largest automaker in the country. Furthermore, with reduced domestic demand caused by the economic recessions, PROTON experienced some growing pains. More significantly, since the company relied on imported parts for its production, the appreciation of the Japanese yen eventually led to substantial increase in production cost, resulting in major losses in the ensuing years. After PROTON took over the management from Mitsubishi, the company made great efforts to grow beyond manufacturing rebadged Japanese vehicles; by the early 2000s, it produced its first indigenously designed and engineered car, albeit still with Mitsubishi engine. Since then, PROTON has produced a mix of locally engineered and badge engineered vehicles. However, the continual operational loss and the alleged dispute over technology transfers forced Mitsubishi to divest its shares to Khazanah Nasional, Malaysia's sovereign wealth fund, and that PROTON stake was later acquired by HICOM, thus marking the end of two-decade partnership with the Japanese automaker (*The Star*, 2005). Besides its alliance with Mitsubishi, PROTON also collaborated briefly with Honda, Suzuki, and French car manufacturer Citroën for the purpose of technology transfers. More notably, in 2004, PROTON reached an understanding with Volkswagen for a strategic partnership that would go beyond the contract manufacturing by allowing the company to access Volkswagen's superior technology and develop new models more quickly. However, when Europe's largest automaker proposed to take 51% of the controlling stake, the negotiation was terminated by HICOM (Whitby, 2013).

In 1996, in an ambitious move for global expansion, PROTON made an opportunistic purchase of Lotus Sports Cars of the UK, hoping to gain not only new market shares but also some sophisticated R&D abilities for its new vehicles. Headquartered in Hethel, Norfolk, England, Lotus Cars is a British automotive company that manufactures sports cars and racing cars. Since the early 1950s, Lotus has been well known for its design, engineering, and production of automobiles with lightweight and fine handling characteristics. In addition to producing sports models such as *Esprit, Elan, Europa, Elise, Exige, Evora*, and *Evija*, the company has had multiple racing successes with its Team Lotus in Formula One motorsport. Lotus traced its beginning to the years after World War II, when British engineer and racing car enthusiast Colin B. Chapman built his first competition car while studying structural engineering at University College in London in 1948 (Lotus Cars, 2019). After joining the University Air Squadron and learning about aviation dynamics, Chapman became an influential English design engineer, inventor, and builder in the automotive industry, and the "most creative designer of racing cars in the history of motor racing," who was known for his simple yet effective design philosophy: "Adding power makes you faster on the straights, subtracting weight makes you faster everywhere" (Crombac, 1986).

During its early decades of operation, Lotus sold cars aimed at private racers and trialists in the UK, Europe and the US, and its sports model was notable for its use of fiberglass bodies, backbone chassis, and overhead camshaft engines. However, by the early 1980s, when faced with a worldwide economic recession, the company encountered serious financial challenges, and its production had dropped from 1,200 units per year to a mere 383 (Lotus Esprit World, 2009a). Amid an investigation for his involvement in a scandal over the use of UK government subsidies, Chapman died of heart attack in 1982, and Lotus was on the verge of bankruptcy. Although the company sought a brief partnership with Toyota Motors, it was later acquired by the General Motors for £22.7 million in 1986 (Lotus Esprit World, 2009b). Regrettably, that affiliation did not last long either. After a few years and a loss of £50 million, GM liquidated its ownership of Lotus for £30 million to a Luxembourg holding company. In 1996, that stake was acquired by DRB-HICOM through the bankruptcy of former owner Romano Artioli, and Lotus became a subsidiary of PROTON, as the Malaysian carmaker was eager to expand in the international market and gain "ready access to research and development capability" (*Reuters*, 1996).

Unfortunately, PROTON's drive to self-sufficiency was premature. The global recession hit the region hard shortly after, the ensuring economic recovery was painfully slow, and the company's business expansion did not proceed as planned. Accordingly, PROTON only produced one fully self-developed vehicle (Gen2 hatchback), and the proposed Proton City was only partially built. Furthermore, the Malaysian government held that in order to compete in the global economy, protectionism was no longer an option, and the local car producers would not survive without partners. Deputy Premier Najib Razak once openly declared in 2006: "To continue shielding our domestic market indefinitely is not a viable long-term strategy. The solution is to have a powerful foreign partner that will open the door for Malaysian-made vehicles to larger markets" (Bursa, 2006). To boost the national economy, the Malaysian government reduced import taxes from 15% to 5% in 2006; with the strong growth in imports and the rise of domestic rivals, PROTON suffered considerably, and its market share fell to below 40% from 65% a decade earlier (*Ibid.*). From the international market's perspective, PROTON still remains an insignificant player. Although the company is an important automobile manufacturer in Southeast Asia, with a poor distribution network and weak residual values, its global position as a budget Asian brand is much weaker than the fast-growing Korean rivals. After the company was privatized in 2012, it no longer held the crown as Malaysia's "National Car" manufacturer. Since then, the company has been facing an identity crisis while struggling for its direction of growth, and DRB-HICOM has been actively seeking an international partner to avoid business collapse. After several rounds of failed negotiations with Volkswagen, PSA Peugeot Citroen, and even China's Chery, Geely Auto has finally emerged as a suitable partner for PROTON.

10.3. Geely's Trajectory of International Expansion in Malaysia

Although Geely and PROTON are both automobile manufacturing enterprises from the emerging economies, the two companies have followed different paths of development. PROTON was first launched as a "National Car" maker with full government support and protective tariffs. While it has some initial successes, the company has struggled for sustainable growth after its privatization. On the other hand, Geely was founded as a private enterprise without government blessing and struggled for its survival during its early development. Nevertheless, the firm has since emerged in recent years as a new and significant player in the global automotive market. Whereas Geely has been expanding its overseas operations, PROTON has also made some efforts to grow beyond the Southeast Asian market. The Malaysian carmaker first entered China in 2007, when it formed a strategic joint venture with China Youngman Automobile Group to sell rebadged *Europestar* marque in China (Tan, 2007). However, that partnership was neither profitable nor very long, as Youngman Group ceased operation a few years later. In the following sections, we will review Geely's first efforts in Malaysia, and then examine its contract negotiation and final agreement with HICOM regarding PROTON and Lotus Cars.

10.3.1. *Geely's initial endeavors in Malaysia*

More than a dozen years before Geely made significant investment in PROTON, the company has already set its eyes on the emerging Southeast Asian market. Shortly after its official approval from the Chinese government for car manufacturing, Geely launched a small-scale export project, first to the Middle East and Africa, and then to Malaysia in 2005. Noted Li Shufu, "2005 was a milestone in the Group's expansion into the international market with the exports of over 7,000 sedans to over 30 countries, accounting for almost half of the total number of sedans exported from China in 2005. In June, 2005, the Group's associate Shanghai Maple signed an agreement with Information Gateway Corporation Sdn Bhd (IGC) to export and assemble Geely sedans in Malaysia, marking the Group's first step to manufacture Geely sedans in overseas location and the export and sales of car-manufacturing technologies to third parties" (Geely, 2005).

Geely Maple's efforts in Malaysia merit special noting. First established in 2000 and acquired by Geely as its budget brand a couple of years later, Shanghai Maple's first vehicle was produced in 2003 based on Citroen ZX of the 1990s. After Geely's rebranding initiatives, Shanghai Maple was fully consolidated into the group holding and replaced by the Geely *Englon* brand in 2010. Back in 2005, after seeing its export increased from 5,000 to 7,000 vehicles, although only accounted for 5% of the sales volume, Geely regarded export a very important part of business development and allocated substantial resources to further explore the overseas markets, with hope of exporting at least 10,000 cars in the following year. More remarkably, Geely made a daring move to launch its first complete knock-down (CKD) manufacturing and product development outside China. On May 30, 2005, Shanghai Maple entered an agreement to export Geely sedans, CKD parts, and components for the CK-1, FC-1, and LG-1 models of right-hand drive sedans to IGC for sales and assembly of Geely vehicles in Malaysia. According to the contract, Shanghai Maple would provide the technical assistance at a fee and authorize the rights to use Geely logo, intellectual property, and know-hows at cost to IGC. This move is significant in the history of Geely, as it marks the first strategic attempt to assemble Geely sedans in overseas locations to further expand sales in overseas markets (*Ibid.*).

CKD is a common practice in the automotive industry, as companies often sell knocked-down kits to their foreign affiliates or licensees for various reasons, including preferable tax treatment for providing local manufacturing jobs (Miller, 2000). Geely's announcement was initially well received in the media, noted *China Daily*: "Employing around 500 Malaysian workers, the plant will turn out 30,000 Geely branded cars next year with components supplied from China... This year, Geely hopes to export 3,000 *Haoqing* compact cars to Malaysia. The plant in Malaysia will be Geely's manufacturing base for Southeast Asia, which will target the whole market in the region" (*China Daily*, 2005). However, after the news was made public in Malaysia, domestic carmakers, including PROTON, lobbied the government for more protective measures, fearing the ultra-cheap Chinese economy brands would crush the local market. As one industry observer noted, "And coming up on the rails are the Chinese — less experienced, but with greater critical mass from a much bigger domestic market. If, as expected, the likes of Chery and Geely get their act together as exporters, Proton may find its meagre export sales squeezed even further" (Bursa, 2006). Consequently, the Malaysian government passed new strict regulations stipulating that any foreign brands assembled in the country were not for local sales but export only, which essentially marked the end of Geely's initial attempt in Malaysia (Wu, 2018). Although its first proposed overseas manufacturing base never materialized, Southeast Asia with its multi-million annual sales remains a key market for Geely's global expansion plan.

10.3.2. *The final agreement with PROTON and Lotus*

Over its history of more than 30 years, PROTON has entered into multiple partnerships with some of the world's leading automakers such as Mitsubishi, Citroën, Honda, and Suzuki. After PROTON's privatization in 2012, its conglomerate owner attempted but failed to revive the company. In 2013, with its successful revitalization of Volvo under consideration, Geely was invited by DRB-HICOM to submit a new partnership proposal with PROTON that was eventually vetoed by Mahathir, as the proud leader was not ready to give up the national carmaker founded by himself two decades ago. The same line of thinking also led to the failed negotiation with Volkswagen years earlier. However, by 2016, PROTON's operation continually deteriorated, and its market share further decreased to 12.5%. As part of the conditions of the government's RM1.5 billion soft loan to the carmaker, DRB-HICOM started an international bidding exercise for a new international strategic partner, which saw 23 global companies vetted. Rumored among those to be in the final running include Renault, Suzuki, GM, Volkswagen, Peugeot, and Geely. After several rounds of tough negotiations, Geely emerged in Spring 2017 as the final winner in the bidding process. Although its quote was lower than PSA, Geely had submitted more concrete plans for the sustained growth of both PROTON and Lotus, which made its proposal more appealing than the other final offers that treated the business merely as an overseas production base. Furthermore, to respect the wishes of Malaysians, Geely has agreed for DRB-HICOM to retain its controlling stake, so that PROTON will keep its status as a national carmaker in Malaysia. In addition to winning the trust and support from its local partner, this compromise is also out of consideration for the long-term growth of Geely in the Southeast Asia market.

On May 24, 2017, Geely Automobile Holdings announced plans to acquire 49.9% stake in PROTON for RM460.3 million (US$148.9 million), of which RM170.3 million is a cash injection while the remaining

RM290 million is from the valuation of Geely's popular SUV, *Boyue*; the remaining 50.1% will continue to be held by DRB-HICOM, meanwhile the conglomerate also completely disposed its stake in British sports automaker Lotus, with Geely taking majority stake at 51% for £51 million (US$90 million) and the remaining share to be bought by Etika Automotive (Leong, 2017). The final signing ceremony took place in Kuala Lumpur on June 23, 2017, with the Malaysian Prime Minister, DRB-HICOM Chairman, and Managing Director in attendance. Geely Chairman Li Shufu, President and CEO An Conghui, and the Chinese Ambassador Huang Huikang also attended the event (DRB-HICOM, 2017a). Commenting on the new partnership with Geely, Syed Faisal Albar noted the agreement was a historic moment for the Malaysian carmaker, "PROTON can now eye the huge Association of Southeast Asian Nations (ASEAN) passenger car market with renewed confidence" (*Ibid.*). In his remarks, Li Shufu expressed the same optimism: "PROTON is an iconic national brand of Malaysia. It is the symbol of Malaysia's national achievement and industrial spirit. We hope that through our cooperation with DRB-HICOM, PROTON will be transformed into the No. 1 independent automobile brand in Malaysia and one of the top three in Southeast Asia. For Lotus, we will increase new product launches and capacity to fully release its brand appeal. PROTON and Lotus will create synergies for Zhejiang Geely Holding (ZGH) to position ourselves as a major player in the ASEAN market, which in turn will enhance our global position and help us achieve sales target of 3 million units by 2020" (*Ibid.*).

In addition to its ownership investment, Geely also acquired the management rights to PROTON. On September 29, 2017, three months after the signing ceremony, Geely and DRB-HICOM jointed announced the corporate restructure and a new board of directors for PROTON Holdings. While Syed Faisal Albar remains as the chairman, he is joined by Li Dongfeng (Executive VP and CFO), Feng Qingfeng (Group VP and CTO), and Yu Ning (Executive VP of International Business) from Geely (DRB-HICOM, 2017b). Moreover, Li Chunrong, an executive with 30 years of experience in automobile industry, was named the new CEO of PROTON, responsible for the whole operations including R&D, production, manufacturing, and marketing (Ho, 2017). After the new leadership in place, the management team has developed a go-getting revitalization plan to restore PROTON as the best-selling brand within Malaysia and a top three ASEAN brand in the coming years. Since the company predominantly relies on its domestic market, PROTON's turnaround plan is to first return to profitability and then regain its international presence.

It is noteworthy that after the announcement, the deal has been strongly criticized by Mahathir, Malaysian political leader, original founder, and long-term serving chairman of PROTON, who slammed the sale to Geely like "losing a child" (Ng, 2018). Nevertheless, both Geely and DRB-HICOM remain resolute. Commenting on the new alliance, Li Donghui remarked: "With PROTON and Lotus joining the Geely Group portfolio of brands, we strengthen our global footprint and develop a beachhead in South East Asia. Geely Holding is full of confidence for the future of PROTON, we will fully respect the brands history and culture to restore PROTON to its former glory with the support of Geely's innovative technology and management resources" (Lye, 2017).

10.4. New Dynamics of PROTON and Lotus under Geely

With significant investment and technical assistance from Geely, PROTON began its efforts in regaining market shares both domestically and overseas. A major step forward was the introduction of the much-anticipated sport utility vehicle based on *Boyue*, one of China's best-selling SUVs. Specifically, as a part of multi-year license agreement with Geely, PROTON secured the intellectual properties to the design, development, manufacture, sale, marketing, and distribution of the Geely *Boyue*, *Binyue*, and *Jiaji* for not only Malaysia but also Brunei, Indonesia, Singapore, and Thailand markets (Tan, 2018). Named PROTON X70 with touches of local design elements for the Southeast Asia market, the new SUV was officially launched by Prime Minister Mahathir Mohamad in December 2018, who was impressed with technological advances of the vehicle and expressed high hopes for PROTON's recovery (Ng, 2018). Since it was priced competitively with Japanese and South Korean brands, the company received strong orders. Given PROTON's distribution network in some key markets in the region, this arrangement has given Geely a practical platform to expand in Southeast Asia, where non-Japanese brands often struggle (*Ibid*). PROTON's first SUV introduced the company to a new market segment, and the first model jointly developed with Geely is thus seen as a key catalyst for the transformation of the brand. As part of its localization plans, PROTON has further invested

RM1.2 billion with the expansion of its Tanjong Malim plant to produce new car models, which pushes forward Geely's plan of making Malaysia a manufacturing hub for right-hand drive vehicles for its global sales (Ridzuan, 2018).

When the Geely–PROTON deal was first announced, most ordinary Malaysians were not familiar with the Chinese carmaker. In the 2000s, when some Chinese-made economy vehicles were first introduced into the Malaysian market, they were poorly received by the locals as being cheap and of low quality. To overcome the public skepticism and enhance its corporate image, Geely has invited scores of automotive journalists, dealers, vendors, investors, and even customers from Malaysia to visit its company headquarters in Hangzhou and the Geely Research Center in Ningbo. Consequently, public perceptions in Malaysia toward Geely began to change — instead of seeing Geely as an unreliable carmaker, people begin to see it as a forward-looking company with advanced technologies, and later more people began to view the PROTON agreement in a positive light.

To restore its early glory and retain its heritage as Malaysia's first national carmaker, PROTON has closely collaborated with Geely in the design and development of new vehicles for both domestic and international markets. With substantial investment of funds and human capital from Geely, PROTON has experienced a strong rebound in 2019. Its introduction of the Geely's Global Key User Interface (GKUI) technology has received rave reviews and remarks from Malaysians, among them Prime Minister Mahathir himself, and the new smart ecosystem has moved PROTON to the forefront of automotive technology advancement in Malaysia. In addition, its X70 has received over 30,000 orders, with more than 20,000 deliveries by the summer of 2019, making it the market leader for SUVs in Malaysia; the company's other models have also undergone some upgrades, including the *Iriz*, *Persona*, and *Exora*, and the total combined sales volume recorded an impressive growth of 50.2% for the first four months of 2019 as compared with the same period a year before (Taquiddin, 2019).

On the international front, PROTON has resumed exports and its vehicles are currently sold in at least 15 countries in Southeast Asia, the Middle East, and North Africa. More notably, in 2019, PROTON has reached an agreement with Alhaj Automotive for a new CKD assembly plant in Karachi, Pakistan, with full support from the Malaysian and Pakistan governments. Designed to make X70 based on Geely technology, the US$30 million greenfield investment is scheduled to begin production in 2021, with a long-term goal of selling 400,000 vehicles by 2027, and it is anticipated that the new automotive plant will create 2,000 direct jobs and another 20,000 indirect employment opportunities in its first three years of operations (*The Sun Daily*, 2019). Undoubtedly, a strong increase in global presence and sales will certainly help the company's long-term growth, but more significantly, the Pakistan deal marks for the first time PROTON will have its own manufacturing plant overseas, which is a clear indication that the Malaysian automaker has begun to turn around and is regaining international recognition. With Geely's support, PROTON is not only reshaping the landscape of Malaysia's automotive industry but also vigorously expanding overseas with great confidence. As one company employee remarked: "We Malaysians have now started to see the positivity behind the marriage between Geely and PROTON. We have begun to see that Geely is 'light-years' ahead in not just its technology adoption rate, but also in its vision and dedication towards the holistic future of the mobility ecosystem. In short, PROTON is in very good hands" (Taquiddin, 2019).

Like its strategic partnership with PROTON, Geely is also working closely with the British sports carmaker to restore the splendor of Lotus brand. When the Geely–PROTON agreement was first announced in 2017, some industry observers expressed their doubts about the future of Lotus. Although Geely has a successful track record in its sensitive management of Volvo, automotive analysts point out the enormous gap between premium and ultra-luxury brands. Since the 1980s, when Lotus first ran into difficulties, the global luxury car market has become increasingly competitive; with each ownership change came a new round of excitement and promises, still each time the hope only led to further disappointment down the road. One commentator noted: "Low volume sports specialists like Lotus might be praised to the heavens for their dynamics and performance by the motoring press and the few hardcore aficionados that buy their cars, but that isn't sufficient to sustain a viable business. The biggest challenge facing Geely is developing a coherent model strategy that will carry Lotus through into the 2020s and beyond" (Adcock, 2017). Since the global market for luxury/prestige crossovers is believed to be around 40,000 vehicles annually, a crossover/Lotus SUV is seen as a possibility for Geely, especially for the Chinese market.

After Geely took over the controlling stake in 2017, Lotus sold 1,600 sports vehicles, an increase of 10% versus 2016, its strongest sales since

2011, and the company also showed a profit for the first time in history (Leggett, 2018). In June 2018, Feng Qingfeng was named the new CEO of Lotus, and it was stated that "Lotus is poised for the next phase of growth under Feng Qingfeng's leadership, where its expertise in light-weight materials and sport cars-engineering will form part of the wider expansion of Geely's automotive portfolio" (*Ibid*). With the new leader-ship in place, it is reported that Lotus' eventual sales target is 10,000 vehicles a year, with both the American and Chinese markets as two key components of the expansion strategy. One of the major challenges with Lotus is that it previously did not have enough funds to allow it to develop its models and fully compete in the global market for luxury sports cars. Since its acquisition, it is reported that Geely has made substantial invest-ment (close to US$2 billion); the iconic British sports carmaker went on a hiring spree and there are rumors about the development of an ultra-luxury super electric vehicle (Gibbs, 2019). Although the company has not formally laid out its masterplan, it is believed that Geely would like for Lotus to become a major player in the luxury market, taking on Porsche, Maserati, and even breaking into the ultra-luxury space to poach customers from Bentley, Aston Martin, Ferrari, and McLaren (*Ibid*).

In January 2019, Geely was reportedly planning to start producing Lotus cars in a new facility in Wuhan, China (Leggett, 2019). By July 2019, Lotus unveiled its first electric hypercar *Evija*, of which only 130 units were produced and cost around US$2 million when deliveries begin in 2020 (Moldrich, 2019). As Lotus' first all-new product in over a decade and the first model under Geely ownership, the electric vehicle is both visually exciting and mechanically extraordinary, with ultrafast charging capability and almost 2,000 horsepower. Although only time will reveal how the future will hold for Lotus, it appears that Geely has made serious commitment to ensure the success of the iconic British carmaker. Built on its engineering legacy, Lotus with Geely funding has apparently begun to realize its ambition of introducing new models and achieve its full poten-tial as a luxury sports brand in the world.

10.5. Conclusion

Over the past two decades, the globalization of the emerging market mul-tinationals has become a growing field of study for business scholars, and Geely is one such example of the so-called dragon enterprises rising from China. While any single theoretical examination may not fully explain the rise and fall of a firm on the global stage, the "Linkage, Leverage, and Learning" Theory and the Uppsala Model can help us better comprehend the phenomenon and further develop our understanding on Geely's globalization strategies. Recent international business literatures have provided us multiple explanations of the determinants of MNC firms' globalization and FDI endeavors, notable among them are the four major motives for internationalization: market-seeking, resource-seeking, asset-seeking, and efficiency seeking. Based on our research, we conclude that Geely's expansion in Malaysia can be defined as mainly market-seeking. Due to intense domestic competition and market stagnation in recent years, Geely regards its internationalization a key growth strategy and an opportunity to expand its operations outside China. New market growth is certainly an important consideration in Geely's strategic thinking. To Geely, the size of the Southeast Asia market with its multi-million annual sales is very attractive, especially since the company does not yet have a strong presence in the right-hand driving sector of the global automobile industry.

Based on the international business (IB) theoretic framework, we can also argue that Geely's acquisition of Lotus is largely a strategic-asset–seeking move. As a latecomer actively seeking global expansion, Geely lacks not only the market presence, reputation, and brand name but also the international experience and knowledge of local cultures, language, and institutions. Therefore, a major motivation is to acquire necessary knowledge and know-hows related to product and technology development. Through its strategic investments, Geely hopes to advance its technological capabilities and achieve a sustainable advantage for long-term growth. As to its mode of entry to the new sector and new market, instead of costly greenfield investment, Geely has chosen to establish its presence through strategic partnerships, which will likely help the company to overcome its "competitive disadvantage" and mitigate risks associated with the "liability of foreignness" (Child and Rodrigues, 2005; Zaheer, 1995).

After its acquisition of Volvo Cars, Geely Auto has begun a new stage of global development. In 2017, the company entered into a strategic partnership with Malaysia's DRB-HICOM to bring the country's first national carmaker, PROTON, and the iconic British sports car brand, Lotus, under its corporate wings. As its first step to revive PROTON, the company has re-engineered its best-selling SUV for the right-hand drive market in Malaysia and Southeast Asia. Geely has closely collaborated with PROTON with the goal of making it the leading carmaker in

Malaysia and one of the top car brands in Southeast Asia within a decade. Furthermore, Geely has made substantial investment in Lotus Cars. Since its acquisition, the company has sponsored major research and development in auto racing technologies and the new model advancement by the iconic British carmaker, hoping to restore its glory as a leading luxury sports brand in the world. With strong support from Geely, both PROTON and Lotus have begun to flourish since the deal was made back in 2017.

References

Adcock, I. (2017). Lotus and a new beginning. Again? *Just-auto.com*, June 30.

Athukorala, P. (2014). Industrialisation through State-MNC partnership: Lessons from the Malaysia's National Car Project. *Working Papers in Trade and Development* No. 2014/06, The Australian National University.

Blomstermo, A. and D. D. Sharma (2003). *Learning in the Internationalisation Process of Firms*. Cheltenham, UK: Edward Elgar.

Bursa, M. (2006). Emerging markets analysis: Can Proton survive without a partner? *Just-auto.com*, October 24.

Child, J. and S. B. Rodrigues (2005). The internationalization of Chinese firms: A case for theoretical extension? *Management and Organization Review*, **1**:3, 381–410.

China Daily (2005). Geely to assemble cars in Malaysia. May 31. Available at: http://www.china.org.cn/english/BAT/130590.htm (accessed September 22, 2019).

Crombac, G. (1986). *Colin Chapman: The Man and His Cars*. Sherborne, UK: Evro Publishing, p. 15.

DRB-HICOM (2017a). DRB-HICOM, ZGH Inks historic agreement. DRB-HICOM Media Release, June 23. Available at: https://www.drb-hicom.com/wp-content/uploads/2017/07/MEDIA-RELEASE-DRB-HICOM-ZGH-INKS-HISTORIC-AGREEMENT.pdf (accessed December 27, 2019).

DRB-HICOM (2017b). Joint Media Statement by DRB-HICOM and Zhejiang Geely Holding Group. September 29. Available at: https://www.drb-hicom.com/wp-content/uploads/2017/09/MEDIA-RELEASE-JOINT-MEDIA-STATEMENT-BY-DRB-HICOM-ZHEJIANG-GEELY-HOLDING.pdf (accessed December 27, 2019).

Felipe, J. (2018). Asia's industrial transformation: The role of manufacturing and global value chains. *ADB Economics Working Paper Series* 550 (July).

Geely Automobile Holding Limited (2005). *Geely Annual Report 2005*. Available at: http://geelyauto.com.hk/core/files/financial/en/2005-02.pdf (accessed September 22, 2019), p. 11.

Gibbs, N. (2019). With Geely's resources, Lotus aims big; Can Volvo owner make tiny sports car brand a player? *Automotive News*, January 7.

Ho, S. (2017). Li Chunrong named CEO of Proton manufacturing arm. *The Edge Markets*, September 29. Available at: https://www.theedgemarkets.com/article/li-chunrong-named-ceo-proton-manufacturing-arm (accessed December 28, 2019).

Johanson, J. and J.-E. Vahlne (1977). The internationalization process of the firm — a model of knowledge development and increasing foreign market commitments. *Journal of International Business Studies*, **8**:1, 23–32.

Leggett, D. (2018). Feng Qingfeng succeeds Gales as Lotus CEO. *Just-auto.com*, June 4.

Leggett, D. (2019). Lotus cars to be produced in China — Report. *Just-auto.com*, January 17.

Leong, T. (2017). China's Geely inks deal to buy stake in Malaysia's Proton. *The Straits Times*, June 23. Available at: https://www.straitstimes.com/asia/se-asia/malaysias-drb-hicom-and-chinas-geely-ink-final-contract-for-proton-lotus-deal#:~:text=KUALA%20LUMPUR%20%2D%20Malaysia's%20national%20carmaker,million%20(S%24148.9%20million). (accessed December 28, 2019).

Lotus Cars (2019). Company History. Available at: https://media.lotuscars.com/en/about/about.html (accessed September 15, 2019).

Lotus Esprit World (2009a). The final Chapman years. Available at: http://www.lotusespritworld.com/EHistory/ChapmanLastYears.html (accessed September 15, 2019).

Lotus Esprit World (2009b). The Toyota and GM link. Available at: http://www.lotusespritworld.com/EHistory/ToyotaGM.html (accessed September 15, 2019).

Lye, G. (2017). Geely to acquire 49.9% stake in Proton, 51% in Lotus — Definitive agreement to be signed before end of July. *Paul Tan's Automotive News*, May 24. Available at: https://paultan.org/2017/05/24/geely-to-acquire-49-9-percent-stake-in-proton-51-percent-in-lotus/ (accessed December 27, 2019).

Mathews, J. A. (2002). *Dragon Multinationals: Toward a New Model for Global Growth*. New York: Oxford University Press.

Mathews, J. A. (2006). Dragon multinationals: New players in 21st century globalization. *Asia Pacific Journal of Management*, **23**:5, 5–27.

Miller, R. R. (2000). *Doing Business in Newly Privatized Markets: Global Opportunities and Challenges*. Westport, CT: Greenwood Publishing, p. 281.

Moldrich, C. (2019). Lotus Evija electric hypercar: What it's like at the limit. *Car Magazine*, December 17. Available at: https://www.carmagazine.co.uk/car-news/first-official-pictures/lotus/evija-electric-hypercar/ (accessed December 29, 2019).

Ng, E. (2018). Malaysia's Proton launches 1st SUV with China's Geely. *Associated Press*, December 12. Available at: https://www.apnews.com/1d5 067608b0e44fbbf52b8fc7f13c21e (accessed September 22, 2019).

Reuters (1996). Lotus purchased by Proton. October 30.

Ridzuan, L. (2018). Proton invests RM1.2b to expand Tanjung Malim plant. *New Straits Times*, October 10. Available at: https://www.nst.com.my/business/2018/10/419947/proton-invests-rm12b-expand-tanjung-malim-plant (accessed December 28, 2019).

The Star (2005). Mitsubishi sells entire 7.9% stake in Proton for RM384 Mil. January 13. Available at: https://www.thestar.com.my/business/business-news/2005/01/13/mitsubishi-sells-entire-79-stake-in-proton-for-rm384mil (accessed September 15, 2019).

The Sun Daily (2019). 1st Proton X70 for Pakistani PM, CKD plant underway. December 26. Available at: https://www.thesundaily.my/gear-up/1st-proton-x70-for-pakistani-pm-ckd-plant-underway-XH1823365 (accessed December 29, 2019).

Tai, W.-P. and S. C. Y. Ku (2013). State and industrial policy: Comparative political economic analysis of automotive industrial policies in Malaysia and Thailand. *Journal of ASEAN Studies*, 1:1, 55–82.

Tan, D. (2018). Proton secures license to produce and sell three Geely models for ASEAN — Boyue, SX11 SUV, VF11 MPV. *Paul Tan's Automotive News,* September 28. Available at: https://paultan.org/2018/09/28/proton-secures-license-to-produce-and-sell-three-geely-models-for-asean-boyue-sx11-suv-vf11-mpv/ (accessed December 27, 2019).

Tan, P. (2007). Youngman to sell Proton GEN2 badged as *Europestar* in China. *Paul Tan's Automotive News*, July 13. Available at: https://paultan.org/2007/07/13/youngman-to-sell-proton-gen2-badged-as-europestar-in-china/#:~:text=Proton%20has%20secured%20a%20deal,through%20its%20Chairman%2C%20Pang%20Qingnian (accessed September 15, 2019).

Tank, A. (1986). Malaysian car parts need new design. *New Scientist*, July 24, p. 36.

Taquiddin, F. (2019). Geely: Through Malaysian eyes. Geely Media Center, August 29. Available at: http://zgh.com/media-center/story/geely-through-malaysian-eyes/?lang=en (accessed September 15, 2019).

Wain, B. (2010). *Malaysian Maverick: Mahathir Mohamad in Turbulent Times*. Cham, Switzerland: Palgrave Macmillan.

Whitby, D. (2013). Automotive Trends in Asia. In *Synthetics, Mineral Oils, and Bio-Based Lubricants: Chemistry and Technology*, L. R. Rudnick (ed.). Boca Raton, Florida: CRC Press, pp. 827–854.

Wu, Y. (2018). *Li Shufu's Secrete Code for Automobiles: Geely's Acquisition of PROTON and Lotus Cars*. Beijing: People's Press, pp. 3–8 (in Chinese).

Zaheer, S. (1995). Overcoming the liability of foreignness. *Academy of Management Journal*, **38**:2, 341–363.

Part IV

The Strategic Transformation for the Future

Chapter 11

Geely's Platform Strategy for Long-Term Growth

Abstract

This chapter provides a much-needed summary on the general introduction of product architecture and quasi-open product architecture by
Chinese carmakers. After noting that Geely's first-stage development
was mainly based on reverse engineering, this chapter investigates the
complex process of changing platform strategy by Geely during the
2010s, i.e. Geely's own platform upgrading (FE, KC, NL), and the co-
development of new Compact Modular Architecture (CMA) platform
with Volvo at the same time. The chapter illustrates Geely's future
ambition on the internalization of platform development capacity in
B-segment Modular Architecture (BMA) and Sustainable Experience
Architecture (SEA), and concludes with the hypothesis of future rationalization of platform strategy by the broader implementation of Volvo's
platforms in CMA, SEA, and Scalable Product Architecture (SPA) to
Geely's car brands when two entities further consolidate their assets in
the coming years.

Keywords: Geely Auto; Volvo; platform strategy; quasi-open architecture;
CMA.

11.1. Introduction

This chapter provides a much-needed summary on the general introduction of product architecture and quasi-open product architecture by Chinese carmakers. After noting that Geely's first-stage development was mainly based on reverse engineering. We investigate the complex process of changing platform strategy by Geely during the 2010s, i.e. Geely's own platform upgrading (FE, KC, NL), and the simultaneous co-development of new Compact Modular Architecture (CMA) platform with Volvo. The chapter illustrates Geely's future ambition on the internalization of platform development capacity in B-segment Modular Architecture (BMA) and Sustainable Experience Architecture (SEA), the former Pure-electric Modular Architecture (PMA), and concludes with the hypothesis of future rationalization of platform strategy by the broader implementation of Volvo's platforms in CMA, PMA, and Scalable Product Architecture (SPA) to Geely's car brands when two entities further consolidate their assets in the coming years.

11.2. Product Architecture and Quasi-Open Product Architecture in China

Research on the product platform development is mainly covered by the literature of the product development and operations management (Wheelwright and Clark, 1992; Meyer and Lehnerd, 1997; Robertson and Ulrich, 1998; Becker and Zirpoli, 2003). Product architecture is not a simple design business but is part of the important corporate strategy. Ulrich (1995) defines five aspects of architecture impact to the strategy: (1) product change, (2) product variety, (3) component standardization, (4) product performance, and (5) product development management.

Fujimoto (2007) analyzes the evolution of product architecture in the automobile industry from the historical perspective and finds two main transitions. The beginning of the automobile industry in the 19th century was the stage of craftsmanship. It was a matter of assembling modified or adapted standard parts mostly from horse-drawn vehicles. This was a form of open modular architecture. Starting from the 1930s, the mass production by some automobile companies moved the whole industry progressively toward close integral product architecture. It can be defined by two main features: one is the high level of vertical integration, i.e.

produce large quantities of components in house; the other is the high centralization of in-house design of components (Langlois, 2002).

The second major architectural change in the automobile industry happened in the 1990s. The main driving force was the increased competition. To maintain a balance between volume strategy and the variety of products, the modular platform strategy at the group level for different brands became mainstream. Modularization goes along with the increasing outsourcing process, thus the evolving relations between original equipment manufacturers (OEMs) and suppliers.

It was not until the early 2000s that key carmakers began to mark their platform strategy via concrete modular platforms. For example, the Volkswagen Group launched MQB (*Modularer Längsbaukasten*) platform in 2012 for different brands of cars. Other main carmakers launched platform strategies include PSA, Renault-Nissan, BMW, Daimler, GM, and Volvo (Table 11.1).

It is worth to note that this modularity remains at the group level, thus it is named closed modular platform. As of writing, an industrial-level open product architecture in the global automobile industry has not yet emerged. The open modular product architecture in some other industries, including PC industry, some software industries, and web design, is the mainstream approach, with the objective of simplifying the domination of plug-and-play functionality between components and/or software.

Heading to the future of the automobile industry, in particular in the segment of electric vehicles, the platform strategy has been also confirmed by key carmakers. The platform strategy can result in the standardization of modules, the reduction of costs via the augmentation of

Table 11.1. Modular platforms by global carmakers.

Carmaker	Year of launching	Modular platform	Segments
Volkswagen	2012	MQB	B, C, D
PSA Peugeot-Citroën	2013	EMP2	C, D
Renault-Nissan	2013	CMF	C, D
BMW	2014	UKL	B, C
Daimler	2014	MRA	D, E, F
General Motors	2015	D2XX	C, D
Volvo	2015	SPA	C, D

Source: Related corporate websites. Compiled by author.

sourcing volumes, and reduced development time (Muffatto, 1999; Suk *et al.*, 2007). Two key factors drive the creation of platforms dedicated to the electric car. One is the significant difference in terms of layout of core modules, including chassis, the placement of engine versus battery pack, and thus related modules, the other one is the high costs of battery. Carmakers have strong motivation to reduce the costs of EVs via the platform strategy and make the car affordable for the mass market. Initial investment for the EV platforms is significant, which becomes a risky bet for the future win of the market (Table 11.2).

In the Chinese automobile industry, Fujimoto (2002) observed a widespread phenomenon of quasi-open architecture during the technology catching-up period in the 1990s. Quasi-open architecture defines the following phenomenon in China: key components of best-selling foreign products were copied through reverse engineering and repetitive remodeling, then produced by suppliers in big volumes, thereby becoming de-facto generic components sold to indigenous producers: "…imitation-turned-versatile parts are being gathered and assembled by numerous companies and this is different from a full-fledged open architecture based on a carefully worked-out plan as seen in various digital products made by American companies" (Fujimoto, 2002, p. 35).

Some foreign companies have also contributed to the expansion of the quasi-open architectural paradigm. By taking the advantage of this specific industry feature in China, for example, Mitsubishi engine, together with Delphi's engine management system, have been packaged together as an industrial-level standardized product and service. According to a research study, at least 21 Chinese carmakers have purchased either the engine or the solution (Wang and Kimble, 2010). The advantage of a quasi-open architecture is the lower entry barriers for Chinese assemblers and component producers. Imitation via reverse engineering has enabled Chinese companies to produce new cars faster and with lower prices (Figure 11.1).

11.3. Geely's Initial Product Architecture: Quasi-Open Product Architecture before 2006

In the early stage of development, with limited capital and technology expertise, Geely, like some other indigenous assemblers, adopted unconventional practices to enter the market, including the adaptation of a

Table 11.2. Modular platforms of electric cars by global carmakers.

Carmaker	Name of platform	Investment (estimation)	Production location	Car types
Volkswagen	MEB	Over €30bn by 2023	Zwickau, Germany (2019); Shanghai, China (2020); Chattanooga, TN, US (2022)	Volkswagen ID3 and ID4; Seat El Born; Audi Q4 e-tron; Skoda Enyaq
GM	Global EV Platform	US$20bn by 2025	Detroit-Hamtramck, MI, USA (2021); Multiple locations in China	Cruise Origin; Cadillac Lyriq; GMC Hummer
Toyota	e-TNGA	US$13bn by 2030	Tianjin, China with FAW	Toyota C-HR; Lexus UX300e
Renault-Nissan	CMF-EV	Over US$10bn by 2022	Flins, France; Smyrna, TN, US; Sunderland, UK; Oppama, Japan	Renault Morphoz concept; Nissan Ariya concept
Hyundai-Kia	E-GMP Global EV Platform	US$87bn by 2025	Multiple, undisclosed	Hyundai 45 and Prophecy; Kia Imagine
Total investment	—	US$160bn by 2030	—	—

Note: Total investment by 2030, estimation according to the corporate announcement.
Source: Corporate announcement of above carmakers. Compiled by author.

Figure 11.1.   The emerging Chinese automobile industry.

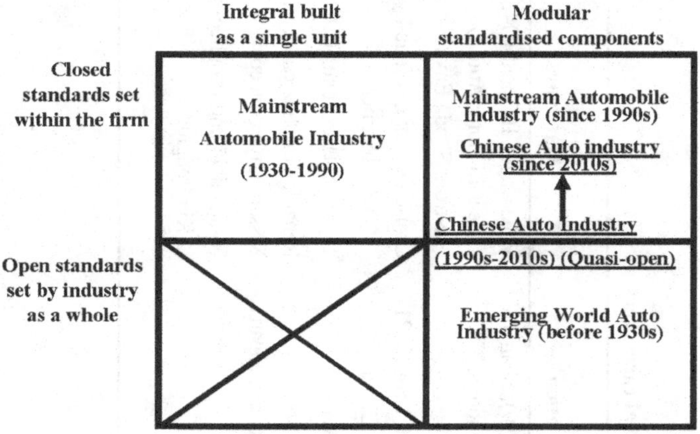

Source: Wang and Kimble (2010, p. 16). Updated by author.

quasi-open product architecture. We will use several car models of Geely to illustrate the growth of its quasi-open architecture.

The earliest car model, the *Haoqing* (豪情), started its production in the 1998 and was based on the Charade model of FAW *Xiali*. The technology of Charade is from Daihatsu, Toyota's affiliate. To produce *Haoqing*, there are three categories of sourcing of components: the original components of Charade, coming from Charade's suppliers, comprised 60% while the copied components was 10%. Thus, 70% of the components were interchangeable with that of the Charade model. The remaining parts of the components were provided by suppliers of other car brands and Geely's own suppliers — some of them previously were in the motorcycle industry (Wang, 2008). The second car model, *Meiri* (Merrie 美日) has the same method of benchmarking on the Japanese cars and sourcing method.

Several years later, with the increasing technology capacity, Geely managed to develop a higher level of mixing-and-matching of components from different car models, resulting in a more complex approach of quasi-open product architecture innovation. In 2002, Geely started production of the third car model *Maple*. This car's product architecture is a mixture of two models: the French Citroën ZX and the Charade, derived from Japanese technology. The body and chassis of the *Maple* was based on the imitation and remodeling of Citroën ZX, while the engine was based on the remodeling of a Toyota engine. Compared to the *Haoqing*, the *Maple*'s quasi-open architecture is more complex.

External competition pressure also forced Geely to internalize the technology of engine. A critical driving force is Toyota. Toyota China first increased the price of its engine from 17,000 RMB (US$1,470) to 23,000 RMB (US$3,382) for the *Meiri* car model, which retailed at 50,000 RMB (US$7,353), and later stopped sales of the engine to Geely, as the Japanese giant very quickly realized the threat of an emerging competitor. Thus, Geely was forced to conduct a reverse engineering of Toyota's engine and then progressively produce its own engine model. The price of Geely's MR4790Q engine is one-third of the price of a Toyota engine (8A model). This is the result of reverse engineering, and the broad use of "imitation-turned-versatile" parts.

After the *Maple*, the logic of quasi-open design was implemented on other car models. The very significant part of the architecture design is the interface between engine and other modules. At least two engines can be used for the same car type, one is the first-generation Geely's engine (as mentioned above), and another one is the better performing Mitsubishi engine. This further leaves the choice to the consumers: either purchase a more price-competitive Geely car (with Geely's engine), or a better performing car (with Mitsubishi engine). A senior manager at Geely explains (Wang, 2009, p. 392): "During the design period, enough space has been reserved for an engine. We've tried to assemble different engines on the same car, and all of them work without the need to change the rest of the car's architecture."

The quasi-open architecture design, via reverse engineering, also requires technological and engineering capability other than simply copying. It requires innovative supply chain management. As a new player in the automobile industry, Geely must have its unique point of differentiation. "We build good cars affordable for the mass people" was the slogan of Geely in the early 2000s. Significant price competitiveness while maintaining reasonable quality proved vital for its initial survival and further growth. From the supply chain perspective, Geely achieved a balance between sourcing low-cost components from its motorcycle business and quality-sensitive components from the suppliers of global carmakers including Volkswagen, Toyota, PSA, Nissan, and General Motors. Among the total 70% of outsourced components, there was roughly an equal split in terms of number of suppliers of the above two categories of suppliers. As the OEM, Geely needs ensure the overall architecture design, and sourcing system management — this is the newly build competency of Geely.

It is worth to point out that this open-architecture design is subjected to the evolution of the Chinese institutional environment change. In the early 1990s, the intellectual property rights (IPR) courts started their establishment in some big cities, and the efforts of protection further intensified before and after the country's accession to the World Trade Organization in 2001. Companies are moving from copying to reverse engineering by respecting IPR. Lawyers and technology specialists in IPR are involved in car design projects. In addition, patents are proactively registered to protect carmakers' innovations. BYD is another indigenous Chinese carmaker taking the approach of quasi-open architecture. The founder of the company, Wang Chuanfu, stated:

> For the development of new (car) product, in fact 60% (of the technology) comes from public literature (without patents), 30% comes from samples, 5% comes from raw materials, etc. …our own research only rests on around 5%. We widely use non-patented technology, and the integration of non-patented technology becomes our own innovation. We should respect intellectual property rights, but we can also avoid the usage of patented technology (Xing, 2009).

As *Haoqing*, *Meri*, and *Maple* cars progressively became obsolete, they had the liability of further reinforcing the negative image of "low price, poor quality" for Geely. The disturbing commercial sales performance between 2004 and 2006 further pushed Li Shufu to make the strategic decision to shift toward advanced engineering and platform strategy by mainstream carmakers.

11.4. Geely's Second Platform Strategy: Plan to Move Toward Forward Engineering

The year 2006 is an important milestone to mark the strategic transition, as illustrated by the arrival of Zhao Fuquan since November, who was appointed as Vice President of Zhejiang Geely Holding Group and President of Zhejiang Geely Automotive R&D Center, in charge of developing forward engineering system, the new product development system of Geely. Dr. Zhao is one of the few Chinese professionals to have global senior leadership experiences in car companies, including Daimler Chrysler.

In 2008, Geely announced an ambitious platform strategy: the development of five core technology platforms (for economic compact car, A level, B level, Premium car, and one light truck respectively), and 15 product platforms and 42 new models by 2015, aiming to reach the shared parts of different models up to 70–80%. Between 2006 and 2010, the R&D team expanded from 360 to 1,400 people; the basic technology system and standards were established, serving as the basic foundation for forward engineering and research, especially in the field of engine and safety technology.

The major challenge for this ambitious platform strategy is the slow development speed of new products and huge investment in R&D. In the past, there was no culture of forward engineering and platform strategy at Geely. After the establishment of the R&D system, re-engineering of the R&D process became necessary, as it was previously driven by reverse engineering. This was the biggest challenge in terms of organizational and cultural change. From the business perspective, there was the pressure of launching new products each year, between 2006 and 2015, so as to ensure enough profit generation to support the ambitious new platform strategy under the leadership of Dr. Zhao. Thus, balance and co-existence of reverse engineering and forward engineering during this critical transitional period needed to be achieved.

It was at this context that Geely's next-generation car model, *Emgrand* EC7, based on the reverse engineering of compact cars of Toyota Corolla 9th generation (E120/130), was developed simultaneously since 2006. This car's exterior design was outsourced to a Korean company. Production started in July 2009 at the plant in Ningbo, Zhejiang Province. *Emgrand* was positioned as the mid-range brand of Geely. It served as a platform for its new wave of internationalization, aiming to penetrate again in the global market. To further improve the quality, large numbers of global suppliers were integrated into the supply chain system — e.g. Siemens for electronic control system; Lear Corporation for seats; and Saint-Gobain for glass. *Emgrand* became a huge commercial success and ranked the best-selling Chinese domestic car model in 2013, or the 14th best-selling car models if including Sino–foreign car models into the ranking. This car project was under the leadership of An Conghui, CEO of Geely, and executed by Feng Qingfeng, director of the project.

From 2006 to 2013, the Geely Group experienced a critical strategic dilemma between the quick development via reverse-engineering–driven quasi-open architecture, and the shift toward the forward engineering platform design, which required time and huge resources. Such a predicament requires a delicate balance between the short-term profitability and long-term development. Industrial competition is fierce: local carmakers, especially the Great Wall and the BYD, continued with their strategy of quasi-open architecture and thus were capable of putting new models quickly on the market, while Sino–foreign joint ventures, based on the platform strategy of foreign partners, can also quickly work out new models each year. Geely was stuck in the middle.

During this period, besides the best-selling *Emgrand* EC7, Geely produced some other new car models, including *Emgrand* EC8 and *Gleagle* GC7, GX7, and *Englon* SX7 sports utility vehicle (SUV) car, but essentially based on the platform of *Emgrand* EC7. The diversification of brands, and the needs of car types within each car brand, further stretched Geely's resources, which, by then, had a big thirst in investment for its forward engineering platform strategy (Figure 11.2).

In May 2013, Dr. Zhao resigned from his position, marking a nuanced result of Geely's indigenous new platform strategy, driven by the logic of

Figure 11.2.   Breakdown of sales by Geely's car models in 2013.

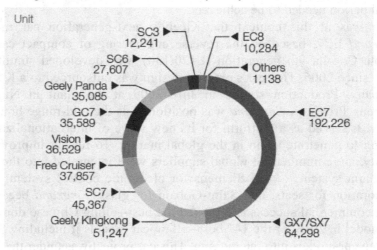

Source: Geely Annual Report, 2013, p. 13. http://www.geelyauto.com.hk/core/files/financial/en/2013-02.pdf (reprinted with permission).

forward engineering. Its initial ambitious strategy announced in 2008 failed to respect the timing of delivery. The acquisition of Volvo and its know-how on platform architecture became the new hope of Geely's platform strategy.

At the same time, the success of *Emgrand* EC7 granted credentials to Feng Qingfeng to become the successor of Zhao Fuquan. During his leadership between 2013 and 2017, Geely finetuned its priority to speed up car sales with better quality and higher price tags. Accordingly, the previous matrix structure of R&D proposed by Dr. Zhao for the development of forward-product-architecture–based platform strategy was abandoned. The R&D team structure went back to the car project team, with some general supporting function of the R&D center. Researchers and engineers were further requested to hear the voice of customers and then translate them into engineering and design.

11.5. Geely's Platform Strategy Compromise: Launch of Three Platforms in 2014 while Still Based on Quasi-Open Architecture

In 2014, Geely's new vision was released — "Making Refined Cars for Everyone." Accordingly, the new branding strategy aimed to centralize resources to build one brand: Geely. Three previous brands, *Emgrand*, *Gleagle*, and *Englon* merged into one Geely brand. In terms of platform, there was a further rationalization into three platforms.

11.5.1. *Framework extensible for compact passenger car*

The Framework Extensible (FE) is a compact passenger car platform, essentially based on the reverse engineering of Toyota Corona technology. It covers the A-/A segment and can produce passenger vehicles (hatchbacks/sedans), crossover vehicles, and SUVs. There is a high percentage of common parts, because of the similar architecture design. Key models include *Vision*, *Emgrand* EC7, and the *Gleagle* GX7. A wide range of engines can be mounted, varied from 1 liter upto 2.4 liter, from turbo to direct injection turbo, or to naturally aspirated engine. The transmission can also vary from 4, 5, 6, and 7 speeds, ranging from manual to automatic, or dual clutch transmission (DCT). A variety of fuels can also be chosen, such as ethanol, alcohol, compressed natural gas (CNG), or liquefied petroleum gas (LPG). The electric power vehicles also include different options, ranging from electric vehicles, extended-range electric vehicles, hybrid electric vehicles, and plug-in hybrid electric vehicles. After the acquisition of Volvo, technology linking with safety, maneuverability, and durability are integrated.

11.5.2. *KC for mid-size passenger car*

The KC platform is a mid-size passenger car platform. According to some analyses, this platform was originally based on the reverse engineering of Toyota Corolla's Global Outstanding Assessment (GOA) car body, the suspension system of Lexus GS, and the engine of Volkswagens EA888 model. The improvement of KC platform was carried out jointly by China Euro Vehicle Technology, AB (CEVT) and Geely Research Institute, with partial technical support from Volvo Cars. Concretely, after the signing of two technology transfer agreements in 2012, the technology of car safety and interior air quality was licensed to Geely and immediately implemented in the two ongoing new car models, *Emgrand* GT and *Boyue* (one SUV). Starting from the project of *Emgrand* GT, Geely began to learn and master the new car engineering standards, including the standard of component, system standard, etc.

The premium cars of B segment, such as the *Emgrand* GT, use this platform and it was on the market since 2014. To further improve the quality, higher portion of global suppliers are integrated into the sourcing system. Among the 113 suppliers, 69 reached the international level.

11.5.3. *NL platform for B-segment SUV*

The NL Platform for B-segment SUV was originally based on the reverse engineering of Toyota Rav4. During the development of *Boyue*, senior management of Geely fixed benchmarking on the Volkswagen Tiguan to further improve the quality. Accordingly, the NL platform is based on the quasi-open product architecture along with higher level of in-house product innovation. This modular platform aims at future expansion in intelligent driving and new energy. This car received some technology support from Volvo, especially the safety technology. Together with *Emgrand* GT, *Boyue* is the strategic product of Geely's premium and volume car strategy (Table 11.3). Under the leadership of Hu Zhennan, the project leader

Table 11.3. Geely's car models, platform, and its reverse engineering objects.

Platform	Class	Car model	Vehicle type	Year of new car launch	Reverse engineering object
N.A.	A00	Panda	Passenger	—	Toyota Aygo
FE	A0	King Kong	Passenger	2015	Toyota Vios, NBC platform
FE	A-	Vision	Passenger	2015	Toyota Corolla 9th generation
FE	A	Gleagle GX7	Passenger	2015	Toyota Corolla
KC	B	Emgrand GT	Passenger	2015	Toyota Corolla GOA car body
NL	B	Boyue Emgrand X7 Sport	SUV	2016	Toyota Rav4

Source: Compiled by author, based on interview and public resources.

and chief engineer, this new car project began in September 2012. Two people played key roles for the successful implementation of the platform strategy and the commercial success of *Boyue*, *Emgrand* GT (Borui), and some other car models during this period. Accordingly, in 2016, Feng Qingfeng was promoted from the Director of Geely Research Institute to CTO, then became the CEO of Lotus in 2018, and Hu became the Director of Geely Research Institute.

11.6. The CMA Platform: Real Forward Engineering with the Support from Volvo via CEVT

The CMA platform is an important milestone for Geely to transform from a reverse-engineering–based, quasi-open architecture toward a forward-engineering–based closed modular product architecture. This flexible and scalable architecture is similar to that of Volkswagen's MQB platform and serves as the mega platform, with higher flexibility and advanced modular parts. This platform can cover cars from B to C segments. It means CMA can replace the previous FE, KC and NL platforms, and car types can vary from sedans, hatchbacks, coupes, SUVs, crossovers, SUV coupes, among others.

The primary advantage of this new architecture is to further increase the parts commonality and thus to explore the economy of scale in terms of sourcing. CMA platform are used by different car models from Volvo

(40 series), Polestar, Lynk & Co, and Geely (for details on vehicle types and sales volumes, please refer Chapter 7). At the operational level, there is the balanced consideration between brand positioning and components differentiation. The first vehicle production was released in 2017, started with Volvo's XC40 and Lynk & Co 01 models. To maintain the differentiation between the two brands, components were planned to have a moderate level of commonality. For example, transmission parts have roughly 50% in common (personal interview with Per Ferdell, VP of CEVT, October 23, 2019).

The CMA platform is the result of Geely's ambition on the globalized R&D, via creation of CEVT in Gothenburg, Sweden, in February 2013. Mats Fägerhag, the former R&D leader of Saab, was recruited as the CEO of CEVT. Over 2,000 engineers, and an important fraction from Volvo, which established the knowledge system of the New Product Development System (NPDS), are the keys to understand the success of CMA. Chinese engineers, despite a small team, have also taken the opportunity to learn the NPD system.

In addition, insights or pressure from Geely, as well as Geely's culture, created new dynamics for the company. Geely has a fixed ambitious objective from the beginning: shorten the development period, with less investment, while maintaining the same quality standard. The result of CEVT was remarkable: compared to the development of the SPA platform, which took 22 months, the CMA platform sketched out the design in 9 months (personal interview, Wei Gang, VP of CEVT, October 21, 2019). Three years later, this CMA platform was officially announced to the market in 2016. Total investment amounted to 12 billion RMB (US$1.8 billion).

11.7. Further Capacity Increase on the Platform Design: BMA and PMA

The B-segment Modular Architecture (BMA) marks the internalization of Geely's platform design capability. It focuses on the range of A0 to A+, with high modularity to cover various vehicle types including sedan, SUV, crossover, wagon, and multi-purpose vehicle (MPV). For the Internal Combustion Engine (ICE) models, BMA can fit various powertrain options, including 1.0T, 1.4T, and 1.5 TD (this turbocharged engine was co-developed with Volvo and can be used for Volvo XC40 crossover).

The platform also offers multiple energy solutions, including plug-in hybrid (PHEV), regular hybrid (HEV), and mild hybrid electric (MHEV) configurations. This platform offers standardized interfaces between power, electrical, chassis and body modules. The car models using BMA platform include *Bingyue*, the small SUV codenamed SX11, the ICON (compact SUV), and then Lynk & Co 06 SUV model in 2020. According to Geely, the rate of interchangeable components for different models reached 70%, which was higher than the CMA platform. For the assembling plant, this design can support the flexible assembling of 15 product varieties on the same production line, with 95% automation.

From the technology perspective, as there was overlap between CMA and BMA, what was the motivation of developing the BMA platform? According to the official announcement, there are two motivations. The first is to complement with CMA for the even smaller A-segment cars. The wheelbases of BMA are between 2,550 and 2,700 mm and track widths between 1,500 and 1,600 mm, smaller than the CMA. The BMA plans to target Eastern and Western Europe, Africa, South America, and the Middle East, where there is huge demand for A-segment cars. This car is aimed at young consumers, who demand more spacious, enjoyable, and personalized experience, especially the experience of Internet and entertainment connectivity. In terms of pricing range, CMA covers the range from 150K–300K RMB, and BMA covers the range of 100-150K RMB. The second motivation is to use this platform to support Geely's independent global expansion, both for Geely's brand and the company's overseas subsidiary brands, including PROTON and Lotus for example, other than Volvo. When CMA was developed by Geely with strong support from Volvo, despite the 100% investment in terms of capital by Geely, the Chinese company still faced difficulty in directly using this CMA platform for Geely's cars, because of Volvo's concerns regarding the major brand gap between Volvo and Geely. It was under this context that Lynk & Co was created. According to our analysis, the second motivation is the real rational choice, both because of Volvo's indirect influence and Geely's ambition of full internalization of new product development platform capacity.

The realization of the BMA platform is more complicated than the downsizing of the CMA model. From the technical perspective, it is possibly based on the benchmarking of Toyota Vios, NBC platform or Corolla platform (Zhihu, 2019), thus its suspension system and fueling system is significantly different from the CMA platform. However, it is not the simple renaming of Geely's previous FE platform either. During the design phase, engine and transmission of Lynk & Co were integrated into the design (as the consumer can even find those components with the logo of Lynk & Co in the *Binyue* car). Electronic systems are shared between CMA and BMA. Security and clean air technology of Volvo were integrated as well (Zhihu, 2019).

The successful development of BMA in China mainly by Geely engineers is an important step in the internationalization of platform design. This BMA project kicked off in 2014, one year after the CMA project, in China. To realize the project, we can observe the innovative organizational arrangement. Mats Fägerhag, the CEO of CEVT, was appointed as the Deputy Director of Geely Research Institute, to support Feng Qingfeng, the Director, and Hu Zhengnan, the project leader of BMA. This leadership structure ensures the transfer of knowledge system of CMA to the BMA. Based on the learning of CMA, the efficiency of R&D further increased. The number of engineers for BMA platform was around 500, versus over 2,000 for CMA. The development time reduced to less than 24 months, almost half of the regular time of development of 40 months. It took over four years to complete the design, with nearly 100 modular architecture experts from over 20 countries.

The Pure electric Modular Architecture (PMA) platform, a strategic platform for pure electric vehicles, was announced by Li Shufu in May 2017 in China. This platform is composed of two sub-platforms, PMA1 and PMA2. The former will launch A and B class, 5–7-seater EVs, and PMA2 is for mini 2-seater EVs. Two brands will first use this PMA platforms: Geely and Lynk & Co. Geely-branded EV cars are for the China market and will cover A+ SUV, A0 Crossover, A sedan, B SUV, and B sedan. Lynk & Co cars are aimed at expanding markets in Europe and the US and plan to have A+/B Crossover, City car, C-Family Crossover, 1+/B High SUV, and A+/B Coupé. In total, 10 car models are planned based on the PMA1. Some of the new cars are expected to be on the market in 2020 or 2021.

The PMA platform will be jointly developed by Geely and Volvo in China, but not at CEVT. In December 2017, the Geely Auto Group and the Volvo Car Group established a new technology joint venture, GV Automobile Technology (Ningbo) Co. Ltd. (GVAT). The registered capital was 60 million RMB (US\$9 million), equally shared by Geely and Volvo (People.cn, 2017). The existing technologies from CEVT will be licensed to all the brands of Geely via this new legal structure. GVAT, and inter-company cooperation between affiliates in Sweden and China, is an important arrangement for the technology transfer from Volvo to Geely in a safe way.

The PMA platform development is under the leadership of Ulrich Schmalohr, the Vice President of Geely Group and Director of Geely EV Research institute (MIIT, 2018). This institute, located at Hangzhou Bay, is the affiliate of Geely Research institute, managed by Hu Zhengnan. In March 2018, Geely announced a total investment of RMB 31.5 billion (US$4.7 billion) at Hangzhou Bay, including the second and third phases of Geely Auto's R&D Center, amounted to RMB 7 billion (US$1 billion). The PMA pure electric vehicle project, with the investment of RMB 14.5 billion (US$2.2 billion) is expected to reach an annual production capacity of 300,000 EVs.

The PMA is upgraded as Sustainable Experience Architecture (SEA) in September 2020. The new architecture has broader scalability, with the capacity to expand to D- and E-segment vehicles, and light commercial vehicles, including specifications of front, rear, and all-wheel drive specifications. By anticipating the future connectivity and intelligence, the SEA includes the Operation System (OS), and open-source collaborative ecosystem as part of architecture design. Geely announced to open this architecture to other OEMs, and some preliminary discussions started. R&D centers in China, Sweden, the UK, and Germany jointly worked on this project, and the technology development was led by Kent Bovellan, Head of Advanced Vehicle Architectures at Geely Holding. The cumulative investment of SEA since PMA is over 18 billion RMB.

According to our observation and analysis, another reason to establish GVAT to develop the EV platform is the consideration of technology and industry proximity of EV industry in China. China is the biggest EV car producer and market and possesses almost the complete supply chain. In 2018, the country's new energy vehicle sales soared by 61.74% to 1.26 million units, according to the China Association of Automobile Manufacturers. The research and development of the EV platform, aiming for the volume sales, is more efficient in China than in Sweden.

Geely has formed joint venture to acquire one of the core assets of EV, the battery. In December 2018, a 49/51% joint venture was established by Geely and Contemporary Amperex Technology (CATL), the leading battery producer in China, with a starting fund of one billion Yuan (€130 million). This joint venture ensures a stable supply of batteries, battery modules, and battery packs with competitive procurement price for

Geely, as the company has the ambition to reach a higher percentage of electrified vehicles in the coming years. Geely Auto's new energy vehicle battery pack project is designed to produce 500,000 sets of battery packs, covering battery, electric control, and electric motor (Gasgoo, 2018). An Conghui, President of Zhejiang Geely Holding Group and President and CEO of Geely Auto Group, said:

> New energy vehicles are a quickly emerging strategic segment in the industry. Geely Auto will work together with partners such as CATL to build a global industrial value chain, become the global leader in new energy and energy-efficient technologies, and continue to create high-value, high-quality new energy and electrified products and services for customers. We aim to reach our 2020 strategic goals in a socially responsible manner through independent innovation, global resource integration, and synergy promotion. (Geely Global Media, 2018)

Interestingly, the first car model based on the PMA2 platform will be the pure electric *smart*, under Benz brand. In January 2020, Mercedes-Benz announced the joint venture with Geely, with 50-50 shares, and equal investment of 2.7 billion yuan (US$388.8 million) to build "premium and intelligent electrified" vehicles under the *smart* brand. The headquarters of the JV is located in Hangzhou, and the manufacturing plant will be located in Xi'an, with annual capacity of around 150,000 vehicles, targeting both China and overseas markets. The EV *smart* car is expected to be launched and sold in 2022. Benz is mainly in charge of overall design, and Geely is mainly in charge of the engineering R&D and manufacturing, with shared work on the supply chain. In the coming years, there is also the possibility to see 2-seater EV cars under the brand of Geely and Lynk & Co (Reuters, 2020).

By this stage, we have not yet managed to further investigate the mechanism of Volvo–Geely collaboration on this PMA platform, and it is worth to continue the study in the near future. In terms of relationship between brand and platform, it is also worth to further observe, how Geely will upgrade *Geometry*, the EV car brand. *Geometry* was first launched in April 2019. According to the official release, it is based on the platform named GE. While this GE platform was not officially communicated on the corporate website, together with BMA, CMA, SPA, and PMA, and based on the car type of *Geometry*, we have the assumption that the car is built on the FE platform, with upgrades to the electrification parts. It is not a pure EV platform. In the near future, there is the possibility that *Geometry* will use the PMA platform.

In summary, the evolution of Geely's platform is a long and complex journey. The first phase was based on the reverse-engineering quasi-open product architecture. When there is an increasing demand for new car models and multiple brands, Geely understands the necessity to build the forward-engineering–based platform strategy. During the transitional period, facing both the pressure of quick success of sales, and huge investment on platform building, Geely had to make concessions and focus on developing new car models based on quasi-open product architecture, with increasing technological improvement (FE, KC, NL, then followed by BMA). The creation of CEVT and the CMA platform is the first systematic learning for Geely with regard to forward engineering and the creation of the platform. While building a brand new pure EV platform, the PMA, it was decided to develop it in China, rather than at CEVT in Sweden, out of consideration for further internalization of R&D capacity by the Chinese engineering team as well as for safer technology transfer from Volvo.

Platform is the core of the competitiveness of a car company. There is a clear indication of Geely's long-term commitment to become a global player and the full master of platform development. In the forthcoming decades, when the business of Volvo and Geely is further consolidated, we can expect the progressive fading out of FE, KC, NL, and BMA platforms, replaced by CMA, PMA, and SPA; a further rationalization of platform strategy; and improvement in product performance of Geely car brands.

11.8. Conclusion

Platform strategy is the hidden but core part to understand the dynamics of corporate competitiveness of Geely. Starting from the approach of quasi-open architecture via reverse engineering based on best-selling foreign car models, Geely gained cost leadership and thus access to the automobile market. This approach is widely accepted by local carmakers such as BYD and Cheery, among others.

Geely has the courage to make the strategic shift toward forward-engineering–based modular platform strategy. The complex business reality that Geely, or any other emerging carmaker, has to face is the trade-off between the steady year-on-year sales growth based on the creation of new car models for the market, while raising significant amount of investment for the creation of new platform that can generate positive impact only years later. This transitional period on the co-existence of quasi-open architecture-based car models, and the creation of CMA platform between 2013 and 2017 reveals the pragmatic approach of Geely to handle the above business complexity.

The creation of CMA at Gothenburg via CEVT is a milestone for Geely on the forward engineering modular platform. This is an important step with regard to asset-seeking and asset creation, with significant support of Volvo. Later, the creation of two platforms, BMA and SEA (former PMA) in China, with the support of Volvo, marks the further internalization of Geely's platform design capability. It is worth to stress the very important phenomenon of reverse technology transfer, i.e. the PMA2 platform to be used by electric version of the smart car, in the framework of joint venture with Daimler. By this stage, Geely definitively takes the leadership in terms of platform capacity compared to other Chinese carmakers who are still heavily dependent on the quasi-open architecture.

A new stage of platform strategy by Geely is illustrated by the stabilization of four platforms: SPA, BMA, CMA, and SEA in 2020. In the coming years, there is the need to further examine the impact of implementation of the platform strategy by Geely — e.g. the economies of scale, the synergy of supply chain system of different car brands of Geely group, the flexibility of producing various models in the same assembling plant, etc.

References

Becker, C. M. and F. Zirpoli (2003). Organizing new product development: Knowledge hollowing-out and knowledge integration — the FIAT Auto case. *International Journal of Operations & Production Management*, **23**:9, 1033–1061.

Fujimoto, T. (2002). Thinking of the Chinese manufacturing sector in architecture context. *Keizai Sangyo Journal*, 34–37. https://www.rieti.go.jp/en/papers/research-review/002.html (accessed March 18, 2020).

Fujimoto, T. (2007). Architecture-based comparative advantage — A design information view of manufacturing. *Evolutionary and Institutional Economics Review*, **4**:1, 55–112.

Gasgoo (2018). Geely Hangzhou Bay Program starts construction with investment of RMB 31.5 billion. March 13. Available at: http://autonews.gasgoo.com/70014349.html (accessed October 26, 2020).

Geely Global Media (2018). Geely Auto and contemporary Amperex technology form JV for new energy vehicle batteries. December 20. Available at: http://global.geely.com/media-center/news/geely-auto-and-contemporary-amperex-technology-form-jv-for-new-energy-vehicle-batteries/ (accessed October 26, 2020).

Langlois, R. N. (2002). Modularity in technology and organization. *Journal of Economic Behavior & Organization*, **49**:1, 19–37.

Meyer, M. H. and A. P. Lehnerd (1997). *The Power of Product Platforms*. New York: The Free Press.

MIIT (2018). Geely gathers international wisdom to promote R&D to create a 'new engine' for development. July 27 (in Chinese).

Muffatto, M. (1999). Introducing a platform strategy in product development. *International Journal of Production Economics*, **60–61**, 145–153.

People.cn (2017). Geely/Volvo jointly develop PMA platform to build more than 10 electric vehicles. November 12. Available at: http://auto.people.com.cn/n1/2017/1112/c1005-29640987.html (in Chinese, accessed October 26, 2020).

Reuters (2020). Mercedes-Benz to build smart brand cars with Geely in China's Xi'an. January 11. Available at: https://www.reuters.com/article/us-geely-daimler-jv/mercedes-benz-to-build-smart-brand-cars-with-geely-in-chinas-xian-senior-exec-idUSKCN1ZA06A (accessed October 26, 2020).

Robertson, D. and K. Ulrich (1998). Planning for product platforms. *Sloan Management Review*, **39**:4, 19–31.

Suk, E., O. de Weck, I. Y. Kim and D. Chang (2007). Flexible platform component design under uncertainty. *Journal of Intelligent Manufacturing*, **18**:1, 115–126.

Ulrich, K. (1995). The role of product architecture in the manufacturing firm. *Research Policy*, **24**:3, 419–440.

Wang, H. (2008). The innovation in the product architecture: A study of Chinese automobile industry. *Asia Pacific Journal of Management*, **25**:3, 509–535.

Wang, H. (2009). Made in China: Joint Ventures and Domestic Newcomers. In M. Freyssenet (ed.) *Second Revolution: Trajectories of the World Carmakers in XXI Century*. New York: Palgrave Macmillan, 383–403.

Wang, H. and C. Kimble (2010). Low-cost strategy through product architecture: Lessons from China. *Journal of Business Strategy*, **31**:3, 12–20.

Wheelwright, S. C. and K. B. Clark (1992). *Revolutionizing Product Development — Quantum Leaps in Speed, Efficiency and Quality*. New York: The Free Press.

Xing, W. (2009). The only way for BYD is innovation and R&D. *China Automobile Headline News*, January 7. Available at: http://tianyongqiu.blog.sohu.com/108151725.html (in Chinese, accessed April 18, 2020).

Zhihu (2019). Disassemble the chassis of Geely Binyue to see how the chassis material is used. January 10. Available at: https://zhuanlan.zhihu.com/p/54580689 (in Chinese, accessed October 26, 2020).

Chapter 12

Corporate Culture and Brand Development

Abstract

As Geely enters a new stage of development, the company has made great efforts to develop its corporate culture by clearly defining its vision and core values. The firm has united its different subsidiaries under the banner of Geely Group toward one common goal: transforming itself into a prominent automaker and technology leader in the global automobile industry. Guided by the notions of *making refined cars for everyone* and *making the safest, most environment-friendly and most energy-efficient vehicles*, Geely has also paid close attention to its brand development, and after some experiments, the company has formulated a single-brand "One Geely" strategy that has contributed to the rise of Geely as a leading national auto brand in China in recent years. To gain a more comprehensive understanding of Geely as a global enterprise, this chapter will first survey the company's mission, vision, core values, and other key concepts of its corporate cultures, then review the stages of its brand development and its current brand and vehicle portfolios, and finally examine its brand management strategies.

Keywords: Geely Auto; corporate culture; corporate social responsibility; brand development; brand management.

12.1. The Evolving Missions and Organizational Cultures of Geely Auto

The British scholar Elliott Jaques was the first organization theorist to describe organizational culture in a factory setting (Jaques, 1951). Since then, multiple scholars have recognized that different organizations often have very differing cultures (Deal and Kennedy, 1982; Schein, 1992; Kotter and Heskett, 1992). Labeled as "corporate personality" by Flamholtz and Randle (2011), organizational culture is defined as values, beliefs, and norms that influence the behavior of people as members of an organization (Flamholtz and Randle, 2014). In the business environment, it is often described as corporate or company culture, which became a widely recognized notion by the 1980s. Rooted in a firm's goals, structure, and approaches to labor, customers, investors, and the greater community, corporate culture encompasses generalized beliefs and behaviors, company-wide value systems, management strategies, employee communication and relations, work environment, and attitudes that define how a company conducts its business. As a core business concept, it is generally believed that corporate culture can grow organically or be shaped intentionally and is influenced by national cultures, traditions, economic trends, international trade, company size, and products. According to the *Harvard Business Review*, the six common, most important characteristics of successful corporate cultures include *vision*, *values*, *practices*, *people*, *narrative*, and *place* (Coleman, 2013). They reach to the core of a company's ideology and practice and affect every aspect of its business.

A firm's culture is largely influenced by its mission statement. As noted in previous chapters, Geely was initially established as a private, grassroots enterprise competing with large state-owned enterprises (SOEs) and powerful joint ventures (JVs) in auto manufacturing. Its first mission was to *make affordable cars for ordinary people* in China, which defined its niche position and ensured its survival as a latecomer in the tough market competition. After some endeavors in reverse engineering and technology catchup through the initial phase of development, Geely found its footing and was able to gradually move upstream up in vertical automobile diversification. In 2014, after the acquisition of Volvo Cars, the company redefined its brand mission to *making refined cars for everyone*, which means building premium products for every consumer segment. Subsequently, Geely further revised its corporate mission to *making the safest, most environment-friendly and most energy-efficient vehicles* (Geely Media Center, 2020a).

Under the leadership of Chairman Li Shufu and President An Conghui, Geely has strived to transform itself into a leading and a forward-looking automobile manufacturer, not only in China but also in the world. Remarking on the joint development of Geely and Volvo, Li shared his view on Geely's corporate culture: "The global corporate culture I mentioned refers to the enterprise model that transcends the borders, nationalities and religions, which is conducive to the advancement of human civilization, people's happy life as well as enterprises' innovation and global adaptability. These advantages can be seen in customers' satisfaction, sense of pride among employees and achievability in management, flexible culture and comprehensive and sustainable development of the company. Under the guidance of this culture, featured by openness, inclusiveness, foresight and sagacity, an enterprise will actively undertake responsibility, have the courage to challenge the peak of science and technology, be brave in the exploration of commercial civilization, and be endowed with an administration concept of legitimacy, fairness, transparency and mutual respect" (Li Shufu, 2014).

Led by this belief, Geely has accordingly outlined its vision as to *bring Geely to the world*, and *let the world be filled with happiness and prosperity*. With a core value of *Happy Life, Geely Drive*, its corporate spirits include *team spirit, learning spirit, innovative spirit, fighting spirit and the truth-seeking spirit, and spirit of excellence* (Geely Media Center, 2020b). More conspicuously, Figure 12.1 illustrates Geely's core value triangle of *technology, society, and environment*, which will be further examined in the following section.

In terms of management philosophy, Li Shufu's leadership role should be recognized for the development of corporate culture and open communication at Geely. In cross-cultural management, Li has a cosmopolitan view following the 16-character philosophy (各美其美, 美人之美, 美美与共, 天下大同): appreciating the culture/values of others as do to one's own, and the world will become a harmonious whole; Everybody cherishes his or her own culture/values, and if we respect and treasure other's culture/values, the world will be a harmonious one (People.com.cn, 2012). This cultural appreciation is clearly reflected in Geely's approach to Volvo after its acquisition, which Li sees as "a tiger in the mountains" and should roam freely in the nature, not "in a cage in a zoo" (Flannery, 2014). Despite very different corporate cultures, with Geely's strategic

Figure 12.1.   Geely's core values, reprint with permission.

support, Volvo was able to operate with China as its second home market and quickly returned to profitability. Along the way, Volvo and Geely also established the China Euro Vehicle Technology AB (CEVT), a joint research center designed to facilitate mutually beneficial learning and innovations (Yakob *et al.*, 2018). While Geely's agility in confronting challenges has a profound impact on the Swedish automaker, Volvo's strong commitment to safety technology and social responsibilities has also helped reshape the corporate mission of Geely: *making the safest, most environment-friendly and most energy-efficient vehicles.*

Since innovation is the key for the long-term, sustainable development, and talents are the primary resource for innovations, Geely has strived to enhance its corporate mission and values by forming a management framework based on four cultural systems: the culture of endeavoring, the culture of problem-solving, the culture of benchmarking, and the culture of compliance. In practice, Geely has designed and continuously implemented its problem-solving ticketing system, which has positively contributed to the improvement of the employee ownership sentiment and achievement over years. In a way it is similar to the "Toyota Way" in production systems and human resource management, a pillar of the leading Japanese automobile manufacturer famed for its quality control mechanism (Saruta, 2006). In 2019 alone, Geely has received more than 666,900 employees' proposals and processed more than 42,500 problem-solving tickets, resulting an increase in revenue of 445 million RMB for the company (*Geely CSR Report*, 2019).

12.2. Core Values of Geely's Corporate Culture and Social Responsibilities

Faced with tough competition both domestically and globally, Geely has recognized the importance of corporate culture as the spiritual pillar of modern enterprises and has committed to advancing its corporate mission and value systems. Notable among Geely's corporate philosophies is its culture of innovation. According to Li Shufu: "the 'core engine' of Geely's development lies in promoting technological innovation so that business units remain robust and maintain their competitive edge" (*Geely CSR Report*, 2019). The culture of innovation includes both social and technology innovations. Guided by its simple yet striking goal of *improving life for all*, Geely has endeavored to "drive and create value for everyone," to make people's daily lives better, with greater convenience, through the use of technology to create superior products and services (Geely Media Center, 2020c). At Geely, the culture of innovation is not only incorporated in its research and development for intelligent factory design to maximize productivity and efficiency, but also reflected in its multiple forward-looking undertakings for mobility solutions. Through a corporate culture that facilities innovations, Geely has obtained 1,933 patents, including 27 international patents,1,552 domestic and foreign trademark applications, and 61 software copyright applications in 2019 alone (*Geely CSR Report*, 2019). In light of the new waves of revolutionary technologies that sweep through the global automotive industries in recent years, Geely has made major efforts to charge forward in the field of social innovation and transportation technology and has begun to lay a new foundation for a three-dimensional mobility ecosystem covering the land, air, and sea. Through multiple partnership endeavors in connectivity, big data, artificial intelligence, and other fields, Geely has already created its own global key user interface (GKUI) smart ecosystem that brings together different products and services into the Internet of Vehicles. By promoting the development of innovative technology, Geely has firmly positioned itself for a strategic transformation from a traditional automaker to a global mobility technology enterprise.

Sustainability is another pillar of Geely's cultural value system. Owing to its firm commitment of going green and becoming an environmentally friendly corporation, Geely has strived to reduce emissions and practice energy conservation while taking concrete steps to ensure its sustainable development. Geely's long-term goal is the mass production of zero-emission pure electric vehicles (EVs); and through its multiple platforms and diversified new-energy vehicle technologies, all its brands have committed to the electrification of their products in the future. At the heart of Geely's socially responsible endeavors is its commitment to the construction of green factories and production lines as well as the development of sustainable and energy-efficient vehicles (Geely Media Center, 2020e). In addition to hybridization, Geely has invested significantly in the development and promotion of new energy such as electrified vehicles, fuel cell technology, or alternative fuels. A core piece of its master plan is the *Blue Geely Initiative*, in which the company promises that 90% of its future sales would come from new-energy vehicles, and consumers would be able to purchase hybrids at the price of traditional models in the coming years (Li, 2018). Guided by its strong belief that the future of the automobile industry resides in electric and new energy vehicles, the company has launched the *Geely Intelligent Power*, a diversified new energy strategy that follows four main technological pathways of hybrid, pure electric, alternative fuel, and fuel cell technologies, with the goal of making Geely a global leader in new energy mobility (Manthey, 2018). In addition to 30 new electric and hybrid models, Geely has also pledged to invest US$5 billion for EVs with an intention of launching its first fuel cell vehicle by 2025. Related to this initiative, Geely has placed great importance in the area of automotive intelligence and pushed forward its iNTEC brand of technologies, a concept to "humanize intelligent drive" with advanced technologies to provide occupants a greater level of safety and convenience when traveling. Currently, the company has employed more than 2,500 professionals to research and develop new energy technologies, and its London Electric Vehicle Company has become a global pioneer in zero-emission capable vehicles in the urban transportation sector. With the launch of its EV-powered *Cao Cao* ride hailing service, Geely has also begun to develop a new energy travel ecology that will actively contribute to the development of a resource-saving and environmentally friendly society.

After its acquisition of Volvo, Geely's corporate value system has been greatly influenced by Volvo's fundamental focus on safety. In line with its vision of *making the safest, most environmental-friendly and most energy-efficient vehicles*, Geely has significantly increased its investment in technological innovation and product improvements in the areas of vehicle safety, powertrain technology, in-car air quality, etc. With safety as a core value and hoping to set a new industry benchmark, Geely has applied and extended the human-based safety and security issues to a concept of "Global Security," covering passive, active, pedestrian, environmental, information, property, and high-voltage power security matters. Inspired by Volvo's track records in safety technology innovation and consumption upgrade, Geely has also developed a comprehensive process of safety improvement encompassing in-depth investigation and evaluation of traffic accidents, reconstructed accident scenarios, and development of a virtual scenario database for testing active safety and autonomous driving functions. Although there is still a quite distance to go before Geely can be recognized as an industry leader in vehicle safety, it is a strategic move in the right direction and will certainly help improve its product lineups, equipped with a higher level of comprehensive standards for safety.

Besides technology and environmental values, Geely has also placed great emphasis on social values that a modern enterprise can and should contribute to the society. In this day and age of corporate social responsibility (CSR), the formation, development, and continued operation of a business is not only to produce economic value but also to create social value. To achieve long-term sustainable growth, an enterprise must go beyond simply complying with laws and regulations and implement high standards of ethics throughout its operation and give back to the society and its customers. Accordingly, Geely has developed a comprehensive social responsibility strategy that is integrated throughout its operations, which in turn lays a solid foundation for the company to grow and become a globally respected enterprise. In particular, its CSR strategy is implemented primarily in the four areas of product, economy, environment, and society, through which Geely aims to connect automobiles to the world, give customers a good life with freedom of mobility, and contribute to the sustainable development of society (*Geely CSR Report*, 2019).

People's wellbeing and happiness is an important part of Geely's corporate culture. Led by its social welfare vision of *letting the world feel love*, Geely's CSR initiatives have been largely focused on education and environmental protection efforts, covering three areas of public interests: education, poverty alleviation, and support for the underprivileged.

Some of its notable undertakings include the "Geely Timely Rain" project that targets poverty alleviation by improving education, creating employment opportunities, and assisting rural regions to develop sustainable agricultural cooperative enterprises; "Geely HOPE — Green Pathways" program, which is designed to help outstanding students in underprivileged areas all around China obtain fair education and development opportunities; 100 People Assistance Charity Activity Series, which provides aid to people in the western part of China through partnership with the Love Charity Foundation; and London Electric Vehicle Company's "Magic Taxi Tour" that takes ailing children to go on a fairytale-like journey to the magical kingdom of their dreams (Geely Media Center, 2020d). Under the umbrella of the Li Shufu Charity Foundation, Geely in recent years has sponsored multiple activities valued over 300 million RMB in poverty alleviation, disaster relief, medical aid, and educational programs. When facing the global pandemic in 2020, Geely also established a fund of 200 million RMB to support the prevention and control of coronavirus.

As Geely transforms itself from high-speed growth to high-quality development, the company has begun to issue its annual CSR reports starting in 2012. Its overall goal is to build Geely into a modern, global enterprise with an inclusive and diversified corporate culture to fulfill its CSR. By pushing technology boundaries and creating social and environmental values, Geely not only aims to take the company to the world and add value to its customers but also hopes the world will experience and benefit from the Geely's spirit of innovation and excellence. Related to its corporate culture development, branding has also played a key role in the rise of Geely. Although Geely has begun its strategic transformation from an automobile manufacturer to a mobility services provider, its core business still remains firmly in the global automobile industry. In the following sections, we will review Geely's vehicle portfolios and its brand development strategies over years.

12.3. Geely's Initial Brand Development

In modern times, branding has been increasingly recognized as a very important tool in product development, marketing, and communication. Brands are used in advertising to generate business recognition and create and store value as brand equity, to the benefit of the brand's customers, its owners and shareholders (Aaker, 1991). In brand development, scholars have noted two distinguished approaches: the Family Brand Strategy (umbrella or single brand strategy) versus Individual Brand Strategy (multiple brands strategy, since the firm create individual brand names for different product categories) (Roberts and McDonald, 1989). Both strategies have been widely used in the automobile industry, with General Motors as a good example of multi-branding management while Audi, Mercedes-Benz, and BMW represent the family branding practice; and each approach has its own strength and weakness in terms of marketing effectiveness, new product development, resource requirement, and risk management. While building a single brand requires a firm to determine its correct branding position, optimize the brand's design, and manage the brand's meaning over time, managing or a group of different brands is a more difficult task, since a collection of brands will have different strengths and limitations (Calkins, 2005). It has been well documented that an effective brand portfolio strategy will have a significant impact on a firm's marketing and financial performance (Morgan and Rego, 2009). Judging from its branding practice, Geely has a brand portfolio that is fairly complex, which we will explore in the sections below.

Over the course of its development, Geely has largely adopted the multiple brands strategy in brand management, although in recent years, the company has moved toward the umbrella branding, made sincere efforts to consolidate different brand names, and enhance the image of the single Geely brand for the group. Like other people around the world, the Chinese always pay close attention to proper names for any business undertakings of significant importance. When Geely was first launched, its name (吉利 *Jili*) means "auspicious" or "lucky" in Mandarin, reflecting the best wishes from its founder. A brief, 40-year timetable of Geely's development can be found on the company website (Geely Global Media, 2018), and its brand history can be roughly divided into three phases.

Phase One of Geely's brand development covers the decade from 1997 to 2007. Similar to other automobile emblems of the time, the first Geely logo was designed with a round frame in hues of blue for the outer ring and the company name printed inside. The inner circle is in the sky-blue background with a metallic triangular symbol resembling a mountain with stripes on it (Figure 12.2). Designed to promote the Asian spirit of conquering challenges and aspiration for success, it represents a crest that indicates high-performance cars. It is believed the inner design also resembles six number 6 grouped together, which is a very auspicious figure for Chinese to embark on new journeys (Wu, 2018). Rolling out from

Figure 12.2.   Logos of Geely Auto (reprinted with permission).

the assembly line in 1998, Geely's first production model HQ (*Haoqing* 豪情) was suitably named *Ambition* in Chinese to reflect the determination and pride of Geely people in automobile manufacturing, although the vehicle was largely based on another Chinese economy brand *Xiali* (夏利), a variant of the 1987 Daihatsu Charade with Toyota engine. Geely's second model was called *Merrie* (MR 美日), which means "happy days" in Chinese; the phrase also suggests America and Japan, implying the top quality represented by the two automobile powerhouses. That model was followed by *Uliou* (MS 优利欧), suggesting it was better than *Xiali* with Japanese technology and *Sail* (赛欧) jointed developed by GM and SAIC (McGregor, 2002). Subsequently, Toyota sued Geely in 2002 for trademark infringement and unfair competition, claiming the company copied Toyota's logo on its *Merrie* saloon and implied in ads that some of the parts were also made by Toyota (Fairclough, 2006).

Likewise, in the ensuing years Geely LC (熊猫) model also faced accusations of similarities to Citroën C1 or Toyota Aygo. Despite the allegations, the weak protection of intellectual property rights in China at that time worked to the advantage of latecomer in technology catching up. Nonetheless, after Geely successfully defended itself in a Beijing court in 2003, the company began to make genuine efforts to outgrow its initial mode of "learning and imitating" in auto design and brand development.

Through partnership with the South Korean carmaker Daewoo, Geely was able to develop its next generation of vehicles that included *Freedom Cruiser* (CK 自由舰) and *China Dragon* (CD 中国龙), which were showcased at the Detroit and Frankfurt Auto Shows in 2005–2006, the first time any Chinese national brand presented at the top international exhibits. However, those models were still produced under Geely's early brand strategy of *building the most affordable vehicles for ordinary people*. Only when the company started to move upstream in vertical automobile diversification and launched its strategic transformation in 2007, Geely entered a new phase of brand management.

Phase Two of Geely's brand development began with a new multiple-brand strategy. Notable models during this period include *Emgrand* (帝豪), which was launched in 2009 as a medium- to high-end luxury brand. *Emgrand* was to feature "luxury, steady, and power" with the core value of "Chinese wisdom, world quality," representing the "new image" of Geely and Chinese automobiles (Geely Media, 2009). For the ultra-economy sector, Geely developed the *Gleagle* (全球鹰) vehicles through its Shanghai Maple brand acquired in 2002, representing style, passion, and dreams (*China Car Times*, 2010). To cover the full spectrum, Geely also developed its *Englon* (英伦) for the mid-priced segment of the auto market, emulating the classic British style and targeting the young, trendy, and ambitious Chinese consumers. The *Englon* emblem was later selected as the new logo for the London Taxi Company after its purchase by Geely (China Auto Web, 2010). Although Shanghai Maple has been fully consolidated into Geely's affordable sector of the auto market, it is noteworthy that in 2019, Shanghai Maple Guorun Automobile Co. under the Geely Technology Group has formed a 50-50 JV with LG Chem of South Korea to engage in the production and sales of batteries for electric vehicles.

As a part of the new marketing initiative, Geely also revealed a new corporate logo through a worldwide design competition in 2007

(Figure 12.2); however, the winning design was soon discontinued due to its similarity to Toyota Auto's emblem. Instead, the runner-up symbol designed for *Emgrand* was selected as the new logo for Geely Auto, although it still bears some similarities to the logo of Cadillac with black and red rectangles decorated in a gold frame in shield-shaped form. After a period of use, the company further improved its logo design with blue and black colors instead, representing sky and earth, respectively, and officially launched its new corporate logo on April 9, 2012 (Wu, 2018). It is believed the six-frame design symbolizes the six-pack muscle, signifying masculine power for its vehicles while the shield shape suggests the safety and personal protection for consumers (Figure 12.2).

12.4. Geely's Brand and Vehicle Portfolios

Phase Three of Geely's brand development began in 2014, when the company announced the plan to consolidate its auto brands. Facing increasing competitions from SOEs and JVs, Geely with its own indigenous brands decided to discontinue *Emgrand*, *Gleagle*, and *Englon* in order to concentrate corporate resources for the promotion of the Geely brand (Shen and Shirouzu, 2014). After brand overhaul, several new models have been developed to better serve the different segments of the auto market, including Geely *Borui* (博瑞 large family sedan), *Boyue* (博越 compact SUV), *Binrui* (缤瑞 compact sedan), *Binyue* (缤越 subcompact crossover), *Xingyue* (星越 SUV coupe), and *Jiaji* (嘉际 compact MPV). Table 12.1 outlines the current series of brand names produced by Geely Auto, with the more recent vehicles listed first, followed by the previous car models that have since been discontinued by the group company.

Table 12.2 lists Geely's recent electric vehicles (EVs) that are equipped with information and communication technology (ICT); such brand initiatives will be further explored in the following section. In addition, this table also provides the information on the car brands by Geely's international partners in auto manufacturing, while vehicles produced before such partnerships were established with Geely are excluded from the listing. As the table illustrates, through its ambitious global expansion efforts via cross-border mergers and acquisitions, Geely has progressively increased its portfolio of car brands, including some well-known, world-class premium brands such as Volvo, London Taxi, and Lotus.

Table 12.1.   Geely's current vehicle brands and previous car models.

Year	Brand	Chinese	Model
New Model Series			
2020	Geely ICON	吉利 ICON	Sub-Compact crossover
2019	Geely Xingyue	星越	Fastback compact crossover
2019	Geely Jiaji	嘉际	MPV
2018	Geely Borui GE	博瑞	D-segment sedan
2018	Geely Binrui	缤瑞	C-segment sedan
2018	Geely Binyue	缤越	subcompact crossover
2016	Geely Boyue	博越	compact crossover
Emgrand (帝豪) Model Series			
2018	New Emgrand	全新帝豪	compact sedan
2018	Emgrand GT	博瑞	D-segment sedan
2016	Emgrand GS	帝豪	compact crossover
2016	Emgrand GL	帝豪	C-segment sedan
Vision (远景) Model Series			
2017	Vision X1	远景	mini hatchback
2017	YuanJing X3	远景	subcompact crossover
2017	Vision S1	远景	compact crossover
2006	Geely Vision	远景	compact sedan
2016	Vision SUV	远景	compact crossover
Previous Emgrand (帝豪) Models			
2011–2014	Emgrand	帝豪	EX7 SUV
2011–2014	Emgrand	帝豪	EC8 2.0 L & 2.4 L sedan
2011–2014	Emgrand	帝豪	EC7-RV 1.5 L & 1.8 L hatchback
2009–2014	Emgrand	帝豪	EC7 — 1.8 L CVVT sedan/hatchback
Previous Englon (英伦) Models			
2010–2014	Englon	英伦	SC3
2010–2014	Englon	英伦	SC5-RV
2010–2014	Englon	英伦	SC6
2010–2014	Englon	英伦	SC7
2010–2014	Englon	英伦	SC7-RV
2010–2014	Englon	英伦	SX5
2010–2014	Englon	英伦	SX7
2010–2014	Englon	英伦	TX4

(Continued)

Table 12.1.   (*Continued*)

Year	Brand	Chinese	Model
Previous Gleagle (全球鹰) Models			
2012	Gleagle	全球鹰	GC7 — 1.8 L four-door sedan
2011	Gleagle	全球鹰	CK — 1.0/1.5 L
2010	Gleagle Panda Cross	全球鹰	GX2 — 1.3/1.5 L
2008	Gleagle Panda	(熊猫)	LC/1.3L & 1.0 L CVVT hatchback
Daewoo-Designed Models			
2008–2011	China Dragon	中国龙	CD/1.8L CVVT coupe
2006–2017	Geely KingKong	金刚	MK/LG/1.5 L & 1.6 L sedan
2005–2012	Freedom Cruiser	自由舰	CK/1.3 L & 1.5 L & 1.6 L sedan
2005–2009	Geely Merrie	美日之星	1.1 L & 1.3 L hatchback
Xiali-Based Model Series			
2003–2006	Beauty Leopard	美人豹	BL/BO 1.5 L coupe
2003–2006	MR/Merrie	美日	hatchback
2003–2005	Uliou	优利欧	MR/MS
2001–2007	PU/Nanny		Rural Nanny/Urban Nanny
1998–2006	Haoqing	豪情	HQ/1.0 L & 1.3 L & 1.5 L hatchback
Shanghai Maple			
2006–2010	Hysoul/Haixuan	海尚/海炫	Maple M206
2005–2010	Hysoul/Haixuan	海尚/海炫	M305 5-door hatchback
2004–2010	Maple Marindo	海域	M303 1.5 L & 1.8 L sedan
2003–2010	Maple Hisoon	海迅	AA & AB 5-door hatchback
2003–2010	Maple Huapu	华普	M203 — 1.5 L 5-door hatchback

Table 12.2.   Geely's new EV brands and partnership models.

Year	Brand	Chinese	Model
Maple Models			
2020	Maple	枫叶汽车	30X SUV crossover
Geometry Models			
2018	Geometry	几何汽车	Geometry A
LEVC			
2017	LEVC	伦敦电动	LEVC TX
smart Model			
2022	smart	司麥特	Mini (Swatch Mercedes ART)

Table 12.2. *(Continued)*

Year	Brand	Chinese	Model
LYNK Model Series			
2019	Lynk & Co	领克	05 A compact crossover
2019	Lynk & Co	领克	04 A compact car
2018	Lynk & Co	领克	03 A compact car
2018	Lynk & Co	领克	02 A compact crossover
2017	Lynk & Co	领克	01 A compact crossover
Volvo Car Models			
2020	Volvo	沃尔沃	V60/XC60
2018	Volvo	沃尔沃	S60
2017	Volvo	沃尔沃	XC40
2016	Volvo	沃尔沃	V90/V90 CC
2016	Volvo	沃尔沃	S90/S90 L
2012	Volvo	沃尔沃	V40/V40 CC
2010	Volvo	沃尔沃	S60/S60 CC
2010	Volvo	沃尔沃	V60/V60 CC
Polestar Models			
2020	Polestar	极星	Precept
2019	Polestar	极星	Polestar 2 Electric AWD
2017	Polestar	极星	Polestar 1 plug-in hybrid
Lotus			
2019	Lotus	路特斯	Evija
PROTON Model under Geely Partnership			
2018	PROTON	宝腾	X70 C-segment SUV
New Transportation Experiment			
2017	Terrafugia	太力飞行汽车	TF-X flying car

12.5. Creating Refined Cars for Everyone

The release of *Borui* in 2014 marked the beginning of a new era for Geely Auto, when the company revised its mission to *making refined cars for everyone*. An Conghui, President and CEO of Geely Auto Group, noted: "Chinese can not only make cars, but are also capable of making good cars" (*Edge Financial*, 2014). Instead of producing the most affordable vehicles for ordinary people, Geely has shifted its focus to making high-quality, high-tech, and high-value cars, and the acquisition of Volvo Cars has greatly facilitated this process. Since then, in addition to its globalized R&D network with four R&D centers located in Gothenburg, Hangzhou, Ningbo, and Coventry, the company has assembled a team of multicultural professional designers to develop new and exciting vehicles, who have been working from all over the world in four key studios based in Shanghai, Gothenburg, Barcelona, and California, turning innovative concepts into reality for Geely.

During a press conference ahead of the 13th Beijing Auto Show in 2014, Geely unveiled its new brand strategy by overhauling its multiple brands to focus on a single Geely brand: "The 'One Geely' brand is founded on the strategy of 'platformisation' and 'universalisation,' which places three platforms under one unified brand. We believe the new approach to the Geely brand will enhance its value, while facilitating more coordinated growth across the markets in which we operate with economies of scale that maximize the efficiency of our R&D function. Our overriding goal is to provide customers with the safest, most environmentally-friendly, and most energy-efficient products possible" (Geely Global Media, 2014). In addition to its commitment to one Geely brand, the company has made new energy vehicles a central pillar of its long-term growth strategy, and such an ambitious determination was on display through its *Emgrand* Cross PHEV concept vehicle designed to meet and lead consumer demands. Shortly after, at the 2016 Beijing Auto Show, Geely unveiled its new product range that marked the arrival of the company's third generation of vehicles, which includes Geely GC9, *Boyue* SUV, and the brand-new *Emgrand* GS SUV (Geely Global Media, 2016).

As a globally focused car brand, Lynk & Co is an excellent case study on Geely's motivation for new brand development. Founded in 2016 based on jointly developed technology by Geely Auto and Volvo Cars, Lynk & Co is a Chinese–Swedish automobile brand owned by Geely Group. Built on the Compact Modular Architecture (CMA) platform developed by CEVT, all Lynk models are positioned between those of the Geely brand and Swedish brand Volvo, and the focus of the new brand is on Internet connectivity and innovative purchasing models in certain markets, targeting the young professional demographic (De Feijter, 2016). Ever since the *Refined Vehicle* Era began in 2014, Geely has made special efforts in the development of the ICT vehicles and has recently begun to reap benefits of its investments in technologies. The introduction of the

GKUI technology powered by ECARX has received rave reviews from international consumers, and its new smart ecosystem has moved Geely to the forefront of automotive technology advancement both in China and globally (*China Automotive News,* 2019). Still, given the company's recent brand strategy, is the creation of Lynk & Co an indication of firm's reduced confidence in its own "Geely" brand, or does the firm simply try to target a higher market positioning? Only time will tell if this new approach will be successful.

First launched in 2015, *Cao Cao* is another brand initiative by Geely for car mobility solution. Cao Cao was a powerful warlord and a central historical figure of the Three Kingdoms period, whose name is often associated with the Chinese adage "Talk of the devil and he comes." Designed for urban residents with busy lifestyles, *Cao Cao* is the first domestic, new-energy-focused mobility service that brings together world-class digital connectivity, Internet of Vehicles, autonomous driving, and new-energy technologies into the field of shared mobility. With the mission of "making every encounter satisfying," it offers ride-hailing with its own dedicated fleet of vehicles and taxis, car rental, concierge, and other services. Utilizing carbon credits, *Cao Cao* is the first low-carbon mobility brand in China to use new-energy vehicles and offer carbon banking for individual and corporate users. It is currently available in more than 50 cities and has been ranked first in user activity among B2C platforms in Hangzhou, Qingdao, Ningbo, Chengdu, Tianjin, Taiyuan, and other cities (Geely, 2020). With more than 4.75 million monthly active users who collectively request over 1.65 million vehicles per day, *Cao Cao* has emerged as the country's leading provider of new mobility services (*Automotive World*, 2019).

In brand development, Geely has determined that the new energy vehicles will be the main driving force of the future automotive industry and endeavored to develop such models in its product lineups. Its *Geometry* A is such a noteworthy undertaking. Designed for the Chinese market, it is reported that the new EV has set its sights on Tesla Model 3 (Duff, 2019). *Polestar* is another striking example. Headquartered in Gothenburg, Sweden, with production taking place in Chengdu, China, *Polestar* is a brand jointly owned by Volvo and Geely, which is named after the Polestar racing team in the Scandinavia Touring Car Championship. As an electric performance car brand, *Polestar* has become the first luxury EV jointed developed by Chinese and international auto manufacturers. Based on the same belief, Geely has also pushed out its LEVC brand in UK. After taking the ownership of London Taxi, Geely has converted the iconic black cabs into electric vehicles that are powered by a full-electric hybrid drivetrain, and LEVC TX has since become the only taxi with zero emissions in London; beginning in 2020, the electric taxi is also available in Japan (Wang, 2019; *China Daily*, 2020). In addition, under Geely's ownership, the British luxury sport car brand Lotus also roared back to life. In 2019, Lotus unveiled its first electric hypercar *Evija*, which is scheduled for production in 2020 of only 130 units and cost around US$2 million with ultrafast charging capability and almost 2,000 horsepower (Moldrich, 2019). Moreover, Geely's new partnership with Daimler also deserves special attention. In 2018, Geely has invested in a 9.7% stake in Daimler and set up a ride-hailing venture in China with the German automaker. Since the *smart* (Swatch Mercedes ART) *Mini* has been losing money for years, Geely has formed a partnership with Daimler to revive the hip brand. The company has received regulatory approval for a China-based JV to make a new generation of electric *smart* vehicles designed by Mercedes, with global sales due to begin in 2022 (Sun and Goh, 2020).

In his "Letter from Chairman," Li Shufu described his vision for Geely brands: "Geely is Geely, Volvo is Volvo, Lotus is Lotus, LEVC is LEVC, Proton is Proton, Polestar is Polestar, Yuan Cheng is Yuan Cheng. Each brand has their own place, with their own brand position, actively participating in the market, and striving to grow their market share" (Li, 2019). Guided by this belief, Geely has recently formulated its design philosophy: *as a Chinese brand competing on the global auto market — Geely does not make global cars but takes Chinese cars global.* Accordingly, the following overarching principles have been established for the future development of Geely Auto brands: *Approachable*: Geely Auto is an independent and authentic Chinese brand that is able to succeed globally; *Bright*: Geely is at the forefront of the Chinese entrepreneurial mindset, optimistic about the future and has the will to succeed; *Stunning*: Geely Auto benchmarks against global designs with refinements that show a hint of its origin; and *Surprising*: the latest technology should not be associated with the price tag, but should be accessible to all and integrated seamlessly into the user's experience (Geely Auto, 2019).

The rise of the Geely brand has been recognized internationally. According to Brand Finance (2019), a leading independent brand valuation and strategy consultancy in the world, Geely Auto is ranked among the top 20 most valuable global auto brands and the highest among the

Chinese auto brands. Its strong growth came on the strength of the brand's third-generation models; more specifically, Geely's *Boyue* and *Emgrand* EC7 are among the top 20 best-selling brands in China (Focus2Move, 2019). Looking forward, An Conghui recently pronounced with confidence: "Our vision for the future is not just to be China's leading brand, but to become the most competitive and respected Chinese auto brand in the world" (Geely Auto, 2020).

12.6. Conclusion

Recognized as an important notion in modern business management, corporate culture encompasses the values, customs, traditions, and meanings that make a company unique. As Geely switches track from high-speed expansion to high-quality development, its vision, mission, and cultural values also evolve along the way. From very early on, Geely's founder Li Shufu has played an active role in shaping its corporate culture. After the company significantly expands its global footprint, its central beliefs have also been greatly enhanced in recent years. From *making affordable cars for ordinary people* in China to *making the safest, most environment-friendly and most energy-efficient vehicles*, Geely's trajectory reflects the growth of the Chinese automobile maker capable competing on the global stage. Notwithstanding the evolving visions and missions, what remain consistent are Geely's commitment to innovation and its organizational agility and adoptability when facing tough challenges. These core cultural values have ensured the initial survival of the Geely Auto and will likely have a continual positive impact on its sustained growth and transformation from a traditional automaker to a mobility technology enterprise and service provider in the global landscape.

Geely's branding progress can be summarized into three stages, with Phase One covering the first decade of its development (1997–2007) that concentrated on the low-cost production of affordable models. In Phase Two, after its strategic transformation in 2007, Geely adopted a multiple-brand strategy to compete on different sectors of the automobile market. After its acquisition of Volvo and influenced by the Swedish carmaker's steadfast commitment to safety technology, Geely revised its corporate mission in 2014 and adopted the "One Geely" strategy in brand management. With its brand mission of *making refined cars for everyone*, Geely has risen to become China's leading privately owned automobile brand. However, the company still has a very complex branding portfolio, and most of its models hold low-tiered brand positions in the auto market, which will likely slow down the globalization of Geely's brand. Based on our observation and analysis, despite its impressive accomplishment as an independent auto brand in China, there is still a long way to go for Geely to become a widely recognized international brand. Nonetheless, the company is certainly moving in the right direction, and the Chinese auto brand's future seems fairly promising. Through its proposed merger with Volvo, Geely may well become China's first global carmaker in the 21st century (Wong, 2020).

References

Aaker, D. A. (1991). *Managing Brand Equity: Capitalizing on the Value of a Brand Name*. New York: The Free Press.

Automotive World (2019). Cao Cao leads Chinese growth in ride-hailing active users. November 7. Available at: https://www.automotiveworld.com/news-releases/cao-cao-leads-chinese-growth-in-ride-hailing-active-users/ (accessed March 17, 2020).

Brand Finance (2019). *Automotive Industry 2019: The Annual Report on the World's Most Valuable Automobile, Tire, Auto Component & Car Rental Services Brands*. March. Available at: https://brandfinance.com/images/upload/automotive_industry_free.pdf (accessed March 21, 2020).

Calkins, T. (2005). Brand Portfolio Strategy. In A. M. Tybout and T. Calkins (eds.) *Kellogg on Branding: The Marketing Faculty of The Kellogg School of Management*. Hoboken, NJ: John Wiley & Sons, 104–127.

China Automotive News (2019). Geely launches GKUI 19 in-car intelligent system powered by first Geely-made SoC." June 4. Available at: http://autonews.gasgoo.com/china_news/70016119.html (accessed March 17, 2020).

China Auto Web (2010). Geely releases all-ew Englon SC5-RV subcompact. November 26.

China Car Times (2010). Englon brand to get major boost in 2011. November 29.

China Daily (2020). China's Geely makes inroads into Japanese electric taxi market. January 11. Available at: https://www.chinadaily.com.cn/a/202001/11/WS5e198148a310cf3e35583ec2.html (accessed March 17, 2020).

Coleman, J. (2013). Six components of a great corporate culture." *Harvard Business Review*, May. Available at: https://www.chinadaily.com.cn/a/202001/11/WS5e198148a310cf3e35583ec2.html (accessed June 28, 2020).

De Feijter, T. (2016). Volvo And China's Geely collaborate on 'connected' car brand, Lynk & Co. *Forbes*, October 20. Available at: https://www.forbes.

com/sites/tychodefeijter/2016/10/20/volvo-and-chinas-geely-collaborate-on-connected-car-brand-lynk-co/?sh=243441b662f4 (accessed March 17, 2020).

Deal, T. E. and A. A. Kennedy (1982). *Corporate Cultures: The Rites and Rituals of Corporate Life.* Harmondsworth, Penguin Books.

Duff, M. (2019). How does the Geely Geometry A measure up to the Tesla Model 3? April 23. *Car & Driver.* Available at: https://www.caranddriver.com/news/a27206051/geely-geometry-a-vs-tesla-model-3/ (accessed March 17, 2020).

Edge Financial Daily (2014). Volvo billionaire owner revamps China's Geely brand. December 18. Available at: https://www.theedgemarkets.com/article/volvo-billionaire-owner-revamps-china%E2%80%99s-geely-brand (accessed September 14, 2019).

Fairclough, G. (2006). Bumper crop: As barriers fall in auto business, China jumps in; Geely aims to be world player, but quality woes linger; cars a new commodity? 'Copycat' accusations fly. *The Wall Street Journal,* November 7, A1.

Flannery, R. (2014). Life after Ford: Volvo turnaround gains speed under Chinese billionaire owner. *Forbes Asia,* November. Available at: https://www.forbes.com/sites/russellflannery/2014/10/27/geely-in-swedish/#18fb61b3999d (accessed September 15, 2019).

Flamholtz, E. and Y. Randle (2011). *Corporate Culture: The Ultimate Strategic Asset.* Stanford, California: Stanford University Press.

Flamholtz, E. and Y. Randle (2014). Implications of Organizational Life Cycles for Corporate Culture and Climate. In B. Schneider and K. M. Barbera (eds.). *The Oxford Handbook of Organizational Climate and Culture.* Oxford: Oxford University Press, 235–256.

Focus2Move (2019). China: The Bestselling Car Models in 2019. Available at: https://focus2move.com/best-selling-cars-models-in-china/ (accessed March 19, 2020).

Geely (2020). Our brands: Cao Cao. Available at: http://global.geely.com/2018/03/13/geely-auto-among-top-20-most-valuable-global-auto-brands/ (accessed March 17, 2020).

Geely Auto (2018). Geely Auto among top 20 most valuable global auto brands. March 18, 2018. Available at: http://global.geely.com/2018/03/13/geely-auto-among-top-20-most-valuable-global-auto-brands/ (accessed March 19, 2020).

Geely Auto (2019). Geely Auto Design Philosophy. Available at: http://global.geely.com/design-philosophy/ (accessed September 14, 2019).

Geely Auto (2020). Our Vision. Available at: http://global.geely.com/our-vision/ (accessed March 21, 2020).

Geely Media Center (2009). Geely Emgrand Brand to Build New Image of Automobile in China. July 28. Available at: https://web.archive.org/web/20110810055449/http://www.geely.com/Brands/international/news/international_news/29224.html (accessed March 19, 2020).

Geely Global Media Center (2014). Geely Auto unveils new brand strategy ahead of Beijing Auto Show 2014. April 18. Available at: http://global.geely.com/media-center/news/geely-auto-unveils-new-brand-strategy-ahead-of-beijing-auto-show-2014/ (accessed March 19, 2020).

Geely Global Media Center (2016). Geely Auto enters into 'refined vehicle era' with all new product range. April 25. Available at: http://global.geely.com/media-center/news/geely-auto-enters-into-refined-vehicle-era-with-all-new-product-range/ (accessed March 19, 2020).

Geely Global Media Center (2018). The forty year journey. December 19. Available at: http://global.geely.com/media-center/story/the-forty-year-journey/ (accessed March 19, 2020).

Geely Holding Group Corporate Social Responsibility Report (2019). Available at: http://zgh.com/social-responsibility-report/?lang=en (accessed June 22, 2020).

Geely Media Center (2020a). About social innovation. Available at: http://zgh.com/about-social-innovation/?lang=en (accessed June 28, 2020).

Geely Media Center (2020b). Geely Culture. Available at: http://zgh.com/geely-culture/?lang=en (accessed June 22, 2020).

Geely Media Center (2020c). Geely Corporate Social Responsibility. Available at: http://zgh.com/corporate-social-responsibility/?lang=en (accessed June 22, 2020).

Geely Media Center (2020d). Geely Social Welfare. Available at: http://zgh.com/geely-social-welfare/?lang=en (accessed June 22, 2020).

Geely Media Center (2020e). Sustainability. Available at: http://zgh.com/sustainability/?lang=en (accessed June 22, 2020).

Jaques, E. (1951). *The Changing Culture of a Factory*. London: Tavistock Publications.

Kotter, J. P. and J. L. Heskett (1992). *Corporate Culture and Performance*. New York: The Free Press.

Li, F. (2018). Geely to ramp up digitalization, new energy efforts. *China Daily*, March 21. Available at: http://www.chinadaily.com.cn/a/201803/21/WS5ab19e3ba3106e7dcc143fbb.html (September 14, 2019).

Li, S. (2014). Global corporate culture will guide the joint development of Geely and Volvo. *Global Times*, April 21, 2014. Available at: http://www.globaltimes.cn/content/855820.shtml (accessed June 22, 2020).

Li, S. (2019). Letter from Chairman: How we find room to grow in a changing world. Available at: https://utahmotorsportscampus.com/news/how-we-find-room-to-grow-in-a-changing-world-new-year-message-from-chairman-li-shufu/ (accessed March 17, 2020).

McGregor, R. (2002). Geely gears up China's first home-grown car. *Financial Times*, April 2, p. 24.

Manthey, N. (2018). Geely presents wide-ranging electric vehicle strategy. *Electrive*, May 30. Available at: https://www.electrive.com/2018/05/30/geely-presents-wide-ranging-electric-vehicle-strategy/ (accessed September 14, 2019).

Moldrich, C. (2019). Lotus Evija electric hypercar: What it's like at the limit. *Car Magazine*, December 17. Available at: https://www.carmagazine.co.uk/car-news/first-official-pictures/lotus/evija-electric-hypercar/ (accessed December 29, 2019).

Morgan, N. A. and L. L. Rego (2009). Brand portfolio strategy and firm performance. *Journal of Marketing*, **73**:1, 59–74.

People.com.cn (2012). Li Shufu. Available at: http://auto.people.com.cn/GB/239017/239575/index.html (accessed September 15, 2019).

Roberts, C. J. and G. M. McDonald (1989). Alternative naming strategies: Family versus individual brand names. *Management Decision*, **27**:6, 31–37.

Saruta, M. (2006). Toyota production systems: The 'Toyota Way' and labour-management relations. Asian *Business & Management*, **5**:4(December), 487–506. DOI:10.1057/palgrave.abm.9200198.

Schein, E. (1992). *Organizational Culture and Leadership: A Dynamic View*. San Francisco, CA: Jossey-Bass.

Shen, S. and N. Shirouzu (2014). China's Geely to consolidate branding, sales. *Reuters*, April 14. Available at: https://www.reuters.com/article/idUSL3N0N61EP20140418 (accessed September 14, 2019).

Sun, Y. and B. Goh (2020). Geely, Mercedes launch China JV to build smart EVs. *Automotive News*, January 8. Available at: https://www.autonews.com/automakers-suppliers/geely-mercedes-launch-china-jv-build-smart-evs (accessed March 19, 2020).

Wang, M. (2019). Chinese company celebrates making its 3,000th electric black cab. *China Daily*, October 25. Available at: https://www.chinadaily.com.cn/a/201910/25/WS5db2b36ca310cf3e35573aec.html (accessed March 19, 2020).

Wong, J. (2020). China's first global car maker is in the works. *The Wall Street Journal*, February 11. Available at: https://www.chinadaily.com.cn/a/201910/25/WS5db2b36ca310cf3e35573aec.html (accessed March 21, 2020).

Wu, Y. (2018). *Li Shufu's Secrete Code for Automobiles: Geely's Acquisition of PROTON and Lotus Cars*. Beijing: People's Press, p. 277 (in Chinese).

Yakob, R., H. R. Nakamura and P. Ström (2018). Chinese foreign acquisitions aimed for strategic asset-creation and innovation upgrading: The case of Geely and Volvo Cars. *Technovation*, **70/71**, 59–72.

Chapter 13

Toward Mobility Solutions: Business Model Innovation for the Future

Abstract

This chapter analyzes Geely's business model innovation and its ambitious expansion toward Mobility as a Service (MaaS) and reviews Geely's four categories of mobility services — low-speed EVs (*Microcity*), economic EVs (*EVcoming*), mid-range cars (*Cao Cao*), and premium cars (*StarRides* with Daimler). They also examine two incremental innovations by Geely, the connection between high-speed train and ride-hailing services, and the launch of low-orbit satellites for the service of high-precision positioning, as well as two radical innovation initiatives, the ultrasonic train and flying cars. The chapter concludes with the analysis of Geely Group's organizational structure that supports business model innovation, while questioning the necessity of rationalization and optimization.

Keywords: Geely Auto; business model innovation; MaaS; mobility service; organizational structure.

13.1. Introduction

This chapter first illustrates Geely's expansion from carmaker to car mobility services provider, further extending into two major categories: ride-hailing and car-sharing business. The ride-hailing business is mainly driven by *Cao Cao*, followed by the new joint venture *StarRides* with Daimler. The car-sharing business is operated by two companies *Microcity* and *EVcoming*. *Cao Cao* has become one of the key players in the Business-to-Consumer (B2C) ride-hailing business segment in China in about four years. We can also observe Geely's initiatives in two incremental and two radical innovations in the field of mobility service. Two incremental innovations include the joint venture for the connection between a high-speed train and ride-hailing services and the launch of low-orbit satellites for the service of high-precision positioning. The radical mobility service innovations include building ultrasonic trains and two flying cars by acquiring American and German start-up companies.

Based on the above observations, we further analyze four layers of business model innovation (BMI) by Geely and its logic of creating a big business cluster of Mobility as a Service (MaaS) in the coming years. This chapter ends with the analysis of the Geely Group's organization that supports the BMI.

13.2. Understanding BMI

The term "business model" has assumed increasing importance in management theory. While Magretta (2002) states that the concept existed already in the 1890s, Morris *et al.* (2005) and Osterwalder *et al.* (2005) trace it back to the mid-1990s, during the so-called "dotcom bubble" period. Therefore, the definition of the term "business model" varies (Zott *et al.*, 2011; Magretta, 2002; Osterwalder *et al.*, 2005; Teece, 2010), while the core converges toward the company's capacity on value creation and value capture at the same time (Chesbrough, 2007). A business model can be described as how a firm "delivers value to customers, entices its customers to pay for value, and converts those payments to profit" (Teece, 2010, p. 172).

The business model per se needs innovation. The reason is explained by Teece: "…in practice, successful business models very often become, to some degree, 'shared' by multiple competitors" (Teece, 2010, p. 179). There are both external factors (institution environment, the market change, etc.) and internal factors (internal capabilities, competitive strategy, organizational culture, and structure) acting as forces of innovation (Bucherer *et al.*, 2012; Morris *et al.*, 2005).

BMI has been popularized by Mitchell and Coles (2003, 2004). "Disruptive technologies" (Bower and Christensen, 1995) and "disruptive innovations" (Christensen, 1997) are two important notions of BMI.

Disruptive technology is a novel technology that is perceived as irrelevant by mainstream competitors that can only satisfy the needs of a niche market. However, this technology later has the potential to become the new mainstream when the sales of related products take off, as incumbent firms fail to catch up and lose the position as market leaders. Christensen also broadens the idea from technologies to general innovations. He notes that: "Generally, disruptive innovations were technologically straightforward, consisting of off-the-shelf components put together in a product architecture that was often simpler than prior approaches ... They offered a different package of attributes valued only in emerging markets remote from, and unimportant to, the mainstream" (Christensen, 1997, p. 15).

Compared to the disruptive technological innovation that is clear cut in terms of technology paradigm, a new business model can be incremental innovation to the previous one, as it "...enlarges the existing economic pie ... business model innovators do not discover new products or services; they simply redefine what an existing product or service is and how it is provided to the customer" (Markides, 2006, p. 20). Thus, the mechanism on higher value creation is the key to BMI.

13.3. Ride-Hailing Business of Geely

13.3.1. *Ride-hailing business in China*

China is the biggest ride-hailing market, valued at US$30 billion, two times greater than the second-largest market, the US, which stands at US$12 billion (Pham, 2018). According to the global consulting firm Bain & Company, the market might more than double in size by 2021, as any large Chinese city is equal to a small country when it comes to ride-hailing (Tsang *et al.*, 2019).

After nine years of competition and consolidation, the Consumer-to-Consumer (C2C) ride-hailing market was featured as a monopolistic market in 2019. *DiDi Chuxing* accounted for 90% of trips. Uber tried to penetrate the China market but decided to quit the fierce competition in mid-2016, selling its operations to *DiDi* and acquiring an 18% stake of *DiDi*.

However, the monopolistic structure of the C2C ride-hailing business is experiencing dynamic evolution, driven by several forces. First, competitors keep on rushing into the market. *Meituan Dianping*, a Chinese Online-to-offline (O2O) e-commerce company, based on its 320 million active users, expanded its services from bike-sharing, food delivery, movie tickets, and flights to ride-hailing services in 2018 and become the second-largest player. The industry is also subjected to higher regulations on passenger safety and driver qualification. It was triggered by the rape and murder of two passengers by *DiDi*'s drivers in 2018. Right after, local authorities began imposing tighter operating-license regulations. More than 200 Chinese cities issued new regulations on platforms, vehicles, and drivers, regulating everything from insurance to drivers' health (Tsang *et al.*, 2019).

Business-to-Consumer (B2C) ride-hailing is the main business approach taken by traditional Chinese carmakers as the driver of business model transformation and strategic move. In 2018, several significant initiatives were made by key players in the industry.

Ford and Zotye's 50-50 joint venture (JV) on mobility solutions with registered capital of US$20 million announced the signing of their MOU in May 2018. A range of affordable all-electric vehicles under a new indigenous brand is expected to be produced and served as the Zhejiang Province's fleet, where the JV is located. (Ford Media Center, 2018).

The Great Wall Motor (GWM), a Chinese leader in the SUV segment, announced its launch of mobility brand *OLA Sharing* in August 2018 with an initial investment of RMB 1 billion (US$149 million), by covering time leasing, ride-hailing cars, and long-term/short-term renting. In the first phase, services will be based in Beijing, Tianjin, Hebei Province, and Xiongan New Area. In the mid-term, the company plans to deploy 200 cities in China by offering a model scale of 200,000 units.

SAIC launched *Xiangdao Chuxing* in December 2018. In the early stage, the business was a car-renting JV with Avis Budget Group in 2002. After full acquisition by SAIC, the company was renamed Anji Car Leasing company. *Xiangdao Chuxing* is the affiliated company of Anji.

BMW Group, the first foreign company, obtaining a ride-hailing license in China, announced its premium mobility brand *ReachNow* in Chengdu — the capital of China's Sichuan Province, in December 2018. The initial operation employs 200 BMW 5 series, with half of them being plug-in hybrid vehicles. This extension of its global mobility service is in line with its strategy.

In December 2018, three Chinese automobile giants, FAW Group, China South Industries Group Corporation (parent company of Changan Automobile), and Dongfeng Motor Corporation, established a JV mobility company named T3, together with Internet giants Tencent and Alibaba, among the others, with a total subscribed capital of RMB9.76 billion (US$1.46 billion). The objective is to develop the next-generation vehicle core systems, modules, and platforms with new energy and intelligent connectivity.

Guangzhou Automobile Group (GAC), Tencent, Guangzhou Public Transport Group, and other investors created a JV on mobility service in June 2019. The total investment was valued at RMB 1 billion (US$150 million). As the most prominent investors, GAC and Tencent own 35% and 25% of the shares, respectively. Cars are sourced from the GAC group, including GAC Toyota's vehicles. The service will first focus on Guangzhou, then expand to the Guangdong–Hong Kong–Macao Greater Bay Area and nationwide (Qiu, 2019).

Facing the quick evolution of the B2C ride-hailing business in China, traditional car renting companies, in partnership with global players, have accelerated their expansion.

Shouqi Limousine & Chauffeur is one of China's leading ride services and rental car companies. The company is part of the state-owned Beijing Shouqi Group, and investors include the Internet giant Baidu. It operates in 59 Chinese cities with 32 million registered customers, served by over 800,000 vehicles at the end of 2019 (Shouqi Limousine, 2020). The partnership with Blacklane in May 2018 allows the company to offer one-stop international transportation solutions in 6 continents, 130 countries, and a total of 1,500 cities around the world. In July, Shouqi raised US$88 million in Series B funding.

Car Inc., established in 2007, is the largest traditional car rental company in China. In 2013, the Hertz Corporate acquired a stake of around 20% and then operated at a co-branded model at Car Inc.'s rental locations, while keeping Hertz's brand and business network independent in China. With over 110 service points in over 300 cities in China and over 100,000 cars owned by the company, expanding the ride-hailing business is a natural strategic move. This new business line is still at the stage of quick expansion (Table 13.1).

In the B2C ride-hailing business segment, *Cao Cao* has become one of the key actors of oligopoly. According to the industry research company Aurora Mobile (NASDAQ: JG), in the third quarter of 2019, *Cao Cao*'s monthly active users (MAU) was 4.75 million, far higher than the next two followers: *Shouqi* with 2.69 million and *DiDi Chuxing* with 2.21 million (Table 13.2). *Cao Cao* also has the leadership with regard to daily active users (DAU), as its average of 780,700 daily active users is

Table 13.1.   Competitors of ride-hailing business in China.

Category of firms	Number of companies	Company names
C2C segment: Duopolists	2	*DiDi* *Meituan*
B2C segment: Top 3	3	*Shouqi* *CAR* Inc. *Cao Cao*
Followers	10+	SAIC: *Xiangdao* FAW, Chang'an, Dongfeng, and others: *T3* GAC, Tencent, *DiDi*, and others: *Ontime* *BMW*

Source: http://www.autoinfo.org.cn/autoinfo_cn/content/news/20190911/1839302.html.

Table 13.2.   Top 3 B2C ride-hailing business companies in China.

MAU			
	Cao Cao	*Shouqi*	*DiDi*
2018Q4	399.1	392	232.8
2019Q1	356.8	321.2	211
2019Q2	405.4	227.8	196.6
2019Q3	475.6	269.9	221.7
DAU			
	Cao Cao	*Shouqi*	*DiDi*
2018Q4	61.7	62.5	25.7
2019Q1	57.4	46.5	22.5
2019Q2	68.1	30.2	21.5
2019Q3	78.7	27.6	23.2

Source: http://talk.cri.cn/n/20191108/8b59261e-d5dd-5db1-9604-d47da348ceff.html.

significantly higher than *Shouqi* with 276,000 and *DiDi Chuxing* with 232,000 daily active users, respectively. However, behind this leadership position of *Cao Cao*, there is a need for caution and further analysis. This study of Aurora Mobile is based on the statistics of the app, excluding other ways of car reservation. The *Cao Cao* fleet size is much smaller than the two other competitors, while the advantage of *Cao Cao* is the development of a booking system almost exclusively based on the app.

13.3.2. *Ride-hailing business: Cao Cao by Geely and StarRides with Daimler*

In 2015, the Geely Group expanded to mobility services by launching a ride-hailing business branded *Cao Cao*. The mission is to make "every encounter satisfying." The company *Cao Cao Zhuanche* was created with an initial registered capital of 1.2 billion RMB (US$179 million). The company obtained the license for ride-hailing services in 71 cities across China. In February 2019, the company was rebranded as *Cao Cao* Mobility (hereinafter *Cao Cao*).

By 2020, *Cao Cao* expanded to over 50 cities in China, including Hangzhou, Beijing, Shanghai, Guangzhou, and Shenzhen. The electric vehicles (EVs) deployed expanded from 32,000 units to over 42,000 from 2018 to 2019, serving a cumulative 31 million registered users across China. This fleet size is still much smaller than two competitors, Shouqi and Car Inc. According to the data of *Cao Cao*, the daily requests from customers were 630,000, and 540,000 rides being completed, indicating demand outpaces actual supply. In 2019, the company raised RMB 1 billion (US$156 million) funds for its Series A round, with an estimated valuation of over RMB 10 billion (US$1.6 billion) (*Automotive World*, 2019).

Starting from the very beginning, Geely takes an integral approach to operation. There are at least three integrations being observed: the use of its cars, the employment of drivers (different to the Uber or Lyft), and the development of in-house software and application. This business model approach, with massive investment, ensures the consistent quality of product and service, and thus increases the level of satisfaction of customers, an essential point of differentiation.

In the early stage, Geely's EV *Emgrand* was the first and the primary car model being used as the fleet. In 2019, the vehicle types further expanded to more than 20 models under the Geely brand, including sedans, crossovers, and multi-purpose vehicles. In the same year, the London taxi car model was deployed in Paris, France, the first overseas *Cao Cao* market.

The selection of drivers goes through a higher-level quality control process. Registered drivers need at least three years of driving experience and undergo stringent criminal record and health checks. Qualified drivers will then participate in the training at *Cao Cao* College. The training content is based on the London taxi driver test's certification system to ensure a higher level of professionalism, service quality, and security of passengers. Drivers also need to maintain a quality assessment through the *Cao Cao* service platform.

The creation of Geely's operation system of ride-hailing is another crucial asset. The company employed hundreds of IT and engineers for the software and hardware development. In less than four years, the mobile-phone–based application upgraded to the 4.0 version, expanding from the pure mobility service to the recommendation of location-based services (food and entertainment). This new feature, dubbed *Cao Cao Zoubei* (Hangzhou), was initiated in Hangzhou city first. This new version is in the early stage of creating a user network by allowing users to follow each other on the application and comment on services.

Paris is the first step of *Cao Cao*'s globalization strategy. Market potential and environmental protection concerns are the two main driving forces for *Cao Cao*'s expansion to Paris, France. The market value of ride-hailing service in France is expected to reach US$2.95 billion by 2023, with double-digit growth in recent years, according to market research firm Statista (Zhang, 2020). French consumers consider air pollution as the most prominent issue of mobility, according to the survey by the French General Commission on Sustainable Development (CGDD). In January 2020, the *Cao Cao* service was launched in Paris. The zero-emission electric London Taxi, produced by Geely subsidiary London Electric Vehicle Company (LEVC), began offering services in Paris. More details about LEVC can be found in Chapter 9 of this book. Unlike the Uber service in Paris, drivers of *Cao Cao* have a high level of selectivity and require the French license for chauffeur-driven cars, known as VTC, or *Voiture de Tourisme avec Chauffeur*. The chauffeur also undergoes additional training on security and etiquette.

The premium ride-hailing business, *StarRides*, is a 50-50 joint venture between Daimler Mobility Services and Geely Technology Group, offering high-end mobility services in select cities in China. The MOU of the cooperation was signed in October 2018, and the JV was established in May 2019, with a registered capital of RMB1.7 billion (US$254 million). In December 2019, the service was officially launched in Hangzhou city.

The premium ride-hailing service branded as *StarRides* (*Yao Chuxing* in Chinese) launched its inaugural services in Hangzhou, a city with a population of more than 10 million. The service team initially consisted of 100 vehicles, including Mercedes-Benz S-class, E-class, and V-class models. According to the plan, the service will expand to other big cities in China, starting in 2020. The car type will also further expand to Geely's other car brands — premium brands like Volvo, Polestar, and Lotus may become the choice.

According to Joerg Lamparter, board member Daimler Mobility AG for Digital & Mobility Solutions: "Premium ride-hailing is an essential element in our mobility ecosystem ranging from multi-year financing contracts to flexible leasing, car rental and subscription models to on-demand mobility. With the Geely Technology Group, we have found an excellent partner to expand our mobility ecosystem in China. *StarRides* will play a significant role in addressing customer needs in the premium ride-hailing segment and solidifying our strong position in the mobility market" (Daimler, 2019).

13.4. Car-Sharing Business: *Microcity* and *EVcoming* by Geely

There are mainly two types of car-sharing business. One is the *point-to-point* car-sharing system and another one is the *free-floating* car-sharing system. The point-to-point car-sharing business is the primary business model of traditional car rental companies like Hertz and Europcar. Users can book a car, pick it up from the company's designated parking space, and pay by the hour, day, month, or even year. After usage, users need to drive back to the parking space designated by the rental company. The free-floating car-sharing system, like Car2Go and *Zipcar*, provides higher flexibility to consumers because users can find the car of their choice (quite often by the nearest distance), and then book and unlock a car via the smartphone app. After the usage, there is the freedom to park the car inside any operating area. There are no obligations to park back to the pick-up point. The payment proceeds via the app as well.

According to our observation, there are at least two point-to-point car-sharing businesses at Geely. One is *Microcity*, started in 2013 by using only A00 type pure EVs, and the other is *EVcoming*, which started its operation from 2018 by using EVs and hybrid cars.

13.4.1. *Microcity*

Hangzhou Microcity Network Technology Co., Ltd. (hereinafter *Microcity*) was jointly established in 2013 by Zhejiang Geely Holding Group Co., Ltd. and Kandi Technology Group Company (hereinafter *Kandi*), of which Geely Holding 97.18%. It is one of the first companies using pure EVs to offer car-sharing business in China. The company started its business in Hangzhou. After five years of operation and development, by 2018, *Microcity* extended its business to nearly 30 cities with more than 42,000 EVs, and over 20,000 cars are in Hangzhou.

Because it is a JV with Kandi, *Microcity*'s primary car model is the Kandi brand A00 pure EV. This car is manufactured by Kandi Electric Vehicle Group Co., Ltd. The registered capital of the company is RMB 1 billion (US$150 million), a 50-50 JV by Zhejiang Kandi Auto Company, the affiliate of Kandi Technology Group (Nasdaq: KNDI), and Shanghai Maple Guorun Automobile Co., Ltd., the affiliate of Geely Automobile Holdings Limited (Hong Kong stock code: 0175). Most of the Kandi EVs produced were sold to *Microcity*. Therefore, there is a very high level of vertical integration between these two companies.

The cruising range of Kandi EV is 60–80 km, and the maximum speed is 80 km/h. By definition, it is de facto a low-speed electric vehicle (LSEV). The rent fee is competitive, 20 yuan (US$3) per hour for two-seater cars, and 25 yuan per hour for four-seater cars. One-year leasing cost is between 11,000–14,000 yuan (US$1,642–2,090). The short cruising range of this car increases its operating costs.

In April 2020, Geely announced a new brand (or a revitalized brand) named *Maple*. The car is manufactured by Fengsheng Automobile Technology Group, which is the former Kandi Electric Vehicle Group Co., Ltd. Geely, through Geely Technology Group, increased its stake to 78% in this new JV. The remaining 22% of the shares belong to Zhejiang Kandi Automobile Co., Ltd. In January 2020, the mass production off-line ceremony of its first model of *Maple*, 30X, was held in Rugao city, Jiangsu Province, the manufacturing base of the car. The production and sales target of this model in 2020 is 30,000 units. In April, the first online-based pre-sale event was launched.

The 30X is a compact SUV with a 70 kW engine based on the architectural design of Vision X3, at the category of A-, based on the FE platform of Geely, equivalent to Toyota Corolla (for platform positioning, please read Chapter 12 on platform strategy of Geely). The cruising range of a full charge is 306 km, significantly longer than Kandi's previous model. The car's price is competitive on the market, starting from 68,800 yuan after subsidies (US$10,269). The *Maple* is expected to be integrated into the fleet of *Cao Cao* in the future. At the same time, the car is also planned to be sold on the market. The *Maple* has signed the contract of the dealership's intension with more than 190 dealers in 2020, of which 105 dealers have paid a cooperation deposit.

In May 2020, *Microcity* was merged with *EVcoming*, and the brand of *Microcity* disappeared from its official website wgjev.com.

13.4.2. *EVcoming*

Geely further expanded its car-sharing venture into a new business entity, named *EVcoming*, via the acquisition of two Chinese start-up companies in January 2018. One is *My Car City*, which was first founded in 2013. Another company, named Ningbo Xuanyuexing EV Service Co. Ltd., was established in 2015 for the business of EV car service. These two companies reached a strategic merging to form *EVcoming*, and Geely became the major shareholder.

Geely's *Evcoming* belongs to point-to-point car-sharing, with two significant specifications: its exclusive use of the new energy vehicles (EVs or hybrid) and short-term and long-term rental services. More precisely, the car's shortest leasing time starts from week, followed by month, quarter, till the longest three- to five-year leasing.

There are also two key features or categories of customers in China that stimulate this new business model's development. One category is car companies. Despite impressive sales figures, China's new energy car market has a hidden structural problem. According to the President of *EVcoming*, Hu Gang, less than 30% of 2 million new energy vehicles in 2019 were sold to households, the rest were sold to car business platforms (Ke, 2020). The car-sharing business of Geely is a way to help car companies to reduce the stock. Another category of customer is end-users. A portion of Chinese consumers, especially in lower-tiered cities (three, four, and below) have lower purchasing power than those in large cities. The car-renting service provides a much competitive price (compare to car purchasing).

By April 2019, the company's business has expanded from Ningbo city, where the company was registered, to over 60 cities, with 40 directly operated shops and 400 franchised shops. The total number of new-energy cars reached 98,000 units, including cars from competitors like BYD, BAC, Zhidou, Tesla, Hozon Auto, etc. According to the business plan, the number is expected to reach 500,000 in the next five years.

In terms of operation, Hu Gang stated the company was still below the breakeven point by 2019, which can be attributed to three factors. The first primary reason is the low rental rate in the early stage of the business, followed by the app and the distribution system's investment; the third factor is the breakeven point measured by the ratio of 1 operation person for 100 cars. The current business situation is 400 operation people for 50,000 cars, slightly better off. In the future, by increasing the size of the fleet and efficiency, Hu expects to reach a profitable business situation — increasing to a ratio of 1 over 170, which is 700 people for 120,000 cars.

To control the operation costs, the smallest unit of the direct-operated shop have 5 staff, with less than 10,000 RMB (US$1,493) business space rental fee. There is at least one type of shop for each city, in charge of asset management and customer relationship management. The franchised shops in the same city, namely the user's experience shop, are in charge of finding customers and the delivery/reception of cars.

New energy cars' mid-to-long term car-sharing business is a niche market, and consumer behavior deserves more in-depth analysis, including the motivation to rent new energy cars instead of classic cars, daily commute distance, usage, and charging behavior. The linkage between rent and purchase is also an interesting point. According to Hu Gang, around 30% of users purchased the car after three years of renting.

In March 2020, during the most challenging period of COVID-19 in China, *Cao Cao* and *EVcoming* created a strategic partnership by extending the ride-hailing business of *Cao Cao* to the monthly car renting business. In Phase One, over 2,000 cars were on the market in 12 cities, with a monthly rent of 999 RMB (US$149), or daily costs of 33 RMB (US$5). In June, *EVcoming* completed A-round funding valued of RMB 687.7 million (US$103 million). This round of financing will be used for R&D — an improvement on the operating systems technologies to expand cooperation with original equipment manufacturers (OEMs) and channel development (*PE Daily*, 2020).

13.5. Other Incremental and Radical Mobility Service Expansion

13.5.1. *Connection of mobility service to high-speed train in China*

In recent years, Geely has further extended mobility solutions to high-speed train passengers in China. In July 2018, a three-party JV was formed by Geely, Tencent, and state-owned China Railway Corp, with a total investment of 4.3 billion RMB (US$642 million), and respective stakes of 39%, 10%, and 51%. This JV, China Railway Gecent Technology Co., Ltd (CRGT), invests in reinforced Wi-Fi hotspots, and both Tencent and Geely's services will be integrated. Besides, this JV is to offer a platform of value-added service through the high-speed rail network. Currently, the first product, a mobile app, is offering a portfolio of services for the users of *Fuxing* high-speed train lines, including parking services, ride-hailing, Wi-Fi access, mobility services, food delivery, leisure content, cultural content, entertainment, news, information, e-commerce, travel services, smart retail services, etc. High-speed rail is an essential means of transportation in China. In 2017, the number of high-speed railway trips exceeded 1.7 billion. This JV will further boost the customer base of *Cao Cao* (He and Li, 2018).

13.5.2. *Low-orbit satellites to provide high-precision positioning services — Geespace*

Geespace (Zhejiang Shikong Daoyu Technology Co. Ltd.) was founded in November 2018, with total registered capital of 500 million RMB (US$75 million). In March 2020, the company announced an investment of 2.27 billion yuan (US$326 million) for a low-orbit satellite manufacturing plant located in Taizhou, where it has car plants. According to the plan, Geely aims to produce 500 satellites a year by around 2025.

The satellite project is part of the new mobility strategy of Geely. The future satellite network would offer high-speed Internet connectivity, precise navigation, and cloud computing capabilities to cars with autonomous driving technology. This technology will benefit Geely's car users and its mobility solutions, including fleet management optimization on ride-hailing, car-sharing management, and future autonomous driving.

For future broader commercialization, the company plans to create a platform named *OmniCloud* by integrating satellite AI data and industrial Internet data. Other car companies and industrial companies can become future clients. According to the Geely Group, the cloud platform can support remote monitoring, control, and maintenance of manufacturing equipment, uncrewed drone flights, and urban management.

13.5.3. *The "supersonic" train initiative — Partnership with China Aerospace Science and Industry Corp*

The "supersonic" train, a radical mobility solution, was launched by Geely in partnership with state-owned China Aerospace Science and Industry Corp. (CASIC), with an agreement of partnership signed in November 2018. This technology was essentially developed by CASIC, based on magnetic levitation (Maglev) technologies and sealed quasi-vacuum tubes. It is close to the Hyperloop concept of Elon Musk, founder of Tesla. The current technology is capable of accelerating trains to 1,000 km/h (620 mph). Geely will contribute expertise in intelligent manufacturing and commercial operations, and CASIC will bring its know-how on core technology, industrial Internet, and smart supply chain (*Global Railway Review*, 2018).

13.5.4. *Flying car — Acquisition of Terrafugia from the US*

An urban air mobility vehicle is another radical mobility solution that Geely has invested in. Terrafugia, a US start-up company, founded in 2006 by five MIT graduates, was fully acquired by Geely in November 2017 with no disclosed pricing. Terrafugia China was established in Hubei Province in September 2018, aiming at the commercial production of the future flying cars, based on the modular design but for the US market. A sub-scale prototype, named Terrafugia TF-2A, completed its ground-related tests and its first air test in December 2019. According to Geely's official communication, the prototype uses electric power, is constructed mainly from composite materials, has a wingspan of 4.5 meters, a designed maximum take-off weight of 60 kg, and a cruising speed of about 100 km/h. In 2020, Terrafugia merged with the Chinese drone developer AOSSCI to form Aerofugia Technologies.

13.5.5. *Flying car — Investment on Volocopter together with Daimler*

Urban flying vehicles based on purely electrified and vertical take-off and landing (VTOL) technologies have become even appealing for Geely, compared to Terrafugia, which requires distance for taking off. In September 2019, Geely jointly invested with Daimler on the German start-up Volocopter in the Series C round, with a total investment of €50 million (US$55 million). Geely received 10% of the company shares and a board seat. At the same time, a JV between Geely and Volocopter is to be established in China. The objective is to produce and sell Volocopters in China in the coming years.

13.6. Analyzing the BMI of Geely

We can observe several layers of BMI from Geely. In summary, Geely has the ambition to create a big business cluster of MaaS in the coming years.

13.6.1. *Four layers of BMI by Geely*

The first layer is the expansion from vehicle production to the mobility services. It includes two point-to-point car-sharing services: the *Microcity* using low-speed electric vehicles launched in 2013, the *EVcoming* using EV or hybrid cars, founded in 2013. These two businesses try to serve the need of carmakers on the sales of cars. In the early stage of EV development, few consumers dared to purchase this innovative product, primarily because of the concern of cruising distance, the convenience of charging, and the life cycle of the battery. Mobility service companies become the main client of EVs during that period.

The third business in this category is the ride-hailing business of *Cao Cao*. It follows the same logic — while the strategy becomes more proactive, from a scene that more innovations are derived from the business, as indicated below. *Cao Cao*'s app can collect rich data on consumer behavior, including the preference for temperature, car ambience, music, seating comfort, work–life behavior, etc. *Cao Cao* helps the R&D center continuously improve the car product by providing data on battery charging, different kinds of car performance, and default and accident information, based on the car's real-time operation. *Cao Cao* contributes to the enrichment of information for the high-resolution map, including important information for EV cars, and the network of EV charging stations. In short, valuable data collected by Cao Cao provide valuable information for Geely, customers, and service providers of the ecosystem.

The second layer is based on combining two existing mobility services and efforts to build a door-to-door, long-distance mobility total solution. It is the case of a three-party JV CRGT. This JV's innovation further extended from mobility solutions to various services on the trip, including the access to Wi-Fi, food, and infotainment offered during the trip.

The third BMI is its preparation for the precise navigation and future autonomous driving by launching low-orbit satellites via Geespace. This ambitious plan has a similar logic to the massive satellite network Starlink by Elon Musk. The big difference is that Geely will not internalize the rocket's business, while Musk owns the company SpaceX.

The fourth is various initiatives of radical mobility solutions — the 1,000 km/h (620 mph) "supersonic" train; the flying car Terrafugia from the US that requires taking off and landing only at airfields; and VTOL technologies based Volocopter. Those three technologies are disruptive to the car industry, as flying cars have certain substitutional relationship with conventional cars, especially in the urban area. "Geely is transitioning from being an automotive manufacturer to a mobility technology group, investing in and developing a wide range of next-generation technologies," said Li Shufu, Geely's Chairman, in a statement. "Our joint venture with Volocopter underlines our confidence in Volocopter air taxis as the next ambitious step in our wider expansion in both electrification and new mobility services" (Lunden, 2019).

13.6.2. *Organization of Geely Technology Group to support BMI*

The Geely Technology Group has managed all the above innovations and is an important affiliate of the Geely Group. The Geely Technology Group is one of the six groups of the Zhejiang Geely Holding Group. The other five are Geely Auto Group, Volvo Car Group, Geely New Energy Commercial Vehicle Group, Mitime Group, and Geely Talent Development Group (Figure 13.1).

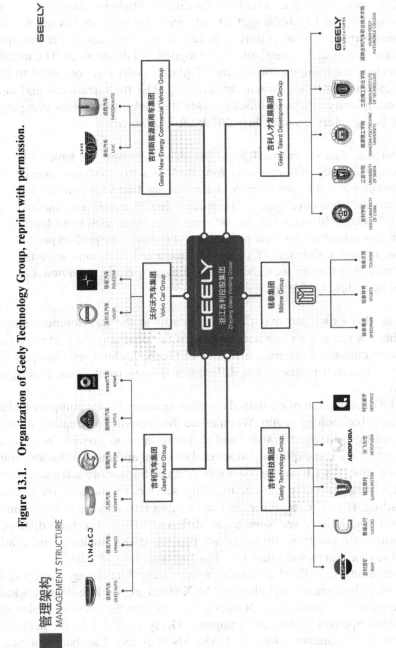

Figure 13.1. Organization of Geely Technology Group, reprint with permission.

This organizational structure facilitates business innovation. As explained by Mr. Liu Jinliang, CEO of Geely Technology Group, the car business' organizational culture is different from the that of the mobility services. Specifically, there are several significant differences. The mobility services are more customer- and IT-platform-driven, compared to the product- and hardware-driven car business. The organizational and cultural complexity is also exhibited inside the mobility services company. When being interviewed in July 2019, Liu explained:

> Our *Cao Cao* environment is not yet an IT company. We have 1000 people, and 300–400 are coming from the IT industry. With a mixture of auto people and IT people in this team, you can find a big mindset. For example, when developing a Taxi product line, IT people are requested to develop software, while this software is not being used immediately and put it aside because car people think it is part of the product portfolio. In such a situation, IT people feel frustrated, and some leave the company as they do not feel quick task delivery (personal interview, Liu Jinliang, July 11, 2019).

Liu also expressed that *Cao Cao* is still at the development stage, and there is not yet a clear new culture of the company. Objectively, the company culture of different affiliates of Geely Technology Group, with different external partners, are different and vary from other groups of Geely.

The organization of car-based mobility services is also complex inside the Geely Technology group. When asked the necessity of creating several legal entities, different brands, and different apps to provide service in different cities, Liu explains that several external and internal factors conditioned this: "In China, the business is sometimes more advanced than the legal regulation. In the car mobility service, regulations on B-to-B car-hailing, B-to-C car-hailing, and car renting business are not the same; regional regulations are sometimes different. Thus, creating different companies are creating 'firewalls' for protecting our business and minimize the risk" (personal interview, Liu Jinliang, July 11, 2019).

According to official communication, Geely Technology Group also holds other businesses, including ECARX (focusing on Intelligent cockpit technologies and products), Qianjiang Motors (the motorcycle business), Joma (the Spanish sportswear company; Geely signed a brand licensing agreement for Greater China and ASEAN regions), Easybao Insurance

Agency, and Geely Travel, among others. It is *de facto* a conglomerate of business, different to the positioning of the Geely Technology Group, as "an incubator for young brands giving them access to Geely global resources."

It is worth noting that the *Maple* brand is integrated into the Geely Technology Group, but not to Geely Auto Group (together with *the Geely* brand, *Geometry* brand, *Lynk & Co*, *PROTON, Lotus*, and *smart*). It is the only exceptional car brand that is being integrated into the Geely Technology Group. This arrangement may create new organizational complexity and brand image confusion. For Geely Technology Group, it means the necessity to create a new team on the traditional car manu-facturing business, overlapping with the Geely Auto Group.

For branding, *Geometry* is a new brand dedicated to pure EVs. The arrival of *Maple*, also in the pure EV segment, raises the need for addi-tional efforts on the brand positioning between *Geometry* and *Maple*.

From the product architecture perspective, the current *Maple* is based on the architecture design of *Vision* X3. The design of these two cars has similarities. There is a need to explain the brand price differences between *Vision* and *Maple*.

At the operational level, *Maple* is not exclusively sold to *Cao Cao* or other car-sharing/car-hailing business units of the Geely Technology Group, and the development of an independent dealership network is a new challenge for the conglomerate, as this is not its core competency.

We observe that Geely wishes to reach different consumer groups through a multi-brand strategy to achieve its goal of two million vehicle sales annually. However, we doubt the effectiveness of this operation, especially by the Geely Technology Group.

13.7. Conclusion

Geely undertook multiple operations to implement its BMI in the scope of mobility solutions. Current mobility services are covering the low-end market by using LSEVs (*Microcity*), economic category (*EVcoming*), mid-range business (*Cao Cao*), and premium business (*StarRides* with Daimler). The ride-hailing business driven by *Cao Cao* is taking shape after company was founded in 2015, while *StarRides* is still in the early stage of development. The car-sharing business is evolving quickly. *EVcoming* merged with *Microcity*. Besides, synergies between the ride-hailing business and car-sharing business create synergies starting from 2020, while keeping these two entities independent.

Besides, the scope of Geely's mobility service is much bigger than most of the carmakers. It is exhibited by Geely's equity JV in the field of mobility connection between Chinese high-speed train and ride-hailing services. The launch of low-orbit satellites is another ambitious project. The supersonic train and two projects of flying cars are radical mobility innovations from the perspective of carmakers.

All the above operations illustrate Geely's audacious ambition to create a much bigger business cluster of MaaS in the coming years, starting from cars, then extending to the high-speed train, supersonic train, and flying cars, with high-precision satellite navigation.

Multiple initiatives on mobility solutions by Geely deserve a future closer look. First, one of the critical points is the dynamic evolution of the core resources and competencies of Geely to ensure various expansions toward MaaS, including core technologies, talents, and new organizational capabilities. It is worth observing how the Geely Technology Group manages to create a new organizational culture that can further boost innovation while simultaneously managing the risk of dilution. Second, by now, there is not yet a clear profit model on the above initiatives. Those services are still in early development; very few are reaching the break-even point. Third, external constraints, such as governmental regulations, maybe strong enough to delay the commercial implementation of some radical transportation like the flying car.

From the organizational perspective, we observe that the Geely Technology Group is more than a mobility service innovation group. It is becoming a business conglomerate with much broader business scope. Some businesses are not linked to the automobile sector at all. The "revitalization" of *Maple* brand and its integration into the Geely Technology Group further creates new challenges in terms of brand portfolio management and operations for Geely. There may be an evolution toward the rationalization and optimization in the coming years.

References

Automotive World (2019). *Cao Cao* leads Chinese growth in ride-hailing active users. November 7. Available at: https://www.automotiveworld.com/news-releases/cao-cao-leads-chinese-growth-in-ride-hailing-active-users/ (accessed October 26, 2020).

Bower, J. L. and C. M. Christensen (1995). Disruptive technologies: Catching the wave. *Harvard Business Review*, **73**:1, 43–53.

Bucherer, E., U. Eisert and O. Gassmann (2012). Towards systematic business model innovation: Lessons from product innovation management. *Creativity and Innovation Management*, **21**:2, 183–198.

Chesbrough, H. W. (2007). Business model innovation: It is not just about technology anymore. *Strategy and Leadership*, **35**:6, 12–17.

Christensen, C. M. (1997). *The Innovator's Dilemma: When New Technologies Cause Great Firms to Fail*. Boston, MA: Harvard Business Press.

Daimler (2019). *StarRides* launches in China. Joint venture between Daimler Mobility and Geely Group. December 3. Available at: https://www.daimler.com/investors/reports-news/financial-news/20191203-geely-starrides.html (accessed October 26, 2020).

Ford Media Center (2018). Ford Smart Mobility and Zotye to form EV solutions JV for China's fast-growing ride-hailing market. May 2. Available at: https://media.ford.com/content/fordmedia/fna/us/en/news/2018/05/02/ford-smart-mobility-and-zotye-to-form-ev-solutions-jv-for-chinas.html (accessed October 26, 2020).

Global Railway Review (2018). Supersonic trains to be developed by Geely Holding and CASIC. November 8. Available at: https://www.globalrailwayreview.com/news/74995/supersonic-trains-geely-holding-casic/ (accessed October 26, 2020).

He, W. and F. Li (2018). Geely, Tencent buy stake in train Wi-Fi firm. *China Daily*, June 8. Available at: http://www.chinadaily.com.cn/a/201806/08/WS5b19d7caa31001b82571ed31.html (accessed October 26, 2020).

Ke, X. (2020). Hu of *Evcoming*: Business affected by COVID-19 but no plan to cut. *Sina Auto*, April 3. Available at: https://k.sina.cn/article_6192937794_1 7120bb42020018nef.html?from=auto&subch=oauto&ab=qiche&http=from http (in Chinese, accessed October 26, 2020).

Lunden, I. (2019). Volocopter raises $55M led by Volvo owner Geely. *Tech Crunch*, September 9. Available at: https://techcrunch.com/2019/09/08/volocopter-raises-55m-led-by-volvo-owner-geely-sets-3-year-timeline-for-its-flying-taxi-service/ (accessed October 26, 2020).

Magretta, J. (2002). Why business models matter? *Harvard Business Review*, **80**:5, 86–92.

Markides, C. (2006). Disruptive innovation: In need of better theory. *Journal of Product Innovation Management*, **23**:1, 19–25.

Mitchell, D. W. and C. B. Coles (2003). The ultimate competitive advantage of continuing business model innovation. *Journal of Business Strategy*, **24**:5, 15–21.

Mitchell, D. W. and C. B. Coles (2004). Business model innovation breakthrough move. *The Journal of Business Strategy*, **25**:1, 16–26.

Morris, M., M. Schindehutte and J. Allen (2005). The entrepreneur's business model: Toward a unified perspective. *Journal of Business Research*, **58**:6, 726–735.

Osterwalder, A., Y. Pigneur and C. L. Tucci (2005). Clarifying business models: Origins, present, and future of the concept. *Communications of the Association for Information Systems*, **15**, 1–25.

PE Daily (2020). *EVcoming* raised 687 million A round funding. June 4. Available at: https://news.pedaily.cn/202006/455821.shtml (in Chinese, accessed October 26, 2020).

Pham, S. (2018). China's $30 billion ride-hailing market could double by 2020. *CNN Business*, May 15. Available at: https://money.cnn.com/2018/05/15/technology/china-ride-hailing-market/index.html (accessed October 26, 2020).

Qiu, Q. (2019). OnTime to boost manufacturing, tech integration. *China Daily*, June 28. Available at: http://www.chinadaily.com.cn/a/201906/28/WS5d15863aa3103dbf1432ad7e.html (accessed October 26, 2020).

Shouqi Limousine (2020). Shouqi Limousine & Chauffeur, the second largest ride-hailing platform in China, has made profits in multiple cities nationwide. 69 News, May 15. Available at: https://www.wfmz.com/news/pr_newswire/pr_newswire_business/shouqi-limousine-chauffeur-the-second-largest-ride-hailing-platform-in-china-has-made-profits-in/article_d6d8121d-10f5-51ec-b418-441d11a80d3b.html (accessed October 26, 2020).

Teece, D. J. (2010). Business models, business strategy and innovation. *Long Range Planning*, **43**:2–3, 172–194.

Tsang, R., D. Cai and H. Liu (2019). The bumpy road to profits in developing Asia's mobility industry. Bain & Company. Available at: https://www.bain.com/insights/the-bumpy-road-to-profits-in-developing-asias-mobility-industry/ (accessed October 26, 2020).

Zhang, J. (2020). Chinese chauffeur-driven ride-hailing platform Caocao launches trial service in Paris as rivalry heats up at home. *South China Morning Post*, January 4. Available at: https://www.scmp.com/tech/enterprises/article/3044522/chinese-chauffeur-driven-ride-hailing-platform-caocao-launches (accessed October 26, 2020).

Zott, C., R. Amit and L. Massa (2011). The business model: Recent developments and future research. *Journal of Management*, **37**:4, 1019–1042.

Chapter 14

Conclusion

Abstract

In less than 25 years, Geely has grown to become a top-selling indigenous brand in China and a rising player in the global automotive industry. The impressive growth of Geely is interpreted by its twin trajectory. One is driven by the technology catching up, the other is the multinational growth. These two simultaneous trajectories were then converged by asset-seeking and asset acquisition via outward foreign direct investment (OFDI). Looking forward, Geely seeks to become a world-class technology-driven mobility service provider. It is definitely worth noting and further studying how these incremental and radical technology initiatives on mobility solutions and its related business model innovations will reshape the global automotive industry for a new and exciting future.

Keywords: Geely Auto; growth trajectory; OFDI; EMNC.

14.1. The Trajectory of Geely's Growth

Geely debuted its automobile business in the late 1990s. In less than 25 years, the company has grown to become a top-selling indigenous brand in China and a rising player in the global automotive industry. Geely ranked the world's 13th largest passenger carmaker by selling 2.178 million units in 2019. The group employs over 120,000 people, operates 14 vehicle manufacturing plants, 9 powertrain plants, and 6 knockdown kit plants. Geely has been listed in Fortune 500 since 2011.

The impressive growth of Geely can be interpreted by its twin trajectory. One is driven by the catching-up trajectory, via technology imitation and reverse engineering of bestselling foreign car models, an innovative approach to quasi-open product architecture that drives low-cost production. As of today, Geely cars based on this approach is still the cash cow for the group. The other is the multinational growth trajectory, first driven by exportation, then the establishment of assembling plants for knocked-down components. The latter has witnessed lesser commercial success, representing less than 5% of the group's total sales volume.

These two simultaneous trajectories were then converged by asset-seeking and asset acquisition via outward foreign direct investment (OFDI). The very typical examples include the acquisition of London Taxi in 2006, the acquisition of transmission system from DSI in 2009, then the acquisition of Volvo Cars in 2010, followed by the acquisition of electric vehicle technology from Emerald in 2014, the Lotus, Volvo AB, and the flying car Terrafugia in 2017, then the financial operation on Daimler in 2018. In comparison, the acquisition of PROTON in Malaysia is mainly a market-seeking operation (Table 14.1).

It is worth pointing out that Geely has experienced more than one decade of cross-border acquisition, increasing its international experience dramatically. The company has demonstrated positive outcomes on post-integration, successful in asset seeking, asset augmentation, and

Table 14.1.   Geely's cross-border acquisitions and motivations.

No	Year	Target company	Country of origin	Equity share by Geely (%)	Motivation
1	2006	MBH–London Taxi	UK	23	Asset-seeking
2	2009	DSI	Australia	100	Asset-seeking
3	2010	Volvo Cars	Sweden	100	Asset-seeking & Market seeking
4	2013	London Taxi (from MBH)	UK	100	Asset-seeking
5	2014	Emerald Automotive	UK	100	Asset-seeking
6	2017	PROTON	Malaysia	49.9	Market-seeking
7	2017	Lotus	Malaysia	51	Asset-seeking
8	2017	Volvo AB	Sweden	8.2	Asset-seeking
9	2017	Terrafugia	US	100	Asset-seeking
10	2018	Daimler AG	German	9.69	Asset-seeking

Source: Compiled by the authors according to Geely's official announcement.

asset creation, which is beneficial for both Geely and the acquired companies.

14.2. Proposal on a New Framework of EMNCs Growth — The Case of Geely

Dunning's eclectic paradigm/OLI paradigm (Dunning, 2000, 2006, 2009) is an effective analytical framework to understand why, where, and how emerging multinational enterprises (EMNEs) create value-added activities via OFDI. The OLI paradigm defines three types of advantages (Dunning, 2009):

O — Ownership advantage refers to firm-specific advantages (FSAs) in terms of resources and capabilities;

L — Location advantage refers to country-specific advantages (CSAs), as accessing and using of host countries' tangible and intangible resources and markets;

I — Internalization advantages refer to internalization of the transaction cost or reducing cost via market such as cross-border mergers and acquisitions (M&A).

Dunning (2006) identifies that Chinese multinational corporations (MNCs) have FSAs, including the financial capacity and privileged access to Chinese markets. On top of that, the combination of O and L resources and assets between acquiring and acquired companies can augment resources for both companies and even create new resources, assets, and capabilities. Both in home and host countries, the O and L advantages need to interact and then be internalized (Table 14.2). These dimensions need to be connected and co-evolutionary to create new dynamic competencies (Narula, 2012).

14.2.1. *Asset augmentation for Geely by the interaction of O and L advantages*

The asset augmentation of Geely is driven by the acquisition of O advantage of Volvo, including brand, technology, and R&D capacity; global sales network; and management expertise. The acquisition of Volvo significantly increased the global visibility and credibility of Geely. It is an important endorsement for Geely's future M&A, including PROTON, Lotus, and Daimler in particular.

Table 14.2.   OLI analysis of Geely–Volvo.

OLI	Geely	Volvo
O	• Financial resource • Capacity to manage low costs on supply chain • Knowledge of China market and customers • Sales network	• Global brand • Technology and R&D capacity • Global sales network • Management expertise • Excellence in car safety
L	• China as the biggest auto market • Regional governments support — land and finance access	• Technology cluster in Sweden in Gothenburg area • Talent pool (engineers and consultants)
I	Reverse Cross-border M&A and OFDI	

Source: Authors' own.

For Geely, the creation of R&D center China Euro Vehicle Technology AB (CEVT) in Gothenburg, Sweden, is an important step for further increasing its product competency by taking advantage of rich talent resources and management know-how from Volvo and its industrial clusters in Europe. The launch of the B-segment Modular Architecture (BMA) platform in China marks the internalization of Geely's platform design capability, based on the technology and talent support from both CEVT and Volvo. Mats Fagerhag, the CEO of CEVT, was appointed as the Deputy Director of Geely Research Institute, to support Feng Qingfeng, the Director, and Hu Zhengnan, leader of BMA. This leadership structure ensures the transfer of the knowledge system of Compact Modular Architecture (CMA) to the BMA. (personal interview with Li Li, VP of Zhejiang Geely Automobile Research Institute, July 11, 2019). The R&D efficiency further improved: the number of engineers for the BMA platform was around 500, one-quarter of that for CMA. The development time was reduced to less than 24 months, around half of the regular time of 40 months.

14.2.2. *Asset augmentation for Volvo by the interaction of O and L advantages*

Volvo's assets were increased globally both in Sweden and China after the acquisition by Geely. In 2019, Volvo Cars' global sales reached the threshold of 700,000, the first time since its establishment in 1927. The sales figure of 705,452 units were also double that of 2010.

Geely invested US$11 billion in Volvo from 2010–2015 to create the Scalable Product Architecture (SPA) platform and increase Gothenburg's production capacity. This growth strategy of Volvo is clearly stated by Li Shufu's metaphor on "tiger": "We should release the tiger to get out of the cage, before, we should sharpen their claws — that is to say, Geely will continue to invest in Volvo to strength their technology by developing Volvo own platform" (Wang and Liang, 2017, p. 249). The new SPA platform makes the new cars like XC90 globally competitive, in terms of car performance, R&D efficiency, and simplification of production.

In China, Volvo's operation expanded from a simple sales company in 2010 to a full original equipment manufacturer (OEM) structure by 2020. There are three assembling plants, one engine plant, one design center, one R&D center, one procurement center, and one sales company. Employees increased from 100 to over 8,000. Volvo China's supply chain system expanded from 0 to over 1,700 suppliers, which can also offer 30% of Volvo global purchasing. A double management system drives this transformation process: each department comprises two directors, one from Sweden and one from China. This management system accelerated Volvo management's transfer from Sweden to China and speeded up the local team's learning and operation. With Geely's strong support, Volvo's sales in China multiplied by five times between 2010 and 2019, expanding from 30,000 units to 161,436 units. Since 2014, China became the single largest market for Volvo with rapid yearly growth.

Cross-culture relations between Geely and Volvo represented an initial big challenge for the post-acquisition integration process, while creating key synergies in the mid-term, essential for the success of deal and explaining the rapid growth that followed, as illustrated in Chapter 6.

14.2.3. *Asset creation for Geely and Volvo by the interaction of O and L advantages*

The creation of CEVT is the illustration of Geely's asset augmentation, while the development of the CMA platform demonstrates asset creation for both Geely and Volvo. This new platform is to be shared by Geely and Volvo Cars, the high synergy between two entities. The Lynk & Co car is another important asset creation strategy. Lynk & Co's branding position is between Volvo and Geely. The sales of Lynk & Co. in 2019 was over 128,000 units. The first showroom in Europe was opened in Amsterdam,

Netherlands, on October 2020, followed by the second one in Gothenburg, Sweden, on January 2021, marking the start of Geely's foray into European markets. This new car further extends the value for both Geely and Volvo.

Asset creation is achieved in China as well. Despite the creation of CEVT and the development of the CMA platform in Sweden, Geely decided to build the Sustainable Experience Architecture (SEA) platform for electric vehicles in China. Geely Volvo Automotive Technology (GVAT), a joint venture (JV) R&D with Volvo in China, will further increase the competitiveness of two companies in smart and connected electric vehicles.

A piece of very important evidence on the broader asset creation that goes beyond the Geely–Volvo relationship is the utilization of the SEA2 platform by smart car, the JV between Geely and Daimler. To a certain extent, this case can also be identified as the reverse technology transfer from Geely to Daimler in the field of compact electric cars (Table 14.3).

The dynamic evolution of Geely drives us to further upgrade the framework of Balcet *et al.* (2012). The early stage of technological catching up and internationalization endeavors is formulated as the "twin trajectories" model. These two trajectories are then quickly converged toward cross-border M&As for the objective of asset seeking, particularly via Volvo's acquisition.

There are mainly five streams of theories to explain the internationalization of companies: (1) OLI model or eclectic paradigm; (2) Institutional theory or institution-based view; (3) Resource-based view; (4) Springboard perspectives; and (5) LLL (linkages, leverage, and learning) models. The first three are the mainstream theories in the scope of international business (IB) and corporate strategy, while the last two are emerging theories (Luo and Zhang, 2016; Luo and Tung, 2018). We adopt the OLI paradigm to conduct the case analysis of Geely.

Asset creation is a step forward of EMNCs globalization (Yakob *et al.*, 2018). New assets and business values are the results of positive interaction and co-creation between acquiring and acquired companies. Based on Geely's new findings, Figure 14.1 proposes an updated framework of Geely's trajectory of growth. The realization of Geely's asset augmentation and asset creation strategy is based on the positive interaction and combination of O and L advantage of acquiring and acquired companies and their respective markets.

Table 14.3. Asset augmentation and asset creation by Geely and Volvo.

OLI Paradigm	Beneficiary	Action	Results
Asset augmentation for acquiring company by the interaction of O and L advantages	Asset augmentation for Geely	In the global market:Branding of Volvo	Easier acquisition of other OFDI cases including Proton and Lotus, etc.
		In the host country (Sweden)	
		The creation of R&D center CEVT in Gothenburg	New platform CMA both for Volvo and Geely's car brands
		In the home country (China)	Improve Geely's car performance and future globalization strategy
		The creation of the BMA platform in China after the CMA platform	
Asset augmentation for the target company by the interaction of O and L advantages	Asset augmentation for Volvo	In the host country (Sweden)	The new SPA platform makes new cars of Volvo like XC90 globally competitive
		Geely invested US$11 billion in Volvo from 2010–2015 to create a SPA platform and increase Gothenburg's production capacity.	By 2020: 3 assembling plants, 1 engine plant, 1 design center, 1 R&D center, 1 procurement center, 1 sales company. Employees increased to 8,000, the supply chain system in China developed
		In the home country (China)	
		Expansion from Volvo sales company in 2010 to full OEM structure by 2020.	
Asset creation for both acquiring and acquired company by the interaction of O and (host and home country) L advantages	Geely and Volvo	In the host country (Sweden)	Develop a CMA platform in 9 months, for both Volvo and Geely cars
		The creation of R&D center CEVT in Gothenburg with the support of Volvo, co-creation of CMA platform	Sales: 128,000 units in 2019. Plan to launch this car in Europe in 2020
		Co-sharing of a new brand: Lynk & Co	
	Geely and Volvo	In the home country (China)	SEA for electric vehicles of Geely
		Design SEA platform in China	SEA2 will be used by smart car
		R&D oriented JV in China: GVAT for electric cars	In the early stage of development

Source: Compiled by the authors according to Geely's official announcements.

Figure 14.1.   Geely's trajectory of growth — An updated framework.

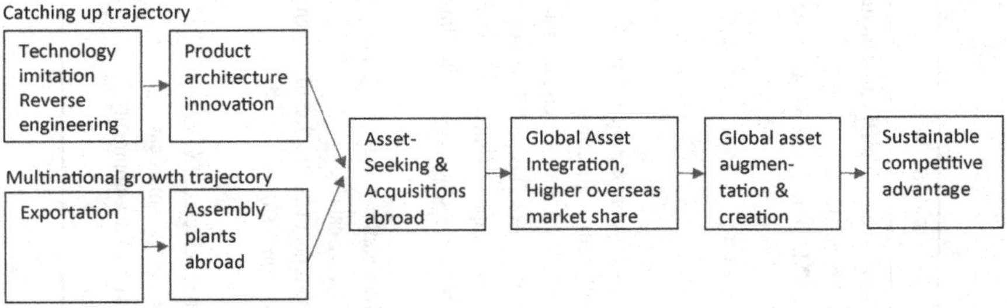

Catching up trajectory

```
┌─────────────┐    ┌─────────────┐
│ Technology  │    │ Product     │
│ imitation   │    │ architecture│
│ Reverse     │ →  │ innovation  │
│ engineering │    │             │
└─────────────┘    └─────────────┘
                                      ┌──────────┐  ┌──────────────┐  ┌───────────┐  ┌─────────────┐
                                      │ Asset-   │  │ Global Asset │  │ Global    │  │ Sustainable │
Multinational growth trajectory       │ Seeking &│  │ Integration, │→ │ asset     │→ │ competitive │
                                   →  │Acquisitions│ │ Higher overseas│ │ augmen-  │  │ advantage   │
┌─────────────┐    ┌─────────────┐    │ abroad   │  │ market share │  │ tation &  │  │             │
│ Exportation │    │ Assembly    │    └──────────┘  └──────────────┘  │ creation  │  └─────────────┘
│             │ →  │ plants      │                                    └───────────┘
│             │    │ abroad      │ →
└─────────────┘    └─────────────┘
```

Source: Compiled by the authors, based on Balcet *et al.* (2012).

14.3.   Future of Global Automobile Industry and Geely's Strategic Move

The global automobile industry is still a volume-driven business. The top five carmakers are Volkswagen, Toyota, Renault–Nissan–Mitsubishi Alliance, General Motors, and Hyundai, all exceeding 7 million sales per year. While industrial leaders strongly believe several paradigm shifts may change the landscape of the future automobile industry, driving forces are mainly "electrified", "autonomous", "connected" and "shared" (PWC, 2019).

Electrified cars signify the car type is expanding from the internal combustion engine-powered car toward hybrid and electric vehicles. The percentage of electric vehicles is expected to exceed 35% of new car registrations for the US, European, and China markets by 2030.

Autonomous cars have a clear technology road map, ranging from Level 1 to Level 5, signifying basic driver assistance to full automation. It is expected that Level 4 autonomous cars being driven in low speed (or less than 50km/h) in restricted areas might be realized in some markets by 2021.

Connected cars heavily depend on the future maturity of 5G technology. V2V (Vehicle to Vehicle), V2I (vehicle-to-infrastructure), V2G (vehicle-to-grid), or more generally, V2X (Vehicle-to-everything) are believed to have the positive output for road safety, traffic efficiency, and energy savings. Between WLAN-based and 5G-based communication technology, the latter has superior performance. According to PWC, the sales of 5G-enabled vehicles may reach 16 million in the EU, US, and China by 2030.

Shared cars already have significant development, as illustrated in Chapter 13. Global players all have made a move toward the provision of mobility services. Currently, mobility services operated by leading car-makers are still a cost center instead of a profit center. PWC research forecasts that 47% of European consumers may use mobility services and give up car ownership in the coming decade.

Based on the above analysis of driving forces, global OEMs are facing several significant changes. The development of shared cars might slow the pace of car sales, and the car park in Europe is expected to decline after reaching a peak of 273 million in 2025. On the other hand, the expenses on mobility by consumers will increase. Electrified and autonomous cars are continuously pushing the costs high while not necessarily increasing the profitability for OEM. The development of connected cars implies the possible shift of value chains, and new players of the V2X ecosystem will capture some values.

Geely has proactively anticipated the automobile industry's future and has made a concrete move into the above four directions.

- Mobility service is the earliest move by Geely. In 2013, Geely accessed this market via *Microcity* by operating micro-electric cars. Later, *Cao Cao* was launched in 2015 and has reached a sizeable operation by 2020. Other initiatives of radical mobility solutions include flying cars, supersonic trains, and low-orbit satellites, as described in Chapter 13. Geely has the ambition to create a big business cluster of Mobility as a Service (MaaS).
- The strategy of electrified cars was launched in 2015, named "Blue Geely Initiative." Key objectives to be reached by 2020 include: 90% of cars sold will consist of new energy vehicles and bring average fuel consumption to 5L per 100 km. However, those objectives are too ambitious to be realized by 2020. The production of future EVs based on SEA may boost the realization of this strategy.
- The autonomous cars project was initiated in 2015. As the main sponsor of the 2022 Asian Games, Geely will install fully autonomous systems in event sites by 2020, a step forward toward a higher level of autonomous drive in a low-speed and closed environment.
- As for the connected cars, the investment in ECARX by Geely is an important step. In 2019, ECARX created one affiliate company named SiEngine in Hubei for the R&D, testing, and production of car chips and modules. By March 2020, users of the GKUI (Geely Smart Ecosystem) 19 system exceeded 1.9 million. We can observe an integral approach taken by Geely to address the future core competency of connected cars (Table 14.4).

Table 14.4. Geely's strategic move toward electrified, autonomous, connected, and shared cars.

Strategic dimension	Electrified cars	Autonomous cars	Connected cars	Shared cars
Key project	**Blue Geely Initiative** Objective: 90% NEV by 2020.	**G-Pilot 4.0+ in 2018** The 4-step strategy of autonomous drive	**GKUI 19** In-car intelligent system	**Cao Cao** Incremental and radical mobility solutions
Real starting year	2015	2015	2016	2013
Chronology	2013: JV on *Microcity*; production on *Kandi* brand A00 pure EV.	2015: *Borui* on the market with ADAS	2014: G-netlink in the new *Emgrand* car.	2013: *Microcity*
	2014: equity participation at Zhidou.	2018: *Borui* GE with L2	2016: ECARX founded by Geely	2015: *Cao Cao*
	2015: EV of *Emgrand* on the market	2019: Automated Valet Parking System	2017: ECARX established a branch in Gothenburg	2017: Terrafugia
	2016: spin-off Zhidou asset	2019: has sold over 450,000 cars with L2 technologies	2018: Proton X70 equipped with GKUI	2018: EVcoming
	2018: Lynk & Co NEV on the market	2020: some volume production of L3 cars	2019: creation of a company named SiEngine in Hubei.	2018: CGRT (high-speed train)
	2019: EV cars Geometry on the market	2020: develop a fully autonomous system in the 2022 Asian Games event sites.	2020: users of the GKUI 19 system exceed 1.9 million by March.	2018: Geespace (Low-orbit satellites)
	2019: control 78% share of Kandi.		2020: launch of low-orbit satellite	2018: Supersonic train (with CASIC)
	2020: EV cars on the market: *Maple*, Lynk & Co and the JV with Daimler on electric smart			2019: *StarRides* (with Daimler)
				2019: Volocopter (with Daimler)
				2020: *Cao Cao* to expand over 50 cities, over 30 million APP users

14.4. Geely's Dynamics and Perspectives

In this concluding chapter, we would like to highlight some of the observations and suggestions for Geely's future sustainable development.

14.4.1. *Entrepreneurship of Li Shufu*

The entrepreneurship of Li Shufu is one of the keys to the stunning business success of Geely. Chapter 4 has illustrated Mr. Li as a visionary and effective leader. As a grassroots businessman, Li demonstrated his determination toward success.

By further decoding his entrepreneurial approach, we can identify the following additional key successful factors of an entrepreneur: (1) having a vision that is in line with the megatrends of one growing industry; (2) using entrepreneurial savvy to combine multiple resources, especially talents to overcome multiple difficulties, and to gain quick wins while approaching the mid-term objective at the same time; and (3) being open and forward-thinking by having strong curiosity and a spirit for innovation and adventure, thus creating a new vision's dynamic perspective.

It is perceived that the essential traits possessed by successful entrepreneurs include passion, resilience, keen sense of self, flexibility, and vision (Rampton, 2014). Mr. Li seems to have all of them, while we would like to provide a new interpretation of the aspect of flexibility.

From the management style perspective, Mr. Li's flexibility can be gleamed from the fact that he respects, trusts, encourages, and support his employees. His management is based on his moral principles and his pluralistic belief system, summarized by the 16-character philosophy (各美其美, 美人之美, 美美与共, 天下大同): appreciating the culture/values of others as do to one's own, and the world will become a harmonious whole; Everybody cherishes his or her culture/values, and if we respect and treasure other's culture/values, the world will be a harmonious one (People.com.cn, 2012). Li cited this philosophy from one leading sociologist in China, Mr. Fei Xiaotong (1910–2005). Based on the shared vision, the process to reach the objective can be decided by experts; the way of thinking and doing can be different according to the specific industrial culture (e.g. automobile versus software industry) and cross-country cultures are different. For us, this pluralistic belief system rooted in the Chinese philosophy is the deep foundation to understand the flexibility of Mr. Li Shufu.

It is perceived that Mr. Li is very media savvy. He can always manage to stay in the news and generate some free publicity for Geely. According to our observation, Mr. Li has become relatively lower profile in the media compared to the early 2000s. Also, Mr. Li's media exposure is mainly in China; there is a necessity to increase his visibility in the global market. The entrepreneurship of Mr. Li Shufu is a great asset, both for Geely and for the Chinese entrepreneurship, a systematic study of which is worthy, both in China and on the global stage, similar to Kiichiro Toyoda for Toyota, Konosuke Matsushita for Panasonic, Inamori Kazuo for Kyocera and KDDI, or Elon Musk for Tesla, among others. From a commercial perspective, the entrepreneurship of Mr. Li Shufu has the potential value to reduce the marketing budget and make the customer loyal. Elon Musk dominates with zero marketing budget, while he is focusing on the product performance, and his customers are also indirectly inspired and attracted by his entrepreneurship.

14.4.2. *Corporate culture and cross-culture management*

From its origins as a Chinese company to transforming into an EMNC, Geely has made great efforts to upgrade its corporate culture by further defining its core values, vision, and mission, as studied in Chapter 12. Geely's core value triangle is composed of technology, society, and the environment. Geely Group's mission is "strategic synergy, promote innovation, and co-creation of value." The latest version of corporate culture in 2020 is "hard working (or fighting), questioning (or truth-seeking), bench-marking, and compliance."

It is interesting to compare the above version of corporate culture in 2020 with the reflection of Mr. Li Shufu in 2014 about his perception of Geely culture: "The global corporate culture I mentioned refers to the enterprise model that transcends the borders, nationalities, and religions, which is conducive to the advancement of human civilization, people's happy life as well as enterprises' innovation and global adaptability. These advantages can be seen in customers' satisfaction, sense of pride among employees and achievability in management, flexible culture, and the company's comprehensive and sustainable development. Under the guidance of this culture, featured by openness, inclusiveness, foresight, and sagacity, an enterprise will actively undertake the responsibility, dare to challenge the peak of science and technology, be brave in the exploration of commercial civilization, and be endowed with an administration concept of legitimacy, fairness, transparency and mutual respect" (Li Shufu, 2014).

Mr. Li's reflection on corporate culture is in line with his 16-character pluralistic belief system. But his thoughts have not yet been systematically interpreted as a corporate culture with simple but powerful message. Today, the Geely Group's cultural statement is not yet the statement for its acquired company. Geely needs to envisage the effective communication and implementation of its culture for all its affiliates, including PROTON, Lotus, and London EV Company (LEVC), if Geely's ambition is to become a truly globalized MNC.

We find out that there is still the margin of improvement on Geely's core values, vision, mission, and corporate culture, and in particular, its interlinkage and consistency. After the acquisition of Volvo, Geely learned technology from Volvo. The systematic learning on a structured management system, starting from value, vision, mission, and corporate culture, will definitively boost Geely to become a truly globalized company.

14.4.3. *The boundary of business*

Geely is more than a car company. The Zhejiang Geely Holding Group was established in 1986, which was followed by Geely Auto in 1997. The Holding Group is divided into five subsidiaries: Geely Auto Group is in charge of the passenger car business (Geely Auto, Geometry, Lynk & Co, PROTON, Lotus, and smart); Volvo Car Group (Volvo Cars and Polestar); Geely New Energy Commercial Vehicle Group is dealing commercial vehicle business (LEVC and Farizon Auto); Geely Technology Group is positioned to take innovative projects including incremental and radical mobility services, *Cao Cao* and flying cars; and Mitime Group, which is Geely's non-vehicle operations (educational institutions, motorsports, tourism business, among others). Geely Automobile Holdings Limited is a listed company with published annual data; Volvo Cars also releases its annual reports, while the visibility of other Geely subsidiaries is weak.

The group in 2019 employed 124,846 people and 52,400 for Geely Auto that generates a revenue of 97,401 million RMB, and 41,517 employees for Volvo Cars globally that generate 274,117 million SEK (208,329 million RMB). There is a big gap in productivity, measured by the revenue per employee, between Geely Auto and Volvo Cars.

As a group with multiple businesses, Geely needs to constantly optimize its business boundary and make the development of the group more efficient and sustainable. In the early stage, Geely and Volvo operated under the motto "Geely is Geely and Volvo is Volvo." After 10 years of M&A, the synergy between the two companies has been exhibited via multiple projects. In February 2020, Geely and Volvo jointly announced the intention to combine their businesses, to accelerate technological and financial efficiencies. This operation is temporally suspended several months later, as Geely planned to be listed in China's Nasdaq-like science and technology board at the Shanghai Stock Exchange, for the interest of bigger funding. Shortly after, we can still expect a much higher synergy between Geely and Volvo.

Future business optimization can be achieved inside the Geely Technology Group. As we mentioned in Chapter 13, this group per se is more than a mobility services innovation cluster. It is becoming a small business conglomerate with much broader business scopes. Some businesses are not linking with the automobile, including the Spanish sportswear brand Joma, one Chinese motorcycle named Qianjiang, and the Maple car. There may be an evolution toward the rationalization and optimization in the coming years. Digging further, Geely's scope of investment is very broad, covering battery, sea car operation system, car chips, satellites, flying cars, and even the education business not linking with the automobile to multiple cities in China.

According to our observations, the priority for Geely is to increase product competitiveness by constantly increasing the percentage of cars using new platforms. Geely cars' current ratio to use CMA, BMA, and SEA in 2020 is only around 20%. Chapter 11 illustrates that Geely is still in the early period of transition from the major utilization of its existing platforms (FE, KC, and NL) toward more sophisticated new platforms. There is no doubt that new platforms will bring a better performance of a product, low costs of component sourcing, and the dilution on the heavy initial investment of platform development.

Another important dimension that Geely needs to improve is the assembly capacity utilization ratio. According to Geely's Annual Report 2019, there are 11 manufacturing plants producing Geely brand cars (excluding Lynk & Co) with a total annual capacity of 2.1 million units. The company sold a total of 1,361,560 units of vehicles (including 128,066 units of Lynk & Co); thus, the overall assembly capacity utilization ratio is 58.7%, far below the global average ratio ranging between

76.7% and 81% between 2012–2017, or 71% for European OEMs in 2019 (Statista, 2020; Vasilash, 2019). Since the automobile is the core business for the Geely Group, and Geely Automobile is a listed company, efficiency of operation and improvement on profitability are definitively top agenda items that need to be addressed.

14.4.4. *Branding strategy*

Based on the comprehensive analysis of Geely's brand management in Chapter 12, we would further highlight the necessity of the future optimization of Geely's branding strategy. After the initial period of selling low-cost affordable car models (1997–2007), and the deliberate choice of multiple brand-strategy periods (2007–2014), Geely officially announced the "One Geely" strategy in brand management in 2014.

Since then, we observe the further increase of brands inside of Geely. For example, at least two brands for electric cars (*Geometry* and LEVC) have been created. During the 2020 Beijing Auto Show, LEVC LX styled by Lorinser is promoted as a "premium tailor-made" electric car for the individual consumers, which is a questionable approach to sell a car with very strong DNA of London taxi.

Besides, the names of car models under the Geely brand is fairly China market-centric. Some of the names are difficult to pronounce or to understand for non-Chinese consumers. A similar case happened for the mobility brand *Cao Cao* and its direct utilization in overseas markets such as Paris.

When interviewing Geely's chief designer, we can read between the lines that branding strategy is beyond his scope and is mainly decided in China. We suggest that the global vision and global practice on brand management need to be one of the top priorities for Geely.

14.5. Future Study

The rise of Geely as a private automaker in China over the past two decades has been a quite impressive feat. Under the entrepreneurial leadership of Li Shufu, Geely has grown to be a successful EMNC with Chinese roots. Geely's achievement drives us to conduct scholarly endeavor from multiple perspectives of International Business, OFDI, Cross-border M&A, Asset Seeking, Asset Augmentation, and Asset Creation Strategy,

Entrepreneurship, Corporate Culture, and Cross-culture Management, Brand Management, Organization Dynamics, Business Model Innovation, Automobile Industry Organization, Technology Catching Up, Product Architecture Innovation, and Platform Strategy.

It will be too ambitious to make each aspect a solid match between the academic and in-depth case studies on Geely. Thus, this book can serve as a call for future collaborative research, and new comparative study will be a worthy undertaking by interested scholars across the globe — e.g. the comparison between Geely and well-established Asian carmakers such as Toyota and Hyundai, Nissan, Honda, and Suzuki, in terms of corporate culture with Asian cultural influence, branding strategy, lean manufacturing, and globalization strategy. The comparison between Geely and Tata on their different globalization approaches, the capacity of asset augmentation, and asset seeking will also make interesting reading.

Looking forward, Geely has made a bold announcement in 2020 that the company seeks to become a world-class technology-driven mobility service provider in the coming years. It is definitely worth noting and further studying how those incremental and radical technology initiatives on mobility solutions and its related business model innovations will reshape the global automotive industry for a new and exciting future.

References

Balcet, G., H. Wang and X. Richet (2012). Geely: A trajectory of catching up and asset-seeking multinational growth. *International Journal of Automotive Technology and Management*, **12**:4, 360–375.

Dunning, J. H. (2000). The eclectic paradigm as an envelope for economic and business theories of MNE activity. *International Business Review*, **9**:2, 163–190.

Dunning, J. H. (2006). Comment on dragon multinationals: New players in 21st century globalization. *Asia Pacific Journal of Management*, **23**:2, 139.

Dunning, J. H. (2009). Location and the multinational enterprise: John Dunning's thoughts on receiving the *Journal of International Business Studies* 2008 Decade Award. *Journal of International Business Studies*, **40**:1, 20–34.

Luo, Y. and H. Zhang (2016). Emerging market MNEs: Qualitative review and theoretical directions. *Journal of International Management*, **22**:4, 333–350.

Luo, Y. and R. L. Tung (2018). A general theory of springboard MNEs. *Journal of International Business Studies*, **49**:2, 129–152.

Narula, R. (2012). Do we need different frameworks to explain infant MNEs from developing countries? Nature of advantages. *Global Strategy Journal*, **204**, 188–204.

PWC (2019). The 2019 Strategy & Digital Auto Report, Time to Get Real: Opportunities in a Transforming Market. Available at: https://www.strategyand. pwc.com/gx/en/insights/2019/digital-auto-report.html (accessed March 15, 2020).

Rampton, J. (2014). Five personality traits of an entrepreneur. *Forbes*, April 14. Available at: https://www.forbes.com/sites/johnrampton/2014/04/14/5-personality-traits-of-an-entrepreneur/#795259083bf4 (accessed December 18, 2019).

Statista (2020). Global automotive assembly capacity utilization from 2012 to 2017. Available at: https://www.statista.com/statistics/266845/capacity-utilization-of-the-global-automobile-production-since-1990/ (accessed April 20, 2020).

Vasilash, G. S. (2019). Plant utilization in Europe: Improving, but... *Additive Manufacturing*, December 2. Available at: https://www.additivemanufacturing. media/articles/plant-utilization-in-europe-improving-but- (accessed April 20, 2020).

Wang, Q. and D. Liang (2017). *The New Manufacturing Era*. Beijing: CITIC Press, p. 41 (in Chinese).

Yakob, R., R. H. Nakamura and P. Ström (2018). Chinese foreign acquisitions aimed for strategic asset-creation and innovation upgrading: The case of Geely and Volvo Cars. *Technovation*, **70–71**, 59–72.

Index

Printed in the United States
by Baker & Taylor Publisher Services